T0330376

The Governance of Socio-Technical Systems

EU-SPRI FORUM ON SCIENCE, TECHNOLOGY AND INNOVATION POLICY

Series Editors: Susana Borrás, *Department of Business and Politics, Copenhagen Business School, Denmark,* Jakob Edler, *Manchester Institute of Innovation Research, Manchester Business School, UK,* Stefan Kuhlmann, *Science, Technology, and Policy Studies, University of Twente, The Netherlands* and Ismael Rafols, *INGENIO (CSIC-UPV), Polytechnic University of Valencia, Spain and SPRU, University of Sussex, UK*

The aim of this series is to present some of the best and most original research emanating from the Eu-SPRI Forum on Science, Technology and Innovation Policy. The typical questions addressed by the books in the series will include, but not be limited to:

- What is the role of science, technology and innovation policy in the 21st century?
- How can policies cope with 'grand social challenges' in the areas of health, energy, security or the environment?
- Are there better ways to link governments' science and innovation policies to other public policies?
- What are the innovation policy rationales and instruments for successfully fostering competitiveness and economic growth?
- Which public policies help to proactively shape responsible and legitimate technological innovation?
- How can public sector research be made more creative and effective?
- How can more intelligent interactions be achieved between investments in research and higher education policies for universities?
- How can the forces of globalisation and localisation be balanced?

The Governance of Socio-Technical Systems

Explaining Change

Edited by

Susana Borrás

Professor of Innovation and Governance, Head of Department of Business and Politics, Copenhagen Business School, Denmark

Jakob Edler

Professor of Innovation Policy and Strategy, Executive Director, Manchester Institute of Innovation Research, University of Manchester, UK

EU-SPRI FORUM ON
SCIENCE, TECHNOLOGY AND INNOVATION POLICY

Edward Elgar

Cheltenham, UK • Northampton, MA, USA

Published by
Edward Elgar Publishing Limited
The Lypiatts
15 Lansdown Road
Cheltenham
Glos GL50 2JA
UK

Edward Elgar Publishing, Inc.
William Pratt House
9 Dewey Court
Northampton
Massachusetts 01060
USA

A catalogue record for this book
is available from the British Library

Library of Congress Control Number: 2014944010

This book is available electronically in the ElgarOnline.com
Social and Political Science Subject Collection, E-ISBN 978 1 78471 019 4

ISBN 978 1 78471 018 7

Typeset by Columns Design XML Ltd, Reading
Printed and bound in Great Britain by T.J. International Ltd, Padstow

Contents

Figures

Tables

Boxes

Contributors

David Barberá-Tomás is Associate Professor at INGENIO, a research institute of the Spanish Council for Scientific Research (CSIC) and the Polytechnic University of Valencia. Before joining INGENIO, he spent seven years as an R&D Project Manager in a Spanish medical technology company, where he led several R&D projects and co-authored three European Patents. His current research uses both quantitative and qualitative approaches for inquiry in several innovation domains, as innovation policy, medical innovation or social innovation, and has been published in journals such as Research Policy, Technological Forecasting and Social Change or European Planning Studies.

Marc Barbier is a Senior Researcher in Sciences and Technology Studies at the National Institute for Agricultural Research (INRA) and director of the Research Unit 'Science in Society'. He manages the CorTexT Platform of the Institute for Research Innovation and Society (IFRIS). His research interests and works contribute to the fields of social studies of knowledge regime in agriculture and of the governance of sustainability transitions under various pressures of change such as pesticide uses, emergent diseases, bioenergy and ecosystem services. Email address: barbier@inra-ifris.org.

Peter Biegelbauer is a Senior Scientist at the Department Innovation Systems at the AIT Austrian Institute of Technology in Vienna and lecturer at the University of Vienna. His research work focuses on public policy analysis, science, technology and innovation policy, social learning in decision-making, knowledge and expertise in decision-making, regulatory impact assessment and qualitative methods. For several years he has concentrated on policy evaluation and the possibilities of learning from experience in policy making. Email address: peter.biegelbauer@ait.ac.at.

Susana Borrás is Professor of Innovation and Governance at the Department of Business and Politics, Copenhagen Business School, Denmark, where she is currently serving as head of Department; she is also visiting professor at CIRCLE, Lund University, Sweden. Her research interests cover the fields of the governance of science and innovation, and European Union governance, with special focus on innovation policy, innovation systems, the new modes of governance, the Lisbon strategy, the role of the Commission, and the patterns of coordination in the EU. Email address: sb.dbp@cbs.dk.

Arthur Daemmrich is an Associate Professor in the Department of History and Philosophy of Medicine at the University of Kansas School of Medicine. His research examines the institutional dynamics of globalization, with a focus on historical and comparative studies of healthcare systems, pharmaceutical regulation, and chemical testing programs. He has published in the history of medicine, science and technology studies, and health policy. He was previously an assistant professor at Harvard Business School and a visiting professor at the China Europe International Business School. He holds a Ph.D. from Cornell University and a B.A. from the University of Pennsylvania. Email address: adaemmrich@kumc.edu.

Aurélie Delemarle is in charge of the Industrial Engineering Department, Ecole des Ponts ParisTech. She is also affiliated to the Institute for Research and Innovation in Society (IFRIS). Her research interests focus on the dynamics of emerging science and technologies with a particular attention to the framing of markets for breakthrough innovations (with the notion of market infrastructures). Email address: aurelie.delemarle @enpc.fr.

Jakob Edler is Professor of Innovation Policy and Strategy and Executive Director of MIoIR (Manchester Institute of Innovation Research) at the Manchester Business School, University of Manchester. His fields of expertise comprise governance of science, technology and innovation systems, responsible research and innovation, analysis and conceptual development of RTDI policies and instrument, including demand based innovation policy, internationalisation of STI Policy and corporate innovation strategies. Jakob has advised the EU, OECD and a range of governments and has led numerous projects for several international funding bodies. In 2013, Jakob was elected to the German National Academy of Science and Engineering (acatech). Email address: Jakob.edler@mbs.ac.uk.

Stefan Kuhlmann is a Professor of Science, Technology, and Society at the University of Twente. Earlier he held positions at the University of Utrecht, the Fraunhofer Institute for Systems and Innovation Research, Karlsruhe, and the University of Kassel. His research is concerned with science and technological innovation as social and political processes, with a special focus on governance. He has published widely in the field of research and innovation policy studies and is, inter alia, editor of 'Research Policy'. Email address: s.kuhlmann@utwente.nl.

Philippe Larédo is Directeur de Recherche at Université de Paris-Est (Ecole des Ponts, IFRIS) and professor at the University of Manchester (MBS, Manchester Institute of Innovation Research). His research interests are on new emerging sciences and breakthrough innovation and on research and innovation policies. Recent work on the latter focuses on the development of new evaluation approaches for assessing societal impacts of public research, and on the development of 'positioning indicators' (with the coordination of a distributed European research infrastructure supported by the EC, RISIS, 2014-2017). Email address: philippe.laredo @enpc.fr.

Daniel Lehner has studied sociology and political science at the University of Vienna and has an ongoing PhD project in the field of political philosophy. He is currently working as an assistant for a Member of the Austrian Parliament. His research interests include the governance of 'Assisted Reproductive Technologies', contemporary political theory and political sociology, with special focus on questions of democracy, European politics and social movements. Email address: daniel.lehner@univie.ac.at.

Allison Loconto is a Research Fellow at the National Institute for Agricultural Research (INRA) and the Institute for Research, Innovation and Society (IFRIS), France; and Visiting Expert at the Food and Agriculture Organization of the United Nations (FAO), Italy. Her research interests include governance by standards, innovations in certification systems, regulatory intermediaries, social innovation and the governance of transitions towards sustainable agriculture. Email address: amloconto@versailles.inra.fr.

Jordi Molas-Gallart is Research Professor and Deputy Director at INGENIO, a research institute of the Spanish Council for Scientific Research (CSIC) and the Polytechnic University of Valencia. Before joining INGENIO, Jordi worked at SPRU, University of Sussex for 13 years. His research interests include the evaluation of science, technology and innovation policies, the use of indicators in evaluation processes, and the evolving characteristics of innovation in the defence industries. He is the author of one book, and of more than 80 articles, book chapters, monographs and reports. He is co-editor of Research Evaluation. Email address: jormoga@ingenio.upv.es.

Peter Stegmaier is Assistant Professor at the Department of Science, Technology, and Policy Studies, University of Twente, the Netherlands and assistant professeur associé at the Université du Luxembourg. He has been trained in sociology, psychology, law, and business studies. His research interests cover the sociologies of knowledge, normativities, and governance, the interactionist view on intermediary organisations and practices in science governance and on discontinuation governance of incumbent sociotechnical systems; furthermore, social theory and explorative-interpretive research methods, sociology of music, improvisation, and mundane phenomenology as proto-sociology. Email address: p.stegmaier@utwente.nl.

Etienne Vignola-Gagné is completing a doctoral thesis on the emergence of translational medicine advocacy and policies and their implications for biomedical innovation systems at the Department of Political Science, University of Vienna. He previously pursued undergraduate training in Science, Technology and Society and Master's training in Urban Studies in Montréal, Canada. Current projects deal with change in oncology clinical research systems in the wake of genomic sequencing advances; argumentative practices in science, technology and innovation policy-making; and the shaping of intellectual and professional trajectories in the life sciences by bibliometric evaluation practices. Email address: etiennevg@gmail.com.

Vincent R. Visser holds a master in 'Philosophy of Science, Technology and Society' and 'Public Administration'. He has an interest in the interactions between science, innovation and policy. For his last thesis project he did an explorative pilot study on the purposeful discontinuation governance of the incandescent light bulb in the EU, under the supervision of Stegmaier and Kuhlmann. At the moment, he is working as a junior lecturer at the Institute of Interdisciplinary Studies (IIS) at the University of Amsterdam. Email address: vincent.ruben.visser@gmail.com.

Preface

The idea behind this book emerged during an informal conversation during one of the coffee breaks at the first conference held by the EU-SPRI forum in Twente in late October 2010, in which we acknowledged some disappointment with the fact that the literature had not really come to grips with the different modes of governance of science and technology and, in particular, with the different ways in which the governance of change in socio-technical systems takes place. Set in motion by this fruitful and stimulating conversation, we arranged a series of further academic initiatives that shaped our discussions and helped to order our ideas a bit more. With funding from the Jean Monnet Center of Excellence at Copenhagen Business School we organized a workshop in Copenhagen in March 2012, entitled 'The Governance of Innovation and Socio-Technical Systems: Theorising and Explaining Change'. Our call for papers received 37 abstracts, far more than we were able to accommodate within our tight program and tight budget. Undaunted, we selected 17 papers. We also invited Alan Irwin and Frank Geels as keynote speakers, who generously shared their time and insights with us. The second opportunity to meet came a few months later, in October 2012, when the Copenhagen Business School hosted the 4S-EASST biannual conference. We seized the opportunity and arranged an open panel on the topic. This allowed us to engage with the broader community of scholars and to go further in our thinking. After this 'double Copenhagen shot' in 2012, we engaged in an intensive process of writing, re-writing and revision of all papers, including our opening chapters (Chapter 1 and Chapter 2) and the concluding Chapter during 2013 and onwards. When embarking in a collective effort and navigating in unknown waters, it takes time and considerable effort to generate synergy. It also takes time to think and re-think, to do and undo.

In this collective project we have discussed many times over the years what 'governance' is, what 'governance of change' is, and how we can analyze it in the complexity of socio-technical and innovation systems. Our thanks go to the team of researchers who worked on this book and to all the participants in our workshops and panels for their input in the project over the years. Our gratitude also goes to the colleagues who have commented extensively on our preliminary ideas, most especially, Jan-Peter Voss, Frank Geels, Alan Irwin, Fabian Schroth, Alexander Wentland as well as our colleagues at the Department of Business and Politics, and at the Manchester Institute of Innovation Research. We would like to thank Katy Roper from, and those at, Edward Elgar Publishing for their encouragement of this project and their patience awaiting its delivery; as well as Stefan Kuhlmann as editor of the new EU-SPRI series at EE, for giving us the opportunity to link our book to EU-SPRI. We are very happy to see this book being part of the EU-SPRI community, as it has benefited extensively from the scholarly work and debates at the annual EU-SPRI conferences in Twente, Karlsruhe, Madrid and Manchester. Last but not least, our special thanks go to Stefanie Edler-Wollstein and Kalle Stahl Nielsen for their extremely effective and efficient editing of the manuscript. Their extraordinary support during the last stages of the manuscript production made this project possible.

Susana Borrás and Jakob Edler
Frederiksberg, Denmark
Manchester, UK

Abbreviations

ACF	Advocacy-Coalition Framework
AKH	Vienna General Hospital of Vienna
ANF	Asia Nano Forum
ANT	Actor-Network Theory
ASC	Anna Spiegel Center
ASTM	American Society for Testing and Materials
BIPM	Bureau International des Poids et Mesures
	(International Bureau of Weights and Measures)
BMBF	German Science Ministry
	Federal Ministry of Education and Research
BMWF	Austrian Federal Ministry for Science and Research
CeMM	Research Center for Molecular Medicine of the
	Austrian Academy of Sciences
CEN	European Standardization Committee
CFL	Compact fluorescent lamp
CoC	Code of Conduct
COMET	Competence Centres for Excellent Technologies
DDT	Dichlorodiphenyltrichloroethane
DIN	Deutsches Institut für Normung
DiscGo	Governance of Discontinuation of Sociotechnical
	Systems
DLR	German Aerospace Centre
ECHA	European Chemicals Agency
EC-JRC	European Commission – Joint Research Centre
(IRMM)	(Institute for Reference Materials and Measurements)
ECOS	European Environmental Citizens Organisation for
	Standardisation
EHS	Environmental Health and Safety
ELC	European Lamps Companies Federation
ETUI	European Trade Union Institute
FDA	Food and Drug Administration
FFG	The Austrian Research Promotion Agency
FLO	Fairtrade International
FSC	Forest Stewardship Council

FWF	Austrian Science Fund
GBF	Gesellschaft für Biotechnologische Forschung
GE	genetic engineering
HACCP	Hazards and Critical Control Points
ICoN	International Council on Nanotechnology
IEC	International Electrotechnical Commission
IFOAM	International Forum of Organic Agriculture Movements
ILB	Incandescent light bulb
IOM	Institute of Medicine
ISEAL	International Social and Environmental Accreditation and Labelling
ISO	International Organization for Standardization
IUPAC	International Union of Pure and Applied Chemistry
JWG	Joint Working Group
MEEuP	Methodology for the Ecodesign of Energy-using Products
MLP	multi-level perspective
MSC	Marine Stewardship Council
MUV	Medical University of Vienna
nanoREACH	Registration, Evaluation, Authorization and Restriction of Chemical Substances at the nanoscale
NBER	National Bureau of Economic Affairs
NIH	US National Institutes of Health
OECD	Organisation for Economic Co-operation and Development
OECD – WPMN	Organisation for Economic Co-operation and Development, Working Party on Nanomaterials
ORA	Open Research Area
PBT	polybutylene terephthalate
PLT	Product Life-Cycle Theory
REACH	Registration, Evaluation, Authorisation and restriction of CHemicals
RTD	Research and Technology Development
SCOT	Social Construction of Technology
SDO	standards development organization
SIDS	screening information data set
ST&I	Socio-Technical and Innovation systems
STI	Science, Technology and Innovation
STIP	Science, Technology, Innovation, and Policy studies
STS	Science and Technology Studies

TAPPI	Technical Association for Pulp, Paper and related Industries
TC229	The Technical Committee 229 'nanotechnologies'
TG	Task Group
TR	Translational Research
TRAIN	Translational Research Alliance in Lower Saxony
TSR	Tripartite Standards Regime
USCC	US Composting Council
USDA	United States Department of Agriculture
VAMAS	The Versailles Project on Advanced Materials and Standards
WHO	World Health Organization
WTO	World Trade Organization
WWTF	Vienna Science and Technology Fund
ZIT	The Technology Agency of the City of Vienna Centre for Innovation and Technology of Vienna

1. Introduction: on governance, systems and change

Susana Borrás and Jakob Edler

1.1 INTRODUCTION

Why do we see so few electric cars on our streets today in spite of the overwhelming positive views on them? Why is it so difficult to introduce electronic patient journals in our hospitals or to phase out fossil-based energy sources? How come mobile telephones were developed and expanded so rapidly in the past two decades? How are integrated transport systems transforming commuting in large cities, and who contributes to that change? At a basic level these questions have to do with the way in which science and technology interact with society. It is commonplace today in social sciences literature that science, technology and society are constantly shaping each other in a truly co-constitutive process. However, these questions also have to do with the elements that form the socio-technical and innovation systems as well as with socio-cultural and economic aspects in the intentionality towards (or against) change. This book argues for the need for a better understanding of governance of change in socio-technical systems and innovation systems. It develops a conceptual framework to understand change and studies governance of change in a range of selected case studies that mobilize this framework.[1]

The notions 'socio-technical system' and 'innovation system' refer to the fact that individual technical artefacts or innovations are not operating in isolation. On the contrary, the functioning of technical artefacts and innovations is highly dependent on specific and complex ensembles of elements in which they are embedded. It is not the individual artefact or innovation as such that has an effect, but its interplay with and embedding in other technical and non-technical elements in society and the economy. To approach the issue, we start with a simple illustration of a socio-technical system: the electric car. The technical solutions for electric cars are developing very quickly (batteries, electric engines, software, and so on), as are the infrastructures for charging batteries and other support services. The development of the electric car system is highly dependent on the opportunities offered by new technical knowledge and consumer demands; by the regulations, soft laws and voluntary standards that frame safety, insurance conditions, and so on for electric cars; and by the societal acceptance and ultimate support to these changes. What we observe over the last decades is a painfully slow process of change towards the electric car system, despite claims of its greatly improved eco-efficiency. This simplified example illustrates the question this book is tackling, namely how the governance of change in socio-technical systems and innovation systems takes place.

It is our humble observation that the way in which the change in socio-technical systems and innovation systems (ST&I systems) is actually governed remains understudied in the social sciences. To be sure, there is a myriad of empirical studies examining the nature of ST&I systems, and the way in which individual artefacts and innovations interact in society and the economy. However, the literature has not come to grips with the intentional nature of the agents' actions that govern the change of these complex systems.[1] During the past decades different disciplines in the social sciences have analysed ST&I systems from very different angles. Scholars in STS (science and technology studies), economics and political science disciplines have been concerned with the complex micro- and macro-level dimensions of the relation between science/technology and society/economics/politics and their mutually shaping interactions. With few exceptions and happy encounters these different disciplinary approaches have run parallel to each other, tending to disregard each other's perspectives.

The various schools of economists have been interested in issues of the role of technical change in economic growth for a long time, at the level of the firm and at the level of national and regional economies. In particular, they have examined the way in which the creation of new knowledge influences the competitiveness of a firm or an economy, and how firms can foster their innovativeness and competitive position in global markets. Sociologists and anthropologists, mostly in the field of science and technology studies (STS), are interested in issues of the co-constitutive relationship between society and science, and in particular in scientific controversies and the critical social contestation of scientific progress. Political scientists for their part are interested in the politics associated with the design of science and innovation policies, the changing role of scientific expertise in advanced democracies, and the implementation, coordination and policy instrumentation of knowledge and innovation policies. These three disciplines in the social sciences have hardly ever explicitly and systematically addressed questions associated with the governance of change or governance altogether. In existing studies 'governance' is rarely the object of study as such, and if it is, it is typically mentioned in a loose manner, becoming a sort of catch-all notion with virtually no explanatory intention. To be sure, the literature on socio-technical and innovation systems offers several possible (largely implicit) understandings of 'governance', but hardly ever as an upfront object of study. This is probably because 'governance' and 'governance of change' do not have a clear conceptual underpinning, making it difficult to operationalize as an object of study in its own right. Hence, there is a need to take a step further and enable a theoretical and empirical advancement on what the processes of governing change are.

This book thus aims to make three contributions to the literature. First, this book will provide a coherent analytical framework based on conceptual clarification on the notion of governance and socio-technical and innovation systems. Our book will contribute by clarifying these crucial conceptual and analytical aspects of governance and governance of change.

Second, this book aims at providing some stepping stones for theory-building about governance of change. The literature offers many exciting empirical case studies on socio-technical systems' and innovation systems' patterns and dynamics, and also implicitly on the systems' governance. However, the eminently empirical nature of these studies has not lent itself towards taking the crucial step into higher levels of abstraction in the social sciences. This book aims at looking at the regularities associated with the governance of change that emanate both from the empirical cases and from core theoretical concepts of governance. This analytical framework for studying the governance of change – as a step towards theory-building – will be defined around the three lead questions above and will thus be based on three pillars, namely:

(1) the relation between opportunity structures and capable agents;
(2) the instrumentation through which intentional definitions of collective solutions are put into practice and
(3) the sources and hindrances of legitimacy in the process of governing change.

These three pillars will structure the theoretical considerations regarding the governance of change in more general and abstract terms and will also determine and structure the collection of empirical analysis of a set of very diverse cases.

Third, the book will bridge the gap between disciplinary fields. It aims at conducting a 'double movement' by bringing the governance approach (which is largely based on the discipline of political science) into the different social science studies on science and technology; and vice versa, bringing the ST&I system approaches into governance studies. This double movement is necessary not only in view of redressing a remarkable blind spot in the social sciences, but most importantly in view of identifying unexplored synergies in terms of the theory-building efforts mentioned above. The empirical area of ST&I systems is very rich and varied, given the broad nature of science and technology and its multiple forms of interaction in society and the economy. Studying how change is governed in these ST&I systems can provide very useful and rich empirical evidence that will help us to better understand the context in which governance operates in our advanced societies. By doing so, the book will contribute to an important mission of social studies of science, technology and innovation – underpinning empirical analyses of systems' change with a theory of governance of change – and at the same time it will further advance the understanding and conceptualization of govern-ance with broader implications for governance studies more generally.

The remainder of this chapter discusses the existing approaches to socio-technical or innovation systems in various strands of social science literature (see section 1.2). This discussion brings to the fore the commonalities, and above all, their differences in the various literature strands in terms of explanatory variables and axiomatic assumptions, particularly those that refer implicitly (or occasionally explicitly) to governance. We reveal the different bases of these theories according to whether they see ST&I systems as being anchored essentially in an economic and market context or a socio-cultural context, and which emphasis they put on the role of agency and the role of institutions. These differences have clear implications on the way the scholars have implicitly addressed issues associated with the governance of change in the systems. Hence, characterizing these approaches is important because while spelling out their alternative views on the systems' dynamics and change processes, the review will unveil the different implicit takes on the question of the governance of change.

After this literature discussion, we develop a working definition of ST&I systems (see section 1.3) and discuss the concept of governance of change (see section 1.4). When doing so, we realize that the notion of governance has been used with different meanings and connotations. While we do not need to analyse these different conceptualizations, as broad and valuable work already exists, we build on this work and present a workable definition in the context of ST&I systems, understanding 'governance of change' as the mechanisms by which societal and state actors intentionally interact and coordinate (see our full definition in section 1.4).

These three steps, discussing antecedents in different strands of literature, defining ST&I systems and then defining governance of change in ST&I systems, serve to demonstrate the need and prepare the ground for our own conceptualization of governance of change that we develop in Chapter 2 of this book. Once this is done, this introductory chapter presents the various case studies presented in the second part of the book.

1.2 SYSTEM, CHANGE AND GOVERNANCE: APPROACHES IN THE LITERATURE

During the past decades many social scientists have analysed the complex processes of science, technology and innovation in their wider context, as phenomena that are intrinsically social, economic and political. In spite of the widespread recognition that these processes are multi-dimensional, the bulk of this literature remains solidly anchored within their own disciplines. In a way, economists, STS scholars, sociologists and political scientists have, each of them on their own terms, developed 'systemic' approaches in their efforts to understand the changes and dynamics of socio-technical and innovation processes. Yet, they have done so in different ways. Reviewing this diversity will allow us to take a further step in developing some theoretical pillars about the governance of change in ST&I systems.

Within the field of economics, the notion of 'system' was coined by evolutionary and institutional economists in a direct challenge to the lineal process view of technical change suggested by neo-classical economists since the 1950s, which assumed a more or less natural and direct relation between the levels of private or public research investments and levels of innovative performance. Founded on notions of bounded rationality and asymmetric information, the evolutionary economists re-examined the role of technical change in economic growth theory, assigning it a central role, and dismantled the 'linear' view (Nelson and Winter, 1982; Dosi, Freeman et al., 1988). Overall, this literature introduced the ideas of evolutionary biology into economics, focusing on variation, selection and retention in the process of technological trajectories and the context conditions under which these processes evolve.

The notion of 'national' or 'regional' innovation systems emerged in the attempt to explain cross-national differences in innovative perform-ance (Lundvall, 1992; Nelson 1993; Braczyk et al., 1998). This was followed by a more knowledge and technology oriented approach under the terms 'technological systems' (Carlsson, 1997) and a more sector related variant with 'sectoral systems of innovation' (Malerba, 2004; Jacobsson and Bergek, 2004). There are some differences, however, regarding the 'narrow' or 'broad' views on systems (Edquist, 2005). Most relevant for us is that some authors put emphasis on the role of institutional frameworks as the rules of the game that shape the behaviour of innovators (Lundvall et al., 2002), whereas others put emphasis on the agents and their inter-organizational relations in networks (Freeman, 1995). As we will see below, this agency-institutional dichotomy on how systems change is not particular to the economic discipline, but extends to other disciplines studying socio-technical and innovation processes.

The literature on Science and Technology Studies (STS) has also dealt with the contextual embeddedness of science and technology in a different, yet related way. We agree with the view that the ontological assumptions of STS and evolutionary economics are 'sufficiently similar' to be considered in the same paper (Geels and Schot, 2010). Drawing from general sociological theories about social action and social systems, particularly from Giddens' structuration theory, the STS scholarly trad-ition has examined the complex and co-constitutive nature of social action and science-technology. The Actor-Network Theory (ANT) devel-oped by Callon and Latour focuses on the local dimension of tech-nological development through actors and networks co-existence (Callon and Law, 1989; Latour, 2005). This development tends to be local and highly ad-hoc, with large elements of heterogeneity and spontaneously organized processes of 'bricolage'. Another central theory in the field of STS is the social construction of technology (SCOT). In their seminal work Trevor Pinch and Wiebe Bijker study how technologies are devel-oped by focusing on social groups' interactions and the social meanings attached to the development of particular artefacts (Pinch and Bijker, 1987). However, it is worth noting that with some exceptions these two approaches within the STS community rarely make use of the notion 'system'. One might argue though, that beneath their understanding of technological development and change, the STS community shares the understanding that socio-technical systems are social systems formed by actors' interdependency relations, where technology and knowledge are recursively co-constituted and translated into meaningful action (Bijker et al., 1987).

However, one of the major differences between evolutionary-institutional economists and the STS scholarship is the tendency of the latter to focus on the socio-cultural context of socio-technical and innovation systems, in contrast to the more economic and market focus of the former. In other words, in spite of some commonalities in the ontological premises regarding agency and institutional frameworks shaping/being shaped by agency, the disciplinary traditions of the evolutionary economists and sociological background of STS continue to echo in their view of what constitutes the wider context of ST&I systems.

These remarks lead to the observation that in this vast literature there are at least two distinct dimensions through which these scholars conceptually approach the change of ST&I systems. The first dimension has to do with this difference, namely between those who focus on the market and economic context where socio-technical changes and innovation happens, and those who focus eminently on the socio-cultural context of such processes. Likewise, and as mentioned earlier, there is a second fundamental dimension that cuts across this large literature, namely the relative emphasis on the role of agency or on the role of institutions in processes of change. To be sure, agency refers here to the organizations and individuals that are agents of action in socio-technical and innovation processes. Institutions, for their part, are the formal or informal rules of the game constraining and enabling agents of socio-technical and innovation processes. This conceptual clarification, commonly accepted in most of the social sciences, allows us to see the analytical differences between those scholars focussing the analysis on individual agents' behaviour and the actual interactions and networks between them; and those putting the focus on the institutional 'rules of the game' as the main mechanism explaining changes in ST&I by means of changing agents' behaviour on what is possible or not.

These two dimensions must be seen as a continuum, rather than as completely separated axiomatic premises. Most of the literature includes agency and institutions, as well as socio-cultural and economic contexts at once. Hence, the differences in the literature reside on nuance and emphasis, rather than on the inclusion or exclusion of these elements. Keeping the gradual and nuanced emphasis on these elements in mind, table 1.1 illustrates the implicit way in which the literature has treated the governance of change in ST&I systems.

Table 1.1   The governance of change of socio-technical and innovation systems: implicit approaches in the literature

	Economy and market context	Socio-cultural context
Agency centred	Entrepreneurialism	Bricolage
Institution centred	Meta-coordination	Institutional coupling

Starting with the cell on the upper left side in Table 1.1, scholars emphasizing the role of agency and operating in contexts that are seen as primarily of economic and market nature tend to look at the change of ST&I systems as being related to the role of entrepreneurialism. Entrepreneurs are in fact key in Joseph Schumpeter's evolutionary view of the 'creative destruction' (Schumpeter, 2005/1942), later refined by evolutionary economists in the 1980s. Economists following this agency perspective tend to see change as the outcome of agents' intentionality (Cañibano et al., 2006) or the result of an explicit action from innovation networks (Schienstock and Hämäläinen, 2001; Freeman and Soete, 1997). Sociologists have also focused on agents' intentionality. One interesting work in this direction is the study by Hargadon and Douglas on the role of Edison. Their argument is that Edison's entrepreneurship generated change as he created robust designs to make a market breakthrough and the subsequent displacement of existing market alternatives socially acceptable (Hargadon and Douglas, 2001). This 'robust design' approach has been used in organizational studies on how the performance of technology-intensive entrepreneurial firms is affected by the design of their business models as boundary-spanning (Zott and Amit, 2007). Therefore, the literature with this agency/market context perspective implicitly tends to see the governance of change as the fruit of entrepreneurialism, or the specific set of entrepreneurial agents' actions and their successful individual 'design' of strategies of change, primarily taking place in the market place. In other words, governance by strong agents often means that economic entrepreneurs who, by carefully designing the introduction of socio-technical novelties and innovations in the market, in fact actively design the change of the entire system. These entrepreneurs might be strong individuals, like Edison, or strong innovation networks collaborating with the same purpose of change.

The second set of the literature, those stressing the role of agency in a more socio-cultural context, put less emphasis on individual entrepreneurs and more on the agents' collective embeddedness in wider set-ups. This is naturally the case in the ANT and SCOT literatures in the

STS scholarship, mentioned above, where the context of the market and the economy in processes of socio-technical relations and change is overshadowed by the socio-cultural aspects of agents' bricolage in terms of various forms of individual and ad-hoc sense-making by combining different elements. Other scholars in organizational sociology have discussed the central role of entrepreneurs as culturally embedded agents in networks who generate change by processes of path creation (rather than path dependency) (Garud and Karnøe, 2003). This relates nicely to a similar view on agents creating niches in a wider social and knowledge-based context (van den Belt and Rip, 1989). These niches can then become strategic pathways in the overall process of socio-technical change and innovation as they become devices that enable broader technological breakthroughs. This has been particularly stressed and analysed in the area of environmental sustainability and the related management of transitions towards sustainability (Nill and Kemp, 2009). More recently, several possible pathways towards transitions have defined several possible processes of change (Smith, Stirling et al., 2005; Geels and Schot, 2007). From this perspective we can say that these scholars implicitly consider the governance of change as the accumulation of specific successful niche solutions and of agents' bricolage.

The third set of the literature, according to our two dimensions, considers ST&I system changes as the result of transformations in the institutional set-up which is operating mainly in an economic context. This literature has taken the complementarity of different sets of institutions as its main explanatory variable. Inspired by the school of 'varieties of capitalism' in the field of comparative political economy, which looks at different modes of coordinating institutions in capitalist economies (Hall and Soskice, 2001), scholars of innovation systems argue that specific forms of institutional complementarities are behind innovative performance and overall socio-technical change (Coriat and Weinstein, 2004; Casper and Soskice, 2004). This is essentially a national or regional perspective on innovation systems, as these institutions are complementary to each other and to the specific knowledge basis of the industrial specialization in a given territory (Asheim and Coenen, 2006). However, the theoretical assumption that liberal market economies (UK, USA, and so on) innovate more radically than coordinated market economies (Germany, France, Austria, and so on) has been empirically challenged (Akkermans et al., 2009). Closely linked with the institutional complementarities axiom is the recent functionalist turn in the innovation systems literature (Edquist, 2005; Hekkert et al., 2007; Bergek et al., 2008). These authors argue that the institutions in a socio-technical and innovation system perform specific functions to enable innovation generation and application (Hekkert et al., 2007). Changes in the nature of the system and its performance are largely related to the (transforming) functional dynamics of the institutions in the system. Taken together, it can be stated that the varieties of capitalism and functionalist scholars view the governance of change as the meta-coordination of the institutions' complementary performance in socio-economic terms.

Last but not least, the fourth perspective, the one based on institutional driving forces in a socio-cultural context, has looked mostly at the role of institutions in innovation systems, and conducted institutional analysis of socio-technical change processes. As with the other approaches, this is not a fully-fledged theory of socio-technical change and innovation process, but rather an analytical approach with a meso-level theoretical range. In this sense, this literature looks at 'how the institutional make up of a society impacts on its innovativeness' (Hollingsworth, 2000, p. 595). Other than considering the structure and cohesion of the institutional set-up, Hollingsworth also takes into consideration the structure and culture of its organizations, as a crucial factor in innovation processes. In a similar vein, the transition approach has initially focused on institutionally-driven evolutionary changes in a broad socio-cultural context (Kemp et al., 2001; Geels, 2002). Recent approaches to institutional analysis of innovation systems have a dynamic view on institutions, as not only do they change through time, but they are also subject to strategic action from the part of agents (Rohracher et al., 2008). These authors see socio-technical and innovation system change as 'institutional coupling', a process used by actors for the alignment and embedding of their strategies. This has assisted the authors in bringing their views closer to the transitions approach (Markard and Truffer, 2008), which examines different transition pathways in the system depending on institutional features in the economy and technologies themselves (Dolata, 2009). These scholars have recently started to examine the issue of the governance of the transitions towards more environmental sustainable socio-technical systems (Kern and Howlett, 2009; Shove and Walker, 2010) and they generally see the governance of change in terms of institutional coupling, or the purposive management of the system's overall institutional set-up towards specific and pre-defined collective goals (that is, sustainability).

1.3 THE NATURE OF SOCIO-TECHNICAL AND INNOVATION SYSTEMS

In our initial example at the onset of Chapter 1, we illustrated the main idea of socio-technical and innovation systems. More formally, we can define socio-technical and innovation systems as:

> *Articulated ensembles of social and technical elements which interact with each other in distinct ways, are distinguishable from their environment, have developed specific forms of collective knowledge production, knowledge utilization and innovation, and which are oriented towards specific purposes in society and economy.*

The main elements of a system are new knowledge and technological artefacts, the individual and organisational actors that produce, adopt, diffuse and use knowledge and technological artefacts, as well as the various forms of infrastructure (physical, market, financial, regulatory, etc) that enable that production, adoption, diffusion and use of knowledge and technological artefacts. Crucially, it is the interactions between those elements that constitute the system. These interactions among the constitutive elements of a system are complex and recurring, stabilising the system and creating specific dynamics. While elements of a system interact with other systems, we can nevertheless define boundaries of a specific system, beyond which interactions and inter-relations are less dense and less relevant for the underlying socio-technical system's purpose. This follows Metcalf (2003) in that to understand systems we need to understand that they are not only defined by their components and the information flow between those components, but that the nature of systems and their internal relations are related to their specific purpose (Metcalf, 2003, p. 65).

There is a range of well-known reasons why ST&I systems become unstable, are changing or are under pressure to change. The production of knowledge and innovation itself is inherently uncertain, we cannot know in which direction technological advancement will go. Equally, there is uncertainty and societal contestation as regards the opportunities and threats that new knowledge and innovation offer for users, for producers and citizens more generally. Pressures for change do not only stem from scientific and technological advancement and the effects actors associate with it, but from a change of societal preferences and a re-interpretation of what the problems and opportunities of new knowledge are and to what ends innovation shall contribute to them. This leads to new demands for certain technological solutions or to the discontinuation of the applications of certain technologies. These demands, however, are often not clear cut and straightforward, exactly because of the uncertain nature of technological and knowledge advancement, because actors and organizations have ambiguous experiences and conflicting expectations themselves as to the contribution of new knowledge and technology to future challenges, and because of the very heterogeneity of societal preferences.

This discussion highlights the importance of the social dimension of ST&I systems. Individuals and organizations have an existing body of knowledge, skills and routines, and they have vested interests, different value systems, take advantage of existing ST&I systems in varied ways and interpret potential change differently. Actors are reflexive, that is, they are conscious about the functioning (or lack thereof) of the ST&I system in relation to its purpose and assign a certain value to its outcomes and elements; all of which has an influence on the way in which society organizes itself, producing and making use of new scientific and technical knowledge. When it comes to change, different stakeholders will attribute different kinds of benefits and costs to new knowledge and innovation, with some actors pushing for change, while others resist, some engaging in change debates, raising their voices and investing resources, while others are passive, choosing not to invest in the debates on change and subsequent change dynamics or are unable to make their voices heard and influence the direction of change. This is a crucial point of departure: the conscious, intentional action of agents, in terms of taking advantage of an existing ST&I system features, in terms of trying to change it, and/or in terms of trying to prevent change from happening.

1.4 THE GOVERNANCE OF CHANGE

As mentioned earlier in this chapter, the literature has generally dealt with the issues of governance of change in the system in an indirect and implicit way. Hence, there remains a considerable conceptual indeterminacy in the literature about what is the governance of change in ST&I systems. Reducing this conceptual indeterminacy of the term will provide a necessary foundation for the development of a conceptual framework to understand governance of change and the subsequent analytical use of the term in the study of this phenomenon.

Our entry point is the origin of the term 'governance' in political science. Despite the diversity of approaches, there are some commonalities in the political science literature on governance. In contrast to the approach on 'steering' by the state, the governance approach of the early 1980s pointed at the fact that an increasing number of empirical cases showed that political institutions have limited capabilities to 'steer' because social systems have dynamics that are determined by all kinds of institutional, cultural, technological and other factors. This observation led to another commonality of governance approaches in political science, namely, that systems are not influenced or changed through political institutions alone (as in 'steering'), but by the interplay of societal and state actors (Benz, 2003; Mayntz, 2003). This means that the boundaries of state and non-state action are becoming blurred (Héritier and Lehmkuhl, 2008; Lyall and Tait, 2005). Some authors tend to see the emergence of new (reflexive) forms of governance as an implicit criticism to specific forms of modern production and social organization (Voss and Kemp, 2006).

To develop our understanding and definition of governance of change in ST&I systems, we want to make two propositions.

First, a general definition of governance must include societal actors, but it must also not neglect the possibility of hierarchical governance mechanisms. Hence, we need to look at two dimensions, namely, the nature of the actors (state or non-state actors) and the nature of the coordination (ranging from hierarchical to non-hierarchical). Table 1.2 represents these two dimensions, depicting the breadth of different modes of 'governance'. The two by two matrix, obviously, is a heuristic simplification of a much more nuanced picture with gradual moves along both dimensions. It represents what is commonly perceived as the broad notion of governance, or 'the multiplicity of *all* forms (processes and structures) of collective regulation of issues of societal relevance, ranging from institutionalized self-regulation of civil society to all forms of interaction and coordination of private and state actors and finally including hierarchical action of state actors' (Mayntz, 2003, p. 72).

Table 1.2   Stylized typology of governance modes

	Driven by state actors	Driven by societal actors
Hierarchical, dominated	Command and control	Oligopoly
Heterarchical, non-dominated	State as primus inter pares	Self-regulation

Our working definition of governance in general is in line with this broad notion, that is, governance as the mechanisms whereby societal actors and state actors interact and coordinate to regulate issues of societal concern. This definition implies that the role of the state can, in the extreme, be minimal ('self-regulation'). This is close to the definition of Peters who defines governance as a particular form of political steering where public sector and private sector in conjunction are capable of providing direction and control to society and economy (Peters, 2012).

Our second proposition is that we need a concept of the governance of change that puts emphasis on the intentionality of different types of actors fostering (or preventing) change. As mentioned earlier in this paper, economists, STS scholars and political scientists are concerned with different aspects of governance in socio-technical systems in a way that puts little explicit focus on the different modes of governing change (described in Table 1.1), and hence on the different forms of agent's expression of intentionality in the various modes of governance. Naturally, in situations in which state actors are driving forces fostering change in a socio-technical system, its intentionality will be expressed in terms of political and bureaucratic strategies and public statements; whereas in situations in which societal actors drive change, that intentionality might be much more diffused and difficult to grasp. To be sure, in a wide concept of 'governance' like ours, the change in a ST&I system might almost always be 'governed' by one or another type of actors and by interaction of actors. But there might be situations in which the self-regulation of change is done in such a diffused coordinated form and by a widely decentralized number and type of actors without any presence of state-actors, that it might be difficult to determine the expression of intentionality in the 'governance' of the change that took place in that ST&I system. Besides, the intentionality of some actors is naturally always contested and hence, the direction that the governance of change (or non-change) takes depends ultimately on political power and economic dominance.

These two propositions lead us to our understanding and definition of governance of change in ST&I systems. In our view, a basic definition of governance of change in ST&I systems is needed and possible. Hence, our working definition of governance of change in ST&I systems is the way in which societal and state actors intentionally interact in order to transform ST&I systems, by regulating issues of societal concern, defining the processes and direction of how technological artefacts and innovations are produced, and shaping how these are introduced, absorbed, diffused and used within society and economy.

This definition needs four further qualifications. First, and without entering into a long discussion regarding the nature of social ontology, it is important for us to mention that the 'intentional' nature of action does not mean we see actors as rational in terms of utility-maximizing their interests. What we are saying is that in the processes of governing change in socio-technical systems, agents have different intentions and considerations according to what they see as desirable or non-desirable 'change', and that these intentions and considerations might be anchored in what March and Olsen see as the logic of consequentiality or the logic of appropriateness (March and Olsen, 1989).

Second, we have made a very conscious choice to define governance as intentional interaction (and coordination) towards some end. We concede that many scholars, especially in the STS tradition, have a broader view of governance of change, including all informal and formal interactions of actors that contribute to transformation, no matter if there is explicit intentionality or not. In this interpretation, all interaction that contributes to or influences change – no matter if actors are conscious and intentional about it – still contributes to governance. While we concede that change of ST&I systems can be spontaneous, 'unguided' and 'ungoverned', in our approach we are interested in governance, that is the way in which actors trigger, seek to influence change or avoid change in ST&I systems. This does not preclude that there are change dynamics that are not governed (that is, not driven by intentional actors). But even in those situations, one can fruitfully analyse the absence of intentionality, the absence of any meaningful intention to stop, alter or accelerate change in socio-technical systems, and thus the failure of actors in a system to purposefully shape the future state of a ST&I system. To label 'governance' any kind of social interaction that leads to some kind of change would render the very concept of governance meaningless. As we do not want to understand dynamics of change per se, but the way in which change is intentionally influenced, we are compelled to include intentionality as a constitutive element of our governance definition.

Third and related to the above, we speak of governance of change, if the governance has made a difference, if there is some sort of transformation in a given ST&I system. This transformation can be judged 'good' or 'bad' by different actor groups, it can contribute more or less to define and solve societal problems. The normative content of the transformation (that is, the outcome of the governance process) as well as the normativity of the process of governance are matters of judgement and not directly relevant for our definition. What is important is the fact that intentional action has transformed something. However, this includes intentional action to stop change that is underway from happening, that is, the transformation here lies in influencing a trajectory, in terminating a specific opportunity for a system to develop in certain directions, triggered by advances in knowledge or by interested stakeholder groups or any other trigger.

Fourth, we understand that governance of change, defined as intentional interaction, might produce tensions between actors (Borrás, 2012). Those tensions originate in different material interests, normative values and perceptions of what change means in relation to specific interests and values. This means that the governance of change might ultimately be related to the exercise of certain forms of political power and economic dominance, reflecting actors' differences in their ability to mobilize resources and support when influencing change (or preventing it). In other words, the tensions and contestations are enhanced in the very process of governance, as governance ultimately entails notions of economic dominance and political power. In some countries and contexts (unfortunately not all) the first is based on fair market competition and the second on democratic processes.

1.5   THE CONTENTS OF THIS BOOK

The book is organized in the following way: Chapter 2 outlines the basic concept of three pillars to understand the governance of change in socio-technical and innovation systems. It develops the building blocks for a conceptual framework of the governance of change in socio-technical and innovation systems (socio-technical systems) by identifying three conceptual pillars: the opportunity structures and capable agents, governance instrumentation and democratic legitimacy. These pillars constitute the theoretical foundations on which a set of specific assumptions to understand the governance of change are developed.

This approach sets the scene for the individual case study contributions of the book. This collection represents a broad variety of different socio-technical systems, discussing different manifestations and combinations of the pillars, and different stories of change and its governance.

Arthur Daemmrich's Chapter 3 on anticipatory markets and technical standards in the development of biodegradable plastics argues that standards are instrumental to the co-production of social systems and markets for new technologies. Standards for novel materials can reduce consumer mistrust and strengthen product claims made by manufacturers. Managed by private organizations rather than government agencies, standardization involves negotiations among experts from industry, government and academic institutions. Daemmrich argues that especially in the course of setting standards for new environmental technologies, these agents undertake a process characterized here as anticipatory market building in which they envision product lifecycles, including raw material sourcing and the manufacture, purchase, use and disposal of products. The case study of BASF's biodegradable plastic Ecoflex sheds light on situations in which the co-production of technology and social institutions is challenged by consumer behaviour which does not align to expectations embedded in the standards. Standardization functions as an open opportunity structure for socio-technical innovation, compared to more rigorous but less flexible environmental or consumer product safety regulation. Technical standardization thus operates as a powerful but flexible instrument for governing change.

In Chapter 4, Allison Loconto and Marc Barbier continue with a focus on standards as governance instruments, focusing on their role in the transition towards sustainability. They start with the observation that a variety of sustainability standards have emerged from social movements that stake claims on different niches in the market for sustainable food and agriculture products. They see the beginning of a transition towards a regime of 'certified sustainability' which is characterized by the use of standards to govern agri-food systems and a second layer of standards to govern the standards. They ask how this regime is constructed and how standards are used to govern the transition to sustainability. Drawing upon a case study of the International Social and Environmental Accreditation and Labelling (ISEAL) Alliance's assurance code development process, they highlight the framing practices that characterize the shape of a multi-layered governance of 'governing by standards'. They discuss how the framing of certified sustainability opens up new issues like the relationship between credibility and legitimacy, the embodiment of skills in auditors or the call for evidence-based systems in order to tame risk.

Chapter 5, by Barberá-Tomás and Molas-Gallart, addresses the dynamic relationship between regulation as a governance instrument and technological change. More particularly, the authors focus on health regulation instruments and their role in shaping the dynamic evolution of medical technologies. By looking at the evolution of a specific technology (hip prosthesis) in the US, they show a dynamic relationship between technical change and regulatory frameworks. Regulatory frameworks are key instruments for the governance of change in socio-technical systems, but the previous literature has typically addressed it from a static perspective. Chapter 5 looks instead at the dynamic interplay between regulatory frameworks and technical change from the perspective of a product life cycle approach. Their case study shows how regulatory frameworks based on assumptions about how radical and incremental innovations are related to risk, lead to undesirable and unexpected outcomes. The history of the hip prosthesis shows how incremental innovation can become riskier and ultimately fail once a technology has entered the mature stages of its evolution. The regulatory framework, which was biased in favour of incremental innovation, prevented more radical innovations in product development.

Stegmaier, Kuhlmann and Visser take a different perspective when looking at the change of systems. They do not focus on the emergence of a new system, but on the governance of the discontinuation of socio-technical systems or regimes. Their lead question is how discontinuation governance targeted at socio-technical systems or regimes can be grasped in its quality and scope. To answer this question, they develop an understanding of 'discontinuation' as purposeful governance action *sui generis* in socio-technical contexts. Their contribution aims at a theoretically driven analysis in the context of science, technology, innovation and policy studies (STIP) and governance and policy studies, looking for junctions and gaps from which the concept 'governance of the discontinuation of socio-technical systems' can be further developed. Stegmaier, Kuhlmann and Visser develop a heuristic of how socio-technical systems can be brought to a halt. They illustrate their approach with the example of the deliberate, purposeful exit from the production and/or usage of incandescent light bulbs in the EU within the framework of the European Commission's eco-design directive.

In Chapter 7, Translational Research: entrepreneurship, advocacy and programmatic work in the governance of biomedical innovation, Vignola-Gagné, Biegelbauer and Lehner focus on change not of entire socio-technical systems, but of key components of those systems, that is, the experimental and organizational practices in research programmes and organizations. Based on empirical case studies of biomedical innovation systems reform they trace the role of selected parameters in this process of transforming existing practices, namely: (1) programmatic statements; (2) their advocacy by entrepreneurs and (3) their interplay with existing and new policy instruments in explaining the governance of socio-technical change. Chapter 7 thus focuses on purposeful actors and research programming as an instrument to drive this change through learning processes. By doing so, the authors add some explanatory power for socio-technical change where policy design and implementation are defining parameters of the process.

Finally, in Chapter 8, Delemarle and Laredo investigate the processes of governing radical change as the development of accepted market infrastructure in an emerging technology, nanotechnology. They conceptualize market infrastructures as the necessary conditions for change, which are in turn developed through the interplay of rules, values and norms. They argue that the market infrastructures are constructed in a number of different but inter-connected arenas, which they define as settings in which 'individual and collective actors interact to define the cognitive and normative dimensions of a problem' (Bonneuil et al., 2008, p. 204). The authors look at five arenas in nanotechnologies, that is, a standard setting body, a working party in the OECD, the international Council on Nanotechnology, the European Code of Conduct for responsible nanosciences and nanotechnologies research and NanoREACH. Delemarle and Laredo show how the market infrastructures developed in the various arenas together form the overall novel governance architecture which then determines the overall direction – and the limits – of market development and change. Chapter 8 develops an exploratory concept to understand what determines the success of arenas to contribute to the overall governance architecture to establish markets for emerging technologies. In doing so, it contributes to a better understanding of the legitimacy and effectiveness of governance processes and instruments.

In a final concluding essay in Chapter 9, Borrás and Edler reflect on how the various chapters mobilize and further enrich the three pillar framework, and how on that basis the theoretical concept should be developed further in the future.

NOTE

1. This book studies the governance of change in socio-technical systems and in innovation systems. For easier reading, the rest of the book will refer to ST&I systems. Occasionally the book might refer only to 'socio-technical systems' or 'innovation systems'. However, it is the intention of the authors to include both systems as an object of study in the conceptual framework put forward by this book.

REFERENCES

Akkermans, D., C. Castaldi and B. Los (2009), 'Do "liberal market economies" really innovate more radically than "coordinated market economies"?: Hall and Soskice reconsidered', *Research Policy*, **38** (1), 181–191.

Asheim, B. and L. Coenen (2006), 'Contextualising regional innovation systems in a globalising learning economy: On knowledge bases and institutional frameworks', *The Journal of Technology Transfer*, **31** (1), 163–173.

Benz, A. (2003), 'Governance – Modebegriff oder nützliches sozialwissenschaftliches Konzept?', in A. Benz (ed.), *Governance. Eine Einführung*, Dreifachkurseinheit der Fernuniversität Hagen, Hagen: Universität Hagen, pp. 13–31.

Bergek, A., S. Jacobsson, B. Carlsson, S. Lindmark and A. Rickne (2008), 'Analyzing the functional dynamics of technological innovation systems: A scheme of analysis', *Research Policy*, **37** (3), 407–429.

Bijker, W. E., T. P. Hughes and T. J. Pinch (eds) (1987), *The Social Construction of Technological Systems: New Directions in the Sociology and History of Technology*, Boston: MIT Press.

Bonneuil, C., P.-B. Joly and C. Marris (2008), 'Disentrenching experiment: The construction of GM – crop field trials as a social problem', *Science, Technology & Human Values*, **33** (2), 201–229.

Borrás, S. (2012), 'Three tensions in the governance of science and technology', in D. Levi-Faur (ed.), *Oxford Handbook of Governance*, Oxford: Oxford University Press, pp. 429–440.

Braczyk, H.-J., P. Cooke and M. Heidenreich (eds) (1998), *Regional Innovation Systems*, London: UCL Press.

Callon, M. and J. Law (1989), 'On the construction of sociotechnical networks: Content and context revisited', in R. A. Jones, L. Hargens and A. Pickering (eds), *Knowledge and Society, Vol 8: Studies in the Sociology of Science Past and Present*, Greenwich, CT: JAI Press, pp. 57–83.

Cañibano, C., M.-I. Encinar and F.-F. Muñoz (2006), 'Evolving capabilities and innovative intentionality: some reflections on the role of intention within innovation processes', *Innovation: Management, Policy & Practice*, **8** (4), 310–321.

Carlsson, B. (ed.) (1997), *Technological Systems and Industrial Dynamics*, Strasbourg: Springer.

Casper, S. and D. Soskice (2004), 'Sectoral systems of innovation and varieties of capitalism: Explaining the development of high-technology entrepreneurship in Europe', in F. Malerba (ed.), *Sectoral Systems of Innovation*, Cambridge: Cambridge University Press, pp. 348–386.

Coriat, B. and O. Weinstein (2004), 'National institutional frameworks, institutional complementarities and sectoral systems of innovation' in F. Malerba (ed.), *Sectoral Systems of Innovation*, Cambridge: Cambridge University Press, pp. 325–346.

Dolata, U. (2009), 'Technological innovations and sectoral change: Transformative capacity, adaptability, patterns of change: An analytical framework', *Research Policy*, **38** (6), 1066–1076.

Dosi, G., C. Freeman, R. R. Nelson, G. Silverberg and L. Soete, (eds) (1988), *Technical Change and Economic Theory*, London: Pinter.

Edquist, C. (2005), 'Systems of innovation, perspectives and challenges', in J. Fagerberg, D. C. Mowery and R. R. Nelson (eds), *The Oxford Handbook of Innovation*, Oxford: Oxford University Press, pp. 181–208.

Freeman, C. (1995), 'The national innovation systems in historical perspective', *Cambridge Journal of Economics*, **19** (1), 5–24.

Freeman, C. and L. Soete (1997), *The Economics of Industrial Innovation*, London: Routledge.

Garud, R. and P. Karnøe (2003), 'Bricolage versus breakthrough: Distributed and embedded agency in technology entrepreneurship', *Research Policy*, **32** (2), 277–300.

Geels, F. W. (2002), 'Technological transitions as evolutionary reconfiguration processes: A multi-level perspective and a case-study', *Research Policy*, **31** (8-9), 1257–1274.

Geels, F. W. and J. Schot (2007), 'Typology of sociotechnical transition pathways', *Research Policy*, **36** (3), 399–417.

Geels, F. W. and J. W. Schot (2010), 'Theoretical backgrounds: Science and technology studies, evolutionary economics and sociology', in J. Grin, J. Rotmans, J. Schot, F. W. Geels and D. Loorbach (eds), *Transitions to Sustainable Development: New Directions in the Study of Long-Term Transformative Change*, London: Routledge, pp. 29–53.

Hall, P. A. and D. Soskice (eds) (2001), *Varieties of Capitalism. The Institutional Foundations of Comparative Advantage*, Oxford: Oxford University Press.

Hargadon, A. B. and Y. Douglas (2001), 'When innovations meet institutions: Edison and the design of the electric light', *Administrative Science Quarterly*, **46** (3), 476–501.

Hekkert, M. P., R. A. A. Suurs, S. O. Negro, S. Kuhlmann and R. E. H. M. Smits (2007), 'Functions of innovation systems: A new approach for analysing technological change', *Technological Forecasting and Social Change*, **74** (4), 413–432.

Héritier A. and D. Lehmkuhl (2008), 'The shadow of hierarchy and new modes of governance', *Journal as Public Policy*, **28** (1), 1–17.

Hollingsworth, J. R. (2000), 'Doing institutional analysis: implications for the study of innovations', *Review of International Political Economy*, **7** (4), 595–644.

Jacobsson, S. and A. Bergek (2004), 'Transforming the energy sector: The evolution of technological systems in renewable energy technology', *Industrial and Corporate Change*, **13** (5), 815–849.

Kemp, R., A. Rip and J. Schot (2001), 'Constructing transition paths through the management of niches', in R. Garud and P. Karnøe (eds), *Path Dependence and Creation*, Mahwah, NJ: Lawrence Erlbaum, pp. 269–297.

Kern, F. and M. Howlett (2009), 'Implementing transition management as policy reforms: A case study of the Dutch energy sector', *Policy Sciences*, **42** (4), 391–408.

Latour, B. (2005), *Reassembling the Social. An Introduction to Actor-Network Theory*, Oxford: Oxford University Press.

Lundvall, B.-Å. (ed) (1992), *National Systems of Innovation: Towards a Theory of Innovation and Interactive Learning*, London: Pinter.

Lundvall, B.-Å., B. Johnson, E. S. Andersen and B. Dalum (2002), 'National systems of production, innovation and competence building', *Research Policy*, **31**, 213–231.

Lyall, C. and J. Tait (eds) (2005), *New Modes of Governance: Developing an Integrated Policy Approach to Science, Technology, Risk and the Environment*, Aldershot: Ashgate Publishing.

Malerba, F. (ed.) (2004), *Sectoral Systems of Innovation: Concepts, Issues and Analyses of Six Major Sectors in Europe*, Cambridge: Cambridge University Press.

March, J. G. and J. P. Olsen (1989), *Rediscovering Institutions: The Organizational Basis of Politics*, New York, NY: The Free Press.

Markard, J. and B. Truffer (2008), 'Technological innovation systems and the multi-level perspective: Towards an integrated framework', *Research Policy*, **37** (4), 596–615.

Mayntz, R. (2003), 'Governance im modernen staat', in A. Benz (ed.), *Governance, Eine Einführung,* Dreifachkurseinheit der Fernuniversität Hagen, Hagen: Universität Hagen, pp. 71–83.

Metcalf, J. S. (2003), 'System failure and the case for innovation policy', in P. Llerena and M. Matt (eds), *Innovatoni Policy in a Knowledge-Based Economy. Theory and Practice*, Strasbourg: Springer, pp. 47–74.

Nelson, R. R. (ed.) (1993), *National Innovation Systems: A Comparative Analysis*, Oxford: Oxford University Press.

Nelson, R. R. and S. G. Winter (1982), *An Evolutionary Theory of Economic Change*, Cambridge, MA: Harvard U.P.

Nill, J. and R. Kemp (2009), 'Evolutionary approaches for sustainable innovation policies: From niche to paradigm?', *Research Policy*, **38** (4), 668–680.

Peters, G. B. (2012), 'Governance as Political Theory', in D. Levi-Faur (ed.), *Oxford Handbook on Governance*, Oxford: Oxford University Press, pp. 19–32.

Pinch, T. and W. E. Bijker (1987), 'The social construction of facts and artifacts: Or how the sociology of science and the sociology of technology might benefit each other', in W. E. Bijker, T. P. Hughes and T. Pinch (eds), *The Social Construction of Technological Systems: New Directions in the Sociology and History of Technology*, Cambridge, MA: MIT Press, 17–50.

Rohracher, H., B. Truffer and J. Markard (2008), 'Doing institutional analysis of innovation systems. A conceptual framework', *Dime Working Paper*, available at www.dime-eu.org/files/active/0/Truffer_Institutional%20Analysis_Aug08.pdf.

Schienstock, G. and T. Hämäläinen (2001), *The Transformation of the Finnish Innovation System: A Network Approach*, Helsinki: SITRA.

Schumpeter, J. A. (2005/1942), *Capitalism, Socialism and Democracy*, London: Routledge.

Shove, E. and G. Walker (2010), 'Governing transitions in the sustainability of everyday life', *Research Policy*, **39** (4), 471–476.

Smith, A., A. Stirling and F. Berkhout (2005), 'The governance of sustainable socio-technical transitions', *Research Policy*, **34** (10), 1491–1510.

van den Belt, H. and A. Rip (1989), 'The Nelson-Winter-Dosi model and synthetic dye chemistry', in W. E. Bijker, P. T. Hughes and T. J. Pinch (eds), *The Social Construction of Technological Systems: New Directions in the Sociology and History of Technology*, Cambridge, MA: MIT Press.

Voss, J.-P. and R. Kemp (2006), 'Sustainability and reflexive governance: An introduction', in J.-P. Voss, D. Bauknecht and R. Kemp (eds), *Reflexive Governance for Sustainable Development*, Cheltenham, UK and Northampton, MA, USA: Edward Elgar, pp. 3–28.

Zott, C. and R. Amit (2007), 'Business model design and the performance of entrepreneurial firms', *Organization Science*, **18** (2), 181–199.

2. The governance of change in socio-technical and innovation systems: three pillars for a conceptual framework

Susana Borrás and Jakob Edler

2.1 INTRODUCTION: THREE PILLARS FOR A CONCEPTUAL FRAMEWORK

Chapter 1 reviewed succinctly the implicit views on governance in the vast literature dedicated to socio-technical change, identified the research gaps associated with conceptual indeterminacy, and clarified and defined a workable notion of 'governance of change in innovation and socio-technical systems'. In this chapter we turn to the exercise of preliminarily developing what we see as a basis for a conceptual framework. With this purpose in mind, we suggest focusing on three pillars: the opportunity structures and capable agents in a system, the instrumentation of governance of change, and the legitimacy and acceptance of change. The reader might immediately ask: why these three and not others? Naturally, this precise line up and combination of pillars is a subjective choice from our side. However, we have two overall arguments for this choice. First, while all three items or pillars can be found already in the literature in various forms, they have never been defined together as part of a consolidated analytical framework focused on the governance of change. Bringing them together not only makes the existing different dimensions of this complex phenomenon of system change more explicit, but gives emphasis to specific axioms that have rarely been put forward and upon which these previous studies are based. We do not imply that all different approaches can be simply juxtaposed. Instead, we aim at putting forward a consistent conceptual framework which allows us to focus on a limited number of dimensions that we think are crucial to understanding the governance of change. Second, and perhaps most relevant for our endeavours, the three pillars together provide a comprehensive view of the key 'governance'-related research question about how system change is coordinated in complex contexts, that is, what are the modes and actors of coordination. The first and second pillars focus on the actual action of the governance of change (opportunity structures and capable agents, as well as instrumentation), the 'who' and 'how' of governance. The third pillar refers to the popular views and support of the socio-technical system (or lack thereof), and to the process of governing change.

The first pillar of our theoretical endeavour deals with:

(1)   the opportunity structures which are offered by the interplay of a specific institutional set-up in a system on the one hand, and new technologies and knowledge on the other hand, and
(2)   with agents' capacity to navigate in complex contexts and align positions for a system change.

This relates to the perennial agency-institution interaction within a system, which is particularly important in processes of governing system change. The second pillar is the governance instrumentation in processes of change of socio-technical systems. The notion of 'governance' brings forward the understanding that collective action entails complex forms of public-private interactions. These interactions are typically conceptualized as 'governance instruments', which have the explicit intention to shape social action in specific ways. Under this prism, governance instruments are the mechanisms put forward by different sets of actors in order to achieve specific goals and therefore are a concretization of the overall opportunity structures mentioned above. The third pillar has to do with the legitimacy and democracy aspects of socio-technical and innovation systems and the process of governing their change. This is a fundamental aspect of governance as a collective social process. Our definition of governance of change underlined the notion of actors' interaction and coordination to regulate issues of societal concern. We see actors as the object and subject of this collective coordination. For that reason we are fully aware of the importance of popular support and of the scientific controversies that can surround processes of governing socio-technical change. We are equally aware that in democratic societies the input forms of legitimacy through representation and participation channels are as important as the output forms of legitimacy in creating effective solutions to real collective problems.

Our analytical point of departure is twofold: first, we believe that these three pillars can provide a clear set of separated analytical tools that allow for opening the 'black box' to analyse processes of governing change in systems. Seen this way, examining each of the pillars one by one can provide a focused study of essential parts that constitute the complex phenomenon of governing change in socio-technical systems. In this sense, each of the pillars allows us to ask questions about the nature and dynamics of change and governance of change, that is, about the 'who', the 'how' and the 'why' of governance of change. Second, we are also aware, however, that an exercise aiming at conceptual framework-building must be able to generate an analytical framework that links these three together. In this sense, each of the pillars accounts for a limited number of theoretical axioms that work as explicit assumptions about the social action related to the governance of change in complex socio-technical systems. Here we would like to revert to our initial notion of socio-technical systems as being intrinsically unstable, and to our understanding that the 'governance' of change is the way in which societal and state actors intentionally and deliberatively interact in order to transform socio-technical systems. Intention and deliberation are crucial notions here. As will be discussed in detail in the coming sections of Chapter 2, we assume generally that the ways in which the change in socio-technical systems is governed varies according to the extent to which capable agents are distributed in the system, the way in which the new knowledge and technologies offer new opportunity structures, the way in which public, private and mixed forms of instrumentation re-define incentives, and last but not least, the extent to which the change and its governance is legitimate (Figure 2.1).

Figure 2.1   Three pillars to understand governance of change in STI systems

The following sections examine each of these aspects one by one, followed by a succinct summary of the main building blocks and their connection in a concluding section.

2.2 OPPORTUNITY STRUCTURES AND CAPABLE AGENTS

The first pillar focuses on a lead question regarding the governance of change in socio-technical systems, namely, who and what drives change? The 'who' and the 'what' are fundamental elements in processes of governing change. Therefore, we define and conceptualize the interaction between opportunity structures and capable agents as a key dimension in those processes. To put it up front, opportunity structures refer to the co-evolution of technology and social institutions, which sequentially or simultaneously generate opportunities for change that agents might take. It is important to underline that we do not see opportunity structures generating change per se. The role of agents is crucial in this regard, in particular agents capable of triggering, directing and inhibiting change in the system by co-creating and/or making the most of the new opportunities.

Looking first at opportunity structures, we must emphasise that we see the interaction between and co-evolution of social institutions and their co-evolving with technology at the heart of the process of the governance of change (Casper and Whitley, 2004). Broadly speaking, this follows the axioms of theories of institutionalism, which underline the role of institutions in the shaping of social order and in its process of the governance of change. This is the social order that forms the core of socio-technical systems. In line with the emphasis of STS scholars during the past decades, we see the production and the use of technology and new (scientific) knowledge as being deeply embedded in social organization. Sociological, historical and anthropological studies have shown that the production and use of new knowledge/technology does not take place in a vacuum, but always in a particular social context defined by social institutions (such as regulation and legislation, normative rules, cognitive frames, worldviews, routines, and so on).

From the above it follows that what we define as opportunity structures is not just technology/new knowledge as such, but the structures that result from the embeddedness of a particular new technology/knowledge into a set of specific social institutions. It is worth noting that new technology/knowledge can be seen in two interrelated perspectives. The first one is to see knowledge as the outcome of a social process. New knowledge is never produced in a mechanistic way, but actively involves socio-cultural and individual dynamics in the process of search and exploration of the unknown. For this reason, the production of knowledge is highly dependent on contextual as well as individual processes. Often these processes are based on human curiosity, the will to unveil the unknown and/or to invent novel technical devices. From sociology of science we know that the Mertonian ideals of disinterestedness and commonality of knowledge production (Merton, 1942/1973) are often met with the reality of individual aspirations for rewards (professional recognition and/or monetary gains) and of the growing commodification of knowledge production processes and outcomes (Callon, 1994). There is a socio-cultural dimension in the production of knowledge in which scientists and technicians are embedded. The second, interrelated, perspective on new technology/knowledge is its ability to open new possibilities for social and human interaction and social organization. This is a perspective focusing on the 'content' of the new technology/knowledge, which characterizes the particular nature of this new knowledge and its potential in relation to possibilities for solving problems or granting new venues for social interaction (Nilsson and Persson, 2012). Economists have tended to distinguish between several types of technology 'content' and the innovation processes associated to them. One such distinction is between enabling/generic technologies, with a horizontal effect over several possible socio-technical systems (including different social organizations and/or industrial sectors), in contrast to some more specific types of technologies with a concrete effect on a more limited set of areas or sectors (Niosi and Reid, 2007). Another such distinction is between network technologies (with different levels of entry barriers and network effects) and non-network technologies (David, 1995). The notion of opportunity structures, with its emphasis on the co-evolution of social institutions and technology/new knowledge production and use, and with its focus on the features that characterize technologies (enabling/specific, networked/non-networked, and so on), sheds light on which specific forms of technology production and use might offer new opportunities and openings for new types of social organization. Hence, we need to understand that technologies have specific features which are deeply ingrained in (new forms of) social organization. It is worth noting that 'opportunity structures' are not necessarily 'good' in normative terms. In other words, 'opportunity' might be normatively/ethically problematic and/or socially contested. As we will see below, this matter has to do with the question of societal legitimacy in the governance of socio-technical change, to be explored in the third pillar of our conceptual framework. Hence, 'opportunity' refers here to the new openings and new venues that this interplay between social institutions and new forms of knowledge might offer to socio-technical systems.

As mentioned above, opportunity structures do not generate governance of change per se. The role of agency is crucial in this regard. Two strands of the literature have addressed the issue of agency in the governance of change. The literature on transitions (towards sustainability) has devoted some attention to the governance of change (or what this literature defines as transition management): 'Governance is therefore carried out through negotiation and bargaining between interested state and non-state actors with interdependent resources relevant to the maintenance and change in the regime' (Smith et al., 2005, p. 1498). This negotiation and bargaining is, however, downplayed when the authors look at governance as the exercise of relational power among interdependent agents of change in the process of generating guiding visions, framing problems and motivating other actors towards change, in what seems to be a more discursive/deliberative approach to the governance of change. Elaborating further on the power aspect of agency in the governance of change, these authors have introduced a very relevant distinction between the 'elite visionary agency' and the 'everyday users' agency' (Smith and Stirling, 2010). The former seems, however, to be more determinant in the process of governing change than the latter because visionary frontrunners enjoy more political authority as they can introduce greater changes than everyday users. This authority is also associated with these powerful agents' capacity to position themselves more favourably in the course of events. Following on from this, we see the governance of change being generated by intentional and capable agents who are strategically positioning themselves in complex set-ups, who are bargaining and negotiating, but who are also framing problems and solutions. In so doing, they are largely interdependent on each other and interdependent on the 'everyday users' in the system. By and large, these visionary powerful agents have also been connected to 'policy entrepreneurs', who develop new ideas, build coalitions, recognize and exploit windows of opportunity, and orchestrate policy networks (Huitema and Meijerink, 2010; Huang and Murray, 2010).

A second strand of literature dealing with agency and change is comparative political economy. Those scholars have not been particularly focused on socio-technical systems per se, but have provided valuable insights in processes of socio-economic change and their governance. Recently, this literature has also been introducing agency-based approaches to change and its governance. This has been prompted by views in the institutionalist and organizational literatures alike, that change is linked to the ambiguity of both, the institutional framework of action and the experience of the agents as such. For Mahoney and Thelen change 'often occurs precisely when problems of rule interpretation and enforcement open up space for actors to implement existing rules in new ways' (Mahoney and Thelen, 2010, p. 4). Hence, they interpret change as being largely dependent on the different degrees of discretion (ambiguity) of those rules, as agents exploit the situation offered by this ambiguity according to their veto power position in the political context. This rational behaviour contrasts, however, with James March's view on ambiguity. Here, the ambiguity is not of the scope of rule enforcement, but of the experience of agency itself (March, 2010). This author suggests that the past and present experience of agents does not provide them with single-minded unilateral lessons, but with multiple possible lessons because that experience is intrinsically ambiguous and can be interpreted in many possible ways. This means that agents are constantly making sense and interpreting their own experience. Any of their positioning or change-attitude is highly related to the way in which the agents have decided to make sense and interpret their experience in the interaction with the social reality. From the perspective of the governance of change in socio-technical systems, these two views are relevant in so far as they recognize that institutions and agent's experiences are ambiguous. However, their very different understanding of social action (utility maximizing vis-à-vis interpretation) results in different views regarding the governance of change. For one school, governance is the dominance of a particular type of utility maximizing agents, whereas for the other, it is the pre-dominance of specific interpretative frameworks. With this, we find ourselves in the classical conundrum of whether social action has one or multiple natures (rationalist or interpretative, or both at once).

Both strands of the literature bring relevant insights to our conceptual framework. Transition scholars bring forward the idea of different types of agency in the governance of change in socio-technical systems; and the comparative political economy literature brings forward the view that ambiguity is an intrinsic element in the agent's perceptions as well as in the way in which social institutions (regulation and legislation, normative rules, cognitive frames, worldviews, routines, and so on) are differently organized and interpreted by the agents.

Yet, acknowledging these contributions does not solve our theoretical problem regarding the nature of social action, nor the nature of agency-institution relations in the dynamics of governing change. We need to be more precise. Our first point of departure is the understanding that in societal and political contexts such as the governance of change in socio-technical systems, agents might chose to operate either under the logic of consequentiality, whereby action is driven by actor's preferences and interest and thus expected outcomes, or under the logic of appropri-ateness, whereby action is driven by the perception of what is necessary and conforms to a given set of norms and rules (March and Olsen, 1989).

Both logics can – and in fact will – co-exist in time. Our second point of departure is the understanding that the agents of change can be everyday agents (civil society organizations, lead consumers, non-governmental organizations, social entrepreneurs, community managers, and so on) as well as more formalized agents (policy entrepreneurs, firms, researchers, inventors, and so on). These agents might have different capabilities in terms of their resources; and these resources might be evenly or unevenly distributed.

An example at hand is the governance of change in the commercial aviation transport system in Europe in the 2000s, with the introduction of an entirely new business model – discount flight companies. This was based on a combination of opportunity structures and capable agents governing change in this specific socio-technical system. First, the co-evolution of a set of socio-political institutions (EU regulations liberalizing the air transport sector aiming to create a single market in Europe) and the advancement of ICT on-line solutions (technology) provided an opportunity structure as an opening. Second, capable agents (newly capitalized aviation companies during the expansive capital markets at the end of the 1990s) made the most of the opportunity by designing a new business model based on cheaper retailing prices, and self-service on-line booking by passengers.

The first pillar of our conceptual framework, opportunity structures and capable agents looks at the ways in which the different nature of opportunity structures (combinations of new technologies and knowledge with institutional frameworks) and different capabilities of actors offer different contexts for the governance of change. Systems in which network-based technologies are dominant will have specific forms of opportunity structures compared to those in which the dominant technologies are more self-contained. In addition, we stress the importance of the interaction with social institutions. Social institutions like regulation, normative rules, worldviews, routines, and so on interact strongly with these technologies/new knowledge, co-evolving in mutual interdependence. Social institutions might enable or constrain the production and use of technologies and hence shape and co-evolve with these technologies. Therefore the main question related to opportunity structure is: what are the ways in which new technologies and knowledge, and their interplay and co-evolutions with social institutions offer different contexts for the governance of change in socio-technical systems?

Our conceptual framework is eminently agency-based. As mentioned above, ambiguity is a constitutive element in agents' experience as well as social institutions. The creation of new knowledge and technology might tend to increase the levels of ambiguity, and therefore to transform the space for individual/collective action as well as for the (re-)interpretation/ re-organization of social institutions. Resources not only in terms of monetary/economic resources, but in terms of other resources like expertise, time, influence, credibility, and so on are also related to the agents' interpretative abilities (as communicative and coordinating devices promoting or hindering change). Resources and interpretative abilities are crucial features defining the level of capability of the agents. For this reason, the distribution of these capabilities in the system is an issue worth studying in the processes of governing change. In sum, the questions related to agency are:

- Who are the primary agents of change?
- What is their capacity to induce/inhibit change?
- What capabilities do they have (resources and interpretative abilities)?
- What is the distribution of the agents' capabilities within the system?

2.3 INSTRUMENTS IN THE GOVERNANCE OF CHANGE

The second pillar is concerned with the *how*, namely with the instruments used in the governance of change, that is, the specific ways and mechanism by which agents induce change in the socio-technical system and are able to design and give direction to that change. Before taking a step further into this discussion, it is paramount to underline that 'governance instrument' is a generic concept referring to different possible types of instrumentation in the process of inducing change. Hence, 'governance instrument' is an umbrella concept that includes the notions 'policy instruments' when those designing those instruments are primarily state agents; and it also includes 'social agent's instruments' designed by non-state agents. For this reason, the notion 'governance instrument' is an umbrella notion focusing on a broad range of mechanisms for social action (Lascoumes and Le Gales, 2007) conducive to governing change in socio-technical systems.

There is a wide scholarly literature on instruments which differs based on the relative importance of either state or societal instrumentation. The different disciplines in the social sciences have their own views on the nature of social action, and also on the expected roles of state and social agents. This means that, traditionally, different social sciences' disciplines have tended to look at specific bundles of governance instruments while disregarding others. Therefore, it is important to take stock of these different paradigmatic views in order to broaden the debate and provide an encompassing and holistic view on governance instrumentation, connecting the traditional public policy with societally-driven instruments.

On the traditional policy analysis end of the spectrum, the literature tends to see state policy as the most prominent actor in the governance of change, because the state has relevant (but not sole) responsibility for 'policy' instruments. Economists share this view in part, particularly on the state as an actor in different modes of hierarchical coordination. In this state-focused view, economists and political scientists have analysed and justified policy instrumentation on the basis of three basic rationales for state intervention: (1) correcting market failure; (2) correcting systems failure and (3) achieve certain missions/goals. The first, market failure, is the most traditional policy rationale for science and technology policy and has mainly been concerned with the need to support public and private investment in science and research in order to address problems of sub-optimal investment ratios due to the limited private incentives and long-term returns (vs. short term returns) of those investments (Arrow, 1959/2002; Nelson, 1959). Correcting system failure is the second rationale of policy instruments. Policy instruments induce change in the system by addressing specific problems, deficiencies, or bottlenecks (Borrás and Edquist, 2013; Smits and Kuhlmann, 2004; Edler and Georghiou, 2007) on the supply side, the demand side, and regarding the interplay of the two. The third rationale for policy instruments has to do with supporting the achievement of specific goals or missions, a rationale becoming increasingly important as illustrated, inter alia, by the move towards public policies instruments to address grand social challenges (Omenn, 2006).

Sociologists have been less concerned with traditional ST&I policy instruments, but tended to focus on social agent's instruments. They have stressed different mechanisms, modes, or 'strategies' of governance within heterarchic governance structures that co-evolve around certain techno-scientific areas and/or around specific concerns or opportunities associated with them. The notion of emergent governance (Kearnes and Rip, 2009) and anticipatory governance (Roco, 2006, Barben et al., 2008) highlights the fluid character of instruments that aim at governing change which has to do with uncertainties in socio-technical systems. Likewise, the notions of adaptive governance (Smith and Stirling, 2010) and distributed governance (Abbott, 2000) highlight the heterarchical, poly-centric nature of instruments, which are essentially social agents' instruments.

Instrumentation in this sociological approach is different from the state-led 'policy instruments' mentioned above because the former comprises social agents' interactions. The bulk of the discussion on governance instruments in the STS tradition has revolved around the ways in which social agents shape and change. One set of social agents' instruments is discursive and relies on stakeholder participation (Joss, 1999; Korthals, 2011; Davenport et al., 2003). Other instruments support the discourse on longer term developments and alternative futures (foresight, Miles, 2010) or around specific technological trajectories and their opportunities and risks (for example, technology assessment). The most comprehensive form of technology assessment, constructive technology assessment (Rip and Schot, 1995) (Schot and Rip, 1997) (Schot, 1991), mobilizes input and feedback on technologies in early design stages and for re-design of technologies from all interested parties (end user, technical experts), thus not only assessing technologies, but influencing and governing the process of change in the socio-technical system. Another set of social agents' instruments are non-binding, voluntary arrangements such as voluntary reporting schemes or stewardship programmes,[1] voluntary self-commitments codified in professional ethics and technology specific codes of conduct (for example, Bowman and Hodge, 2009; Webb, 2004; Koutalakis et al., 2010). Those instruments 'harness market, peer and community energies to influence behaviour, and draw on the infrastructure of intermediaries such as industry associations, standards organizations and non-governmental organizations for rule development and implementation' (Webb, 2004, p. 4).[2] They codify norms and establish a soft form of accountability.

From the above it can be seen that the literature has looked at the issue of instruments, either by focusing on state-led policy instruments or by focusing on societal-led social agents' instruments. Some scholars, however, have aimed at integrating both views on state and social agents. The transition management literature (Kemp and Rotmans, 2004; Kemp and Loorbach, 2006; Loorbach, 2010) has captured the various roles the state plays in systemic governance of change (Kemp et al., 2006, p. 394), by partly integrating it with social agents' instruments.

In this chapter, our view is that we need a broader perspective on governance instruments (an umbrella concept that covers the state-led policy instruments and the socially-led social agents' instruments) for understanding the governance of change in socio-technical systems. This broader perspective of the instruments for the governance of change is needed for three reasons: first, it is an empirical question as to what degree the state-led policy instruments in the governance of change in socio-technical systems are effective in influencing the direction of change and the motivation and ability of agents to change a socio-technical system. Second, the design and implementation of most of the governance instruments (both policy instruments and social agents' instruments) is important for explaining the process of governing change. And third, it is worth noting that traditional policy instruments have increasingly been underpinned and accompanied by social agents' instruments, whereby state and social actors design different but complementary instruments that interact to govern change in the system. In other words, different instruments are combined in specific mixes, some of which might collectively induce change, while others might not.

To sum up, the study of instruments needs to bring forward questions related to who is designing, shaping and using the instruments; how the instruments are shaped in the first place and by whom, and how those instruments are put into practice and implemented. The co-existence of the state-led policy instruments and social agents' instruments lends itself to see how these types of instruments interact, and how potential tensions are resolved, or the instruments' different goals coordinated. These remarks suggest that it is worth going beyond studying the effectiveness of instruments in the traditional evaluative sense (impact assessment) and to study as well the instruments' broader benefits. Here the notion of 'public value', recently put forward by authors in the field, might be a good starting point to grasp that broader view (Bozeman and Sarewitz, 2011). Likewise, one must avoid a 'linear' understanding of governance instrumentation, as if instruments were invariably having a direct and unidirectional effect on the governance of change in socio-technical systems. In this sense, it is important to understand the complex and reflexive design and use of instruments, for example, the ways in which societal actors shape and re-shape the orientation, sense-making and cognitive frames in the reflexive process of designing and using instruments in the governance of change. This is particularly visible in the context of social contestation and scientific controversies, when the non-neutrality of the policy and social agents' instruments become more exposed. With this in mind, we turn now to the issue of legitimacy.

2.4 LEGITIMACY OF THE GOVERNANCE OF CHANGE IN SOCIO-TECHNICAL SYSTEMS

The third pillar has to do with the question of why socio-technical systems are (or are not) accepted, and why the process of governing change is (or is not) accepted. In our view, the concept of legitimacy must be at the heart of discussions about the governance of change in socio-technical systems, both in terms of its normative content and in terms of an analytical framework for an analysis of the nature and scope of the social acceptance of the change in socio-technical systems. To be sure, socio-technical systems are legitimate if they enjoy wide social acceptance and support. The process of governing change must also be legitimate.

The reasons for the need to focus on legitimacy are threefold. The first reason has to do with the uncertainty of the challenges inherent in any change or transition because of the 'unfamiliarity among stakeholders with the new activity and disputed conformity to existing institutional rules' (te Kulve, 2010, p. 18). The uncertainty and related contestation of scientific and technological change necessarily asks for grounding legitimacy in the decisions that shape that change. The second reason is the inherent political nature of all change, since shaping the direction of science, technology and innovation inevitably affects the interests (and material benefits) and value systems (ethical, normative preferences) of all stakeholders, no matter if they are actively involved in the governance process or not. The third reason has to do with the claim that new governance approaches will lead to binding decisions and socially shared direction. It is derived from the notion that socially shared legitimacy beliefs serve to create a sense of normative obligation that helps ensure voluntary compliance with undesired rules or decisions of governing authority, (Scharpf, 2009, p. 5). While Scharpf refers initially to the more traditional role of the state and its authority, his remarks are also applicable to the broader concept of governance, as the voluntary compliance with the outcome of collective decisions and coordination processes is at the very heart of governance approaches.

The various literature strands on change of socio-technical systems and their implicit views on the governance of that change share a – largely implicit – normative consensus about the need for legitimacy, but there is not much of an explicit conceptualization of legitimacy as such (Borrás, 2006b; Sylvester et al., 2009). Rather we find many claims about the lack of legitimacy, about the problems to achieve it, or about the ways to create more of it. However, the concept of legitimacy itself is rarely defined explicitly in terms of concrete analytical and normative dimensions, resulting in a lack of proper operationalization of the research design on questions related to the societal acceptance and democracy in the governance of change in socio-technical systems.

One starting point for conceptualizing legitimacy is the general notion of David Easton whereby systems are legitimate if they enjoy popular support, both in terms of the process by which the decisions were taken (input legitimacy) and in terms of the support of the system's outcomes (output legitimacy) (Easton, 1965). Input legitimacy refers to the popular support that a particular social community grants a political system (a specific set of political institutions) to channel collective problem-solving for that community. Several decades of political science studies have distinguished between different ways of 'channelling'. Normative theories of liberal democracy see input legitimacy essentially as an issue of traditional forms of political representation through free political party contestation, elected into a democratic parliament with real legislative powers (Cunningham, 2002). The social community is represented in a political body with specific powers to make decisions about how to solve collective problems. Those decisions are socially accepted and democratically legitimate in so far as they entail forms of negotiation that represent the different interests within the community. For their part, normative theories of deliberative and participatory democracy see input legitimacy as a form of direct participation of the community (citizens, civil society organizations, and so on) into formal and informal processes of decision-making that are not based on political negotiations or direct contestation, but essentially on deliberation and consensus-building processes (Bohman and Rehg, 1997). The decisions are socially accepted and democratically legitimate in so far as the process to reach them has been inclusive, open to deliberative considerations and directly engaging those affected by the decisions. Naturally, these normative theories of democracy view input legitimacy differently. However, it is important to understand that both give considerable attention to the process of decision-making. In other words, democratic theories tend to be procedural in nature, looking at the mechanisms of representation/participation in the input-side of the legitimacy of a system.

Output legitimacy is the 'success' that governance delivers, the effectiveness to solve problems and to achieve what is perceived as being in line with main societal preferences. In other words, output legitimacy is the popular support given to a system due to its real capacity to solve collective problems. By the same token, the lack of problem-solving capacity potentially de-legitimises processes and the system as such (Scharpf, 1999).

When looking at the input legitimacy aspects, the STS literature is very rich and suggestive in its focus on the roles of citizens and experts and their participation, engagement and consensus-making in socio-technical systems, or the lack thereof. The burgeoning literature on science and democracy takes into consideration the different models of democracy mentioned above, as alternative institutions of voice (Ron, 2011), or through more elaborated and hybrid forms of representation and participation (Fischer, 2011). Deeply entrenched in these discussions are issues related to preferences towards the empowerment of citizens or the empowerment of scientific experts as the best mechanisms to secure legitimate scientific-related decision-making (Borrás, 2012 for a review). Among the former, we find arguments that fostering the public understanding of science among citizens (Miller, 2001) will allow for an informed public debate on crucial science–technology decisions; and that constituting 'science citizens' will engage them in participatory mechanisms that generate deliberation (Hagendijk and Irwin, 2006; Liberatore and Funtowicz, 2003). Those advocating the empowerment of experts instead see the delegation of decision-making to non-majoritarian independent regulatory agencies based on 'sound academic science' as an important mechanism of legitimacy (Majone, 2010). Another perspective on empowering experts argues that widening the scope of who is an expert, including conventional academic science as well as knowledgeable experts from civil society, will generate 'socially robust knowledge' that legitimates decision-making (Nowotny, 2003). However, even if directly related to legitimacy, much of this rich literature does not refer explicitly to the notion of legitimacy, and therefore has so far not been able to connect to the political science discipline dedicated to these matters. There is therefore a gap between the view on legitimacy from normative theories of democracy on the one hand, and the discussions about citizens' and experts' democratic role in socio-technical systems on the other.

Something similar can be observed with respect to output legitimacy. By and large, the traditional literature on policy analysis and economics in socio-technical systems has so far been concerned with questions of effectiveness and efficiency, with what is being delivered. The scholars studying the effectiveness of science, technology and innovation (STI) policies and evaluating the performance of particular socio-technical systems have never discussed issues of performance and effectiveness in terms of legitimacy. Therefore this literature does not have too much to offer in terms of the legitimacy debate around socio-technical systems. In any case, one important remark in this literature has been recently put forward by Smith and Stirling (2010). They see a dilemma between promoting (effective) transitions in socio-technical systems on the one hand, and the democratic aspects of (input legitimacy) in the political representation/participation in decision-making on the other:

[i]t is unclear how these [transition management processes] sit in relation to prevailing policy institutions and political activities. Transition management is not unique in this regard, as other participatory approaches share this dilemma. However, given ambitions to transform the structures of our

everyday lives, this unclear relationship is especially problematic because the basis for authority, legitimacy and accountability in transition governance will ultimately rest on the way it engages. (Smith and Stirling, 2010, p. 11)

Seen from the input-output legitimacy perspective mentioned above, this seems to be a redundant dilemma because input and output legitimacy are two sides of the same coin. There are two reasons for that. First, as Mayntz suggests, in heterogeneous societies the '... very difficulty of defining what constitutes a legitimating output thus emphasizes the importance of input legitimacy' (Mayntz, 2010, p. 11). The point is that, even if outputs are supported by majorities, the ability of the minority to accept that output still rests on the perception that the processes that defined the outcome were participative, open and transparent. Second, the complex nature of socio-technical systems makes the participatory and effective governance of change in socio-technical systems more dependent on the knowledge of citizens and experts alike, precisely because the nature of 'effective outputs' might be contested. This means that the most effective solutions are often those that have been based on a participatory/representative process of decision-making. This, however, might be challenged in contexts of high scientific controversies or contexts with high levels of uncertainty.

The analysis of the governance of change in socio-technical systems is confronted with a challenge it has yet to master, and thus we see that more appropriate approaches to study the legitimacy in the governance of change in socio-technical systems are needed. Hence, our first point of departure is that there is a need to bring forward more analytical and empirical efforts when studying the legitimacy of socio-technical governance in general and of governance of change in socio-technical systems in particular. Questions of legitimacy are intrinsically normative, because they are ultimately based on normative theories of democracy and social order. However, the pleas towards more analytical endeavours on issues of legitimacy (Wessels, 2003) can also be applied to this particular topic. We can illustrate the directions in which this should go with three examples. The first example is the recent effort to test the argument that more participation of stakeholders has generated more input legitimacy. This was studied in the case of a specific new policy instrument in the EU used in STI policy-making (Borrás and Ejrnæs, 2011). A second example for this more empirical endeavour is to focus on certain elements of the governance systems (regulatory bodies) and to analyse their embeddedness in different 'legitimacy communities'. This enables the scholar to develop an analytical concept to actually understand the link (or lack thereof) between strategic behaviour and input/output legitimacy (Black, 2008). In a similar vein, other authors have analysed the input legitimacy of regulatory agencies by looking comparatively at the different levels of stakeholders networks' involvement in decision-making processes (Borrás et al., 2007) and the input-output legitimacy of complex regulatory systems like the patent system (Borrás, 2006a). Last but not least, another example of analytical efforts has been put forward by Geels and Verhees (2011). These authors study 'cultural legitimacy' as a combination of cognitive and normative dimensions of legitimacy. This allows them to study longitudinally the 'framing struggles' for cultural legitimacy in a specific socio-technical system (nuclear energy).

Our second point of departure is that the ways in which socio-technical systems are governed have become much more diffused, with hybrid and heterogeneous arrangements, and are evolving rapidly. For that reason, the aspects of legitimacy need a much more careful consideration because, following Scharpf, the perception of legitimacy is related to the readiness of societies to contribute to the process and to comply with directions taken. With the emergence of complex governance forms, the rules of the game and the mechanisms of inclusion/exclusion in partici-pating are becoming less clearly defined. Hence, questions regarding the sources of legitimacy need to be asked more consistently and sharply:

- How are the conventional mechanisms of parliamentarian represen-tation and non-parliamentarian forms of deliberation balanced and managed?
- If there is participation in deliberation around specific technologies, how are access and exchange organized, and how are results of deliberations channelled? (Davenport et al., 2003)

All in all, the above discussion has shown that a conceptual framework to understand governance of change in STS systems needs to put questions of legitimacy at its core. This leads us to the formulation of a set of building blocks and then allows the formulation of lead questions. First, input and output dimensions of legitimacy cannot be disconnected from each other in the process of governing change in a system, as both are needed to grant legitimacy to the process of governing change. If one is absent, the process of governing change will be compromised in terms of legitimacy. Second, governance of socio-technical systems and their change is legitimate when it is characterized by a normatively appropriate process (defined by the different theories of democratic legitimacy mentioned above – liberal-representative, participatory and deliberative) and by socially endorsed processes (defined by levels of social support) through mechanisms of participation and representation. This is linked to social views and expectations about the outcomes of the change in the socio-technical systems that are widely shared cognitively and normatively (Scott, 1995) in open and explicit reflexive processes in society.

This allows the formulation of concrete analytical questions:

- What are the challenges for legitimacy emerging from the combination of specific actor arenas and the poly-centrality of governance?
- What is the cultural embedding of governance instruments that are applied and how does it change over time?
- How socially accepted are the governance processes and outcomes, and why is this?
- How is contestation of outcomes and processes dealt with?

All of these questions have an analytical and a normative dimension. On that basis, empirical analysis could feed back more explicitly into normative theoretical issues, providing more fine-grained and empirically-grounded normative understandings of the general standards regarding input and output legitimacy of socio-technical governance and its change in contemporary societies. It goes without saying that an analysis of legitimacy as suggested here needs the multidimensional perspective that is at the heart of the rationale for our conceptual framework in the first place.

2.5   CONCLUSIONS

The overall goal of this Chapter 2 has been to address the issue of the governance of change in socio-technical systems. Taking the vast literature in the field of socio-technical and innovation systems as our point of departure, (see Introduction to this volume), we have aimed at conceptualizing governance of change in socio-technical systems. This conceptualization heavily draws on the political science background on these matters. By drawing from the political science disciplinary insights, Chapter 2 has provided a first attempt to bridge the gap between different approaches through conceptual development, through bringing those literatures together and through identifying concrete empirical questions ahead. In so doing, we have dared to take a careful step forward in our effort to provide a consistently analytical framework. We call this preliminary conceptual framework-building. We believe that our three pillars offer a clearer structuration of the central dimensions related to the governance of complex socio-technical systems, and that this offers a novel angle on these matters because it brings key issues from political science into this multi-disciplinary scholarly community that otherwise has not been in contact with the governance disciplinary discussions. Our true ambition has been to structure those lines of inquiry into a coherent whole, to identify analytically relevant issues and to pose questions that were partly disregarded and need further empirical work.

Having said that, however, we can summarize our main assumptions from this first step into the endeavour of theorising the governance of change in socio-technical systems:

- Change in socio-technical systems is driven by the interplay between the opportunity structures (defined by the co-evolution of new technology and knowledge with institutional framework conditions) and the actions and reactions of different agents of change.
- The governance of change in a socio-technical system is essentially the governance of institutional frameworks (which define the opportunity structures for agents) and the subsequent transformation of the agents' behaviour.
- The agents of change can both be elites (that is, policy entrepreneurs, specifically large firms) or everyday agents, depending on their respective capacities and on the top-down or bottom-up social dynamics in the socio-technical system.
- As change inserts uncertainty, the compliance discretion of institutions and the agents' past experience are intrinsically ambiguous. For that reason, the governance of change is rarely an uncontroversial or smooth process. Battles over the specific interpretations of institutional frameworks and over societal and stakeholder costs-benefits characterize the process of socio-technical change and its governance.
- To understand the 'how' of governance of change, it is important to develop a broad perspective on instruments (beyond the traditional 'command and control'), including public, private and joint instrumentation.
- The policy analysis tradition (interested in the effectiveness of policy instruments in a more traditional, evaluative sense) is not sufficient to understand the governance of change. Therefore we include a broader understanding of the dynamics and processes of governance. By doing so, we can better grasp how instruments are shaped in the first place, better explain why they do or do not 'work', and how they interact with societally driven governance mechanisms.

- Various forms of governance instruments include the state-led policy instruments (designed and implemented by public authorities) and the socially-lead instruments (designed and used by societal actors). The governance of change in socio-technical systems is usually characterized by specific mixes of different instruments, sometimes working in the same direction of change, sometimes not. We need to better understand how these specific combinations of instruments induce change (or not).
- The ways in which socio-technical systems are governed have become much more diffused (with hybrid and heterogeneous institutional arrangements and multiple instruments) and have become more rapidly evolving. Those complex and rapid changes are more subject to societal contestation than before. For these reasons, the aspects of legitimacy are at the core of our understanding of change and its governance.
- Our framework brings forward the argument that we need more analytical and empirical efforts in the study of the legitimacy of socio-technical governance in general and of governance of change in socio-technical systems in particular. We differentiate input and output dimensions of legitimacy, which cannot be disconnected from each other, as both are needed to grant legitimacy to a socio-technical system. Input legitimacy (which is more procedural) is intrinsically linked to the perceptions of effectiveness of change (the output legitimacy). The governance of change in socio-technical systems is intrinsically related to developing a process that underpins input legitimacy as well as output legitimacy.

Against this background of core assumptions and principles, we can formulate a set of basic analytical questions to understand specific situations of governance change. Figure 2.2 below summarizes the concrete questions that need to be answered to support the three core pillars of our framework. This is at the same time a – simplified – guide to the understanding of the empirical examples in the following chapters of this book.

Our conceptual framework shall serve as a guide to understand concrete change processes and their governance. However, we see this as a first step in the development of a mid-range theory of the governance of change. To work towards such a theory, a set of further steps will be needed.

Concrete studies of the governance of change in socio-technical systems might help us to better understand the interdependence of the three pillars. The empirical findings will provide solid grounds to identify

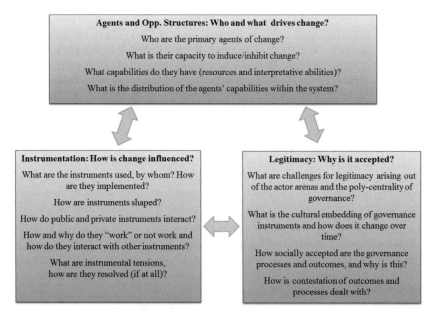

Figure 2.2   Key analytical questions stemming from the conceptual framework

patterns of recurrence in the interrelations of these pillars. For example, do we see a specific relationship between certain characteristics of new knowledge and new technologies (such as the level of uncertainty and disruption, or the network-nature of technology in question) and certain patterns of agency of change (policy entrepreneurs, or large firms' agents of change)? Can we also see linkages between the types of agents of change (elite or everyday agents) in relation to the forms of input legitimacy of the governance of change process? Or can our empirical studies identify a link between certain features of the opportunity structures (defined by the new technology and the institutional set up), with specific mixes of social and policy instrumentation? Likewise, can we identify a link between specific instrumentation mixes and with particular forms of output legitimacy (effective solutions and their widespread acceptance in the society)?

Having a substantial amount of empirical material from which to identify patterns of interactions and co-existence, our theoretical framework would need to take a further step looking into the overall process of learning and reflexivity in the governance of change processes. Our advanced societies are constantly engaged in processes of governing change in socio-technical systems. With the three pillars we have identified some building blocks for a better understanding of the governance of that change. However, we would also need to study the conditions under which this governance of change is characterized by learning processes and if there are some patterns of collective self-reflexion of these governance processes. This would also include the need to understand situations in which learning and reflexion does not take place, resulting in repeated situations of 'lock in' in the different processes of governing change. It is our understanding at this preliminary stage that low levels of learning and reflexivity reduce the collective and individual capacity of agents of change to induce and govern change. The nature and extent of learning from past experiences in the (perceived as successful/unsuccessful) governance of change might enhance or hinder possibilities of further change.

Last but not least, the future development of a meso-range theoretical framework on the basis of empirical analysis and on considerations at meta-level (reflexivity and learning in governance processes) will provide a sound basis for the definition of a series of recommendations for the design of strategies to govern change in socio-technical systems. Those recommendations would naturally have a normative nature in the sense that they would be a series of theoretically and empirically-informed recommendations about specific courses of action.

NOTES

1. For illustration: DEFRA (2008).
2. Examples of broader codes in the area of Nano are examples of the Responsible Nano Code http://www.responsiblenanocode.org/ in the UK or the EU Nano Code http://ec.europa.eu/nanotechnology/pdf/nanocode-rec_pe0894c_en.pdf.

REFERENCES

Abbott, F. M. (2000), 'Distributed governance at the WTO-WIPO: an evolving model for open-architecture integrated governance', *Journal of International Economic Law*, **3** (1), 63–81.

Arrow, K. J. (1959/2002), 'Economic welfare and the allocation of resources for invention', reprinted in P. Mirowski and E.-M. Sent (eds), *Science Bought and Sold. Essays in the Economics of Science*, Chicago: University of Chicago, pp. 165–180.

Barben, D., E. Fisher, C. Selin and D. H. Guston (2008), 'Anticipatory governance of nanotechnology: Foresight, engagement, and integration', in E. J. Hackett, O. Amsterdamska, M. E. Lynch and J. Wajcman (eds), *Handbook* of *Science and Technology Studies*, Third Edition, Cambridge, MA: MIT Press, pp. 979–1000.

Black, J. (2008), 'Constructing and contesting legitimacy and accountability in polycentric regulatory regimes', *Regulation and Governance*, **2**, 137–164.

Bohman, J. and W. Rehg (eds) (1997), *Deliberative Democracy: Essays on Reason and Politics*, Cambridge, MA: MIT Press.

Borrás, S. (2006a), 'The governance of the European patent system: Effective and legitimate?', *Economy and Society*, **35** (4), 594–610.

Borrás, S. (2006b), 'Legitimate governance of risk at EU level? The case of GMOs', *Technological Forecasting and Social Change*, **73** (1), 61–75.

Borrás, S. (2012), 'Three tensions in the governance of science and technology', in D. Levi-Faur (ed.), *Oxford Handbook of Governance*, Oxford: Oxford University Press, pp. 429–440.

Borrás, S. and C. Edquist (2013), 'The choice of innovation policy instruments', *Technological Forecasting and Social Change*, **80** (8), 1513–1522.

Borrás, S. and A. Ejrnæs (2011), 'The legitimacy of new modes of governance in the EU: Studying stakeholders' support', *European Union Politics*, **12** (1), 107–126

Borrás, S., C. Koutalakis and F. Wendler (2007), 'European agencies and input Legitimacy: EFSA, EMeA and EPO in the post-delegation phase', *Journal of European Integration*, **29** (5), 583–600.

Bowman, D. M. and G. A. Hodge (2009), 'Counting on codes: An examination of transnational codes as a regulatory governance mechanism for nanotechnologies', *Regulation and Governance*, **2** (3), 145–164.

Bozeman, B. and D. Sarewitz (2011), 'Public value mapping and science policy evaluation', *Minerva*, **49** (1), 1–23.

Callon, M. (1994), 'Is science a public good?', *Science, Technology and Human Values*, **19** (4), 395–424.

Casper, S. and R. Whitley (2004), 'Managing competences in entrepreneurial technology firms: A comparative institutional analysis of Germany, Sweden and the UK', *Research Policy*, **33** (1), 89–106.

Cunningham, F. (2002), *Theories of Democracy. A Critical Introduction*, London: Routledge.

Davenport, S., S. Leitch and A. Rip (2003), 'The "user" in research funding negotiation processes', *Science and Public Policy*, **30** (4), 239–250.

David, P. A. (1995), 'Standardization policies for network technologies: The flux between freedom and order revisited', in R. Hawkins, R. Mansell and J. Skea (eds), *Standards, Innovation and Competitiveness: The Politics and Economics of Standards in National and Technical Environments*, Cheltenham, UK and Northampton, MA, USA: Edward Elgar, pp. 15–35.

Easton, D. (1965), *A Systems Analysis of Political Life*, New York: John Wiley and Sons.

Edler, J. and L. Georghiou (2007), 'Public procurement and innovation: Resurrecting the demand side', *Research Policy*, **36** (7), 949–963.

Fischer, F. (2011), 'Participatory governance', in D. Levi-Faur (ed.), *The Oxford Handbook of Governance*, Oxford: Oxford University Press.

Geels, F. W. and B. Verhees (2011), 'Cultural legitimacy and framing struggles in innovation journeys: A cultural-performative perspective and a case study of

Dutch nuclear energy (1945–1986)', *Technological Forecasting & Social Change*, **78** (6), 910–930.

Hagendijk, R. and A. Irwin (2006), 'Public deliberation and governance: Engaging with science and technology in contemporary Europe', *Minerva*, **44** (2), 167–184.

Huang, K. G. and F. E. Murray (2010), 'Entrepreneurial experiments in science policy: Analyzing the Human Genome Project', *Research Policy*, **39** (5), 567–582.

Huitema, D. and S. Meijerink (2010), 'Realizing water transitions: The role of policy entrepreneurs in water policy change', *Ecology and Society*, **15** (2).

Joss, S. (1999), 'Public participation in science and technology policy- and decision-making – ephemeral phenomenon or lasting change?', *Science and Public Policy*, **26** (5), 290–293.

Kearnes, M. and A. Rip (2009), 'The emerging governance landscape of nanotechnology', in S. Gammel, A. Lösch and A. Nordmann (eds), *Jenseits von Regulierung: Zum Politischen Umgang mit der Nanotechnologie*, Berlin: Akademische Verlagsgesellschaft.

Kemp, R. and D. Loorbach (2006), 'Transition management: A reflexive governance approach', in J.-P. Voss, D. Baunecht and R. Kemp, *Reflexive Governance and Sustanable Development*, Cheltenham, UK and Northampton, MA, USA: Edward Elgar, pp. 103–130.

Kemp, R. and J. Rotmans (2004), 'Managing the transition to sustainable mobility', in B. Elzen, F. W. Geels and K. Green (eds), *System Innovation and the Transition to Sustainability: Theory, Evidence and Policy*, Cheltenham, UK and Northampton, MA, USA: Edward Elgar, pp. 137–167.

Koutalakis, C., A. Buzogany, and T. A. Börzel (2010), 'When soft regulation is not enough: The integrated pollution prevention and control directive of the European Union', *Regulation and Governance*, **4**, 329–344.

te Kulve, H. (2010), 'Emerging technologies and waiting games: Institutional entrepreneurs around nanotechnology in the food packaging sector', *Science, Technology and Innovation Studies*, **6** (1): 7–31

Lascoumes, P. and P. Le Gales (2007), 'Introduction: Understanding public policy through its instruments: From the nature of instruments to the sociology of public policy instrumentation', *Governance*, **20** (1), 1–21.

Liberatore, A. and S. Funtowicz (2003), '"Democratising" expertise, "expertising" democracy: what does this mean, and why bother?', *Science and Public Policy*, **30** (3), 146–150.

Loorbach, D. (2010), 'Transition management for sustainable develoment: A prescriptive, complexity-based governance framework', *Governance*, **23**, 161–183.

Mahoney, J. and K. Thelen (eds) (2010), *Explaining Institutional Change: Ambiguity, Agency and Power*, Cambridge: Cambridge University Press.

Majone, G. (2010), 'Foundations of risk regulation: Science, decision-making, policy learning and institutional reform', *European Journal of Risk Regulation*, **1** (1), 5–19.

March, J. (2010), *The Ambiguities of Experience*, Ithaca, N.Y.: Cornell University Press.

March, J. G. and J. P. Olsen (1989), *Rediscovering Institutions: The Organizational Basis of Politics*, New York: Free Press.

Mayntz, R. (2010), 'Legitimacy and compliance in transnational governance', *MPIfG Working Paper*, 10/5, available at www.mpifg.de/pu/wp06-11_en.asp.

Merton, R. K. (1942/1973), 'The normative structure of science', reprinted in R. K. Merton, *The Sociology of Science: Theoretical and Empirical Investigations*, Chicago: University of Chicago, pp. 267–278.

Miles, I. (2010), 'The development of technology foresight: A review', *Technological Forecasting and Social Change*, **77** (9), 1448–1456.

Miller, S. (2001), 'Public understanding of science at the crossroads', *Public Understanding of Science*, **10** (1), 115–120.

Nelson, R. R. (1959), 'The simple economics of basic scientific research', *The Journal of Political Economy*, **67** (3), 297–306.

Nilsson, M. and Å. Persson (2012), 'Can Earth system interactions be governed? Governance functions for linking climate change mitigation with land use, freshwater and biodiversity protection', *Ecological Economics*, **75** (0), 61–71.

Niosi, J. and S. E. Reid (2007), 'Biotechnology and nanotechnology: Science-based enabling technologies as windows of opportunity for LDCs?', *World Development*, **35** (3), 426–438.

Nowotny, H. (2003), 'Democratising expertise and socially robust knowledge', *Science and Public Policy*, **30** (3), 151–157.

Omenn, G. S. (2006), 'Grand challenges and great opportunities in science, technology, and public policy', *SCIENCE*, **314** (Dec 2006), 1696–1704.

Rip, A., T. J. Misa and J. Schot (1995), *Managing Technology in Society: The Approach of Constructive Technology Assessment*, London: Pinter.

Ron, A. (2011), 'Forms of democratic governance', in D. Levi-Faur (ed.), *The Oxford Handbook of Governance*, Oxford: Oxford University Press.

Scharpf, F. W. (1999), *Governing in Europe: Effective and Democratic?*, Oxford: Oxford University Press.

Scharpf, F. W. (2009), 'Legitimacy in the multilevel European polity', *MPIfG Working Paper*, No. 09/1, available at http://econstor.eu/bitstream/10419/41652/1/610149423.pdf.

Schot, J. (1991), Maatschappelijke sturing van technische ontwikkeling: Constructief technology assessment als dedendaags luddisme, Ph.D. thesis published in the WMW publication series, *Faculteit Wijsbegeerte en Aatschappijwetenschappen*, University of Twente.

Schot, J. and A. Rip (1997), 'The past and future of constructive technology assessment', *Technological Forecasting and Social Change*, **54**, 251–268.

Smith, A. and A. Stirling (2010), 'The politics of social-ecological resilience and sustainable socio-technical transitions', *Ecology and Society*, **15** (1), 11.

Smith, A., A. Stirling and F. Berkhout (2005), 'The governance of sustainable socio-technical transitions', *Research Policy*, **34** (10), 1491–1510.

Smits, R. and S. Kuhlmann (2004), 'The rise of systemic instruments in innovation policy', *International Journal of Foresight and Innovation Policy*, **1** (1–2), 4–32.

Sylvester, D. J., K. W. Abbott and G. E. Marchant (2009), 'Not again! Public perception, regulation, and nanotechnology', *Regulation and Governance*, **3** (2), 165–185.

Webb, K. (2004), 'Understanding the voluntary Codes phenomenon', in K. Webb (ed.), *Voluntary Codes: Private Governance, the Public Interest and Innovation*, Ottawa: Carleton University, Carleton Research Unit for Innovation, Science and Environment, pp. 3–32.

Wessels, W. (2003), 'Reassessing the legitimacy debate: A comment to Moravcsik', in J. H. H. Weiler, I. Begg and J. Peterson (eds), *Integration in an Expanding European Union: Reassessing the Fundamentals*, Oxford: Blackwell Publishing.

3. Anticipatory markets: technical standards as a governance tool in the development of biodegradable plastics

Arthur Daemmrich

3.1 INTRODUCTION: STANDARDIZATION AND TECHNOLOGY GOVERNANCE

Standardization is never only a process of forcing uniformity and predictability onto measurements, products or services. Instead, standards act also as coordinators of system change, and standard setting involves the co-production (Jasanoff, 2004) of scientific knowledge, technology and social institutions. Furthermore, standards offer industry, academic institutions and government a more flexible form of technology governance than is typical with either precautionary or risk-based regulation. Intriguingly, the process of negotiating even what appear to be narrow technical standards also creates opportunity structures (Borrás and Edler, 2014) for broader system change.

This chapter focuses on a complex system change underway that involves switching from stable but environmentally persistent plastics to novel biodegradable materials. Beyond innovations in materials science, this switch requires the development of new markets for biodegradable plastics and changes to consumer behaviour and waste processing systems. I find that key capable agents (Borrás and Edler, 2014) undertook a co-production of technical standards, novel plastics and waste systems but failed to account for consumer behaviours that put the entire initiative at risk. Yet the use of technical standards as a coordination device for broader systemic change allowed for flexibility in the market uses for biodegradable plastics, contributing to their still-emergent success.

In recent years, standards have multiplied at the national and international level. For example, the International Organization for Standardization (ISO) has published 1,200 new standards annually since 2001, compared to an average of only 140 per year dating back to its first international standard in 1951 (International Organization for Standardization, 2012). A complementary array of industry-sponsored and independent certification organizations has emerged to validate that specific products meet standards. These groups inspect manufacturing sites, test materials, trace products from raw materials to consumer disposal, and license the use of their logos and certification stamps (Conroy, 2007). A new era of standardization and certification emerged even as classic command-and-control regulation was criticized for slowing innovation and interfering with beneficial competition (Blind, 2004). Standardization is also drawing renewed attention from scholars in science and technology studies (STS) who focus on scientific practices associated with standards in order to explore hierarchies of power and authority embedded in socio-technical systems (Crease, 2011; Russell, 2013).

This chapter extends the study of standards by analyzing their role as a coordinating device for contemporary technology and innovation management systems. Specifically, the case described here involved the writing of new technical standards as an integral part of introducing new biodegradable polymers to the market. New standards were a crucial component of an anticipatory market spanning the manufacture of novel plastics, their processing into useful consumer products, notably thin-film shopping bags, and their eventual breakdown in industrial-scale compost systems. As technical standards for the new materials shifted from categorizing plastics based on their raw material source to differentiating them based on their environmental fate, an accompanying set of business models, consumer uses and waste processing were put into place by the manufacturer and government officials in a significant socio-technical system change.

Standards have important similarities and differences from regulations when employed as instruments of technology governance. Both rely on formal testing against stated requirements for market authorization. Likewise, both respond to demands for transparency or challenges to their institutional authority by invoking the power of science and technology as embodied in experimental methods and the expertise of capable agents. Regulation and standardization differ, however, in their enforcement power and flexibility. Regulators can inspect manufacturers or products and typically act as market gatekeepers. Standards agencies instead operate as discursive power brokers who influence technical definitions and promote their widespread uses. To succeed, standards must draw upon capable agents from industry and academia that can combine general knowledge (for example, of biodegradation) with specific product knowledge (for example, of polymer chemistry). Chapter 3 therefore considers how capable agents interacted with the institutionalized practices of standardization to advance system change.

The analysis of standards for biodegradation developed here is based on an empirical case study of Ecoflex, a biodegradable polymer invented and manufactured by the German chemical company BASF. Ecoflex's innovation pathway included collaboration between the firm's scientists and academics studying biodegradation, and the company's direct involvement with standard setting processes in Germany and internationally. Fundamentally, BASF co-created technical standards for biodegradation, the product Ecoflex and a market for new plastics coupled to their environmentally benign disposal. However, the anticipated market proved unwelcoming of biodegradable plastic bags due to challenges of waste separation and processing. The company then developed several secondary user groups into more significant markets while also supporting the adoption of biodegradation standards internationally. As the case exemplifies, a co-production of knowledge, technology, and social institutions, with standards as the primary coordinating mechanism, generated greater stability in the market than would otherwise be the case for a technology encountering post-market challenges.

Findings presented here draw on diverse sources that establish an account of product development at the firm and the standard-setting process. Ecoflex was chosen for a case study for several key reasons: it was the first of a new generation of plastics intended for use with large-scale compost systems; it was built on a petrochemical rather than plant base, making pro-environmental claims more complex; and it offered a test case of the relationship between standards and markets in new product development. Research included in-person interviews, site observations, and the analysis of archival records, other primary source documents and published scientific papers. Interviews were carried out at several locations in Germany, including BASF's headquarters in Ludwigshafen, the academic Gesellschaft für Biotechnologische Forschung's (Society for Biotechnology Research) laboratories in Braunschweig and at the Berlin headquarters of the German Institute for Standardization (Deutsches Institut fur Normung, or DIN). Insights gained from interviews and primary sources were supplemented through observations of waste pickup, transportation and processing at a large-scale compost facility.

The sections that follow first provide a brief history of synthetic polymer development and the regulatory context in which biodegradable plastics attracted research investments by chemical firms. Second, the chapter describes Ecoflex's invention and product development, and the process of setting standards for biodegradation in Germany that were subsequently harmonized internationally. The next section analyses the firm's launch and subsequent market repositioning for the biodegradable plastic. Beyond the specific focus on standards in technology governance, the chapter sheds light more generally on green product innovation and the ways in which firms anticipate markets during product development.

3.2 POLYMERS FROM DURABLE TO DEGRADABLE

From their origins in the late nineteenth century, synthetic polymers were designed to resist wear from human uses and environmental breakdown. Measures of successful innovation in plastics included reduced solubility, resistance to breakdown by sunlight, simultaneous flexibility and hardness, and other features to extend product life. Since the early 1990s, however, efforts have been made to create plastics that will break down into harmless natural materials. This transition is profound, not just for its scientific and technical developments, but also because it has involved designing new systems for waste collection and processing as well as greater information generation and validation than in the past.

Leo Baekeland's invention of Bakelite in the early 1900s brought to the market a chemically synthetic high temperature 'thermoset' resin of incredible durability. It soon found applications ranging from electrical insulation to jewellery. New generations of polymers were invented over the following decades, including synthetic rubber, vinyl chloride, polystyrene, and perhaps most famously, nylon. Post-war advances in catalysts took polyethylene from a laboratory oddity to mass production, and its uses soon ranged from thin-film bags to thick-walled containers (Morris, 1986). By the mid-1970s, polymers and plastics outsold steel by volume; today plastic has become more common in construction than steel, aluminium and copper combined. In food packaging, plastics have almost entirely displaced other materials (Meilke, 1995). Low weight, high durability, and ease of manufacturing and use stimulated steady growth of plastics sales globally to $770 billion globally in 2012. The most widely used plastic, polyethylene, has an annual production volume of approximately 80 million metric tons (C&EN, 2013).

For manufacturers of most packaging, especially thin films used in plastic bags and food wrappers, the market's maturity by the early 1990s offered few rewards for innovation. A small number of high-volume producers competed primarily on price, not value-added features. Companies selling kitchen trash bags tried to differentiate their products through the addition of scents or greater stretch to avoid breakage, but the underlying materials were largely identical.

The durability and environmental persistence of plastics, however, drew sustained attention from environmentalists in the 1990s. Concerns focused on landfill space and toxic runoffs, the costs and inefficiencies associated with polymer recycling, and tremendous amounts of plastic debris found floating in the ocean (Day et al., 1990). Yet when advocating for changes to commodity plastics and their uses, environmentalists encountered both technical and social system challenges. The few biodegradable plastics available at the time were brittle and melted at temperatures that made them unsuitable for food packaging or plastic bags (Van de Velde, 2002). While recycling systems in Europe and the United States involved consumers in the separation of glass, plastics and paper from other waste, thin-film plastics were typically discarded and ended up in landfills. The firms that made plastic bags and other materials were unwilling to risk a transition to new materials or to make major fixed investments into untested production processes (Iles and Martin, 2013).

Nevertheless, several policy and socio-technical trajectories came together over the course of the 1990s in Europe, notably in Germany, to generate the possibility of a sustained market for biodegradable plastics. First, studies projected that landfills would be at capacity in five to ten years, and state and local governments began examining options for waste-to-energy, recycling and other alternatives. With the Green Party above the five percent vote threshold for participation in the German federal parliament (*Bundestag*) and also active nationwide in the states (*Bundesländer*), regulatory policy shifted to mandated waste separation, recycling and the construction of large-scale composting facilities. New policies coupled incentives, including funds for research into alternative materials, to regulations that mandated the removal of organic materials (for example, kitchen scraps) from waste streams (Yamamoto et al., 2002; Bilitewski et al., 1994).

Second, a 1991 federal law made companies responsible for recycling the packaging associated with their products and follow-on legislation established new rules for what materials were accepted at landfills. By the mid-1990s, initiatives were under way in Germany and Austria to engineer systems that included the curbside pickup of waste, large-scale composting of materials and transfer of the final compost to farmers and gardeners (Favoino et al., 2003). In addition to numerous local, regional and national policies, a 1999 European Union Directive mandated that member states reduce the amount of biodegradable municipal waste entering landfills by 65 percent within fifteen years.[1]

The process of envisioning new waste management approaches and the demands of environmentalists for bioplastics together created opportunity structures for technology change (O'Rourke, 2005). As conceived by leading agents, firms would invent and market biodegradable plastics, consumers would use them to carry groceries home and then re-use them to bag kitchen waste and other organic materials, trash collectors would pick up organics separate from other waste, industrial-scale compost facilities would convert materials into useable soil and finally, consumers and even farmers could use the final compost for gardening and agriculture. But to succeed, the model required verifiably compostable plastics and alignment by all parties to a particular set of actions with otherwise mundane and ignored plastic bags.

3.3   ECOFLEX INNOVATION PROCESS

BASF, a global chemical and plastics manufacturer headquartered in Germany, carried out a feasibility study for new materials in the early 1990s as the firm grew aware of policy changes being proposed in Germany concerning waste handling. Initial findings suggested the firm could invent and manufacture new plastics that would fit with existing manufacturing equipment but would decompose organically. Founded in 1865, BASF is a diversified manufacturer of organic chemicals, including agricultural chemicals (fertilizers, insecticides and pesticides), polymers (especially plastics and synthetic fibres), specialty and performance products (for example, antioxidants and lubricant additives) and nutritional compounds. BASF has been the world's largest chemical company for decades when measured by overall sales and employee numbers, although it was only in 2007 that it overtook US competitors in chemical sales alone (Tremblay, 2007; C&EN, 2012).

Anticipating a modest initial market for biodegradable polymers that would grow slowly over time, BASF's management determined that any new material would have to fit with existing manufacturing equipment. Responsible for major facilities to synthesize, package and ship polymers in bulk, senior executives were unlikely to support new pilot plants or capital investments in product-specific manufacturing equipment. But the firm did assign several people to a project team for recyclable and biodegradable plastics.

Over the course of a series of brainstorming sessions that included technical experts and applications-focused scientists, the team advanced the idea of a biodegradable trash bag that consumers could use in their kitchens and then place outside for curb side pickup. Specific requirements included 'properties similar to polyethylene, producible using conventional starting materials available on an industrial scale, if possible with backward integration into BASF's raw materials ... [and] utilization of existing BASF polymerization technologies/plants'. (BASF, 2004, p. 9)

3.3.1 From the Field to the Laboratory

Additional support for research into new biodegradable polymers came from German government funds targeted to supporting industrial biotechnology (Giesecke, 2000). Concerned with low investor support for non-medicinal biotechnology, the government seeded a variety of new institutes in the 1990s and supported competitions among regions to foster biotech clusters. One grant recipient was the restructured Gesellschaft für Biotechnologische Forschung (GBF) at the University of Braunschweig in central Germany. The launch of GBF, previously an academic institute for molecular biology, included a shift to applied work on fermentation and molecular decomposition. Pulling together an interdisciplinary group of chemists and biologists, the GBF began laboratory and field experiments on biodegradation.[2]

Initially, the group carried out studies that brought the analysis of composting processes from the field into the laboratory. In the past, compost researchers put experimental materials into test piles outdoors and measured their volume, temperature, moisture and other properties at regular intervals for up to six months. The scale and process was analogous to backyard composting as carried out by the general public, but not reflective of large-scale industrial composting as was being developed by municipalities. The GBF group pioneered novel protocols for biodegradation, including isolation of microorganisms, measures of enzymatic activity and biological conversion, and other changes in physical and chemical structure that could be measured in tests as brief as 20 seconds in duration (Augusta et al., 1992; Urstadt et al., 1995). Initial tests based on titration (hydrolysis in water or salt water solutions) and plating (suspending the polymer powder in the agar of a petri dish) proved challenging to replicate and standardize. Rolf-Joachim Müller and his colleagues at GBF (Müller et al., 1992; Müller et al., 1994) thereupon modified the so-called 'Sturm test', which uses carbon dioxide emissions as a measure of biological activity. The GBF team thus incrementally developed a controlled system for testing polymers that relied on CO_2 emissions to determine the degree of biological degradation.

In parallel with the development of new protocols and increasingly standardized laboratory tests for biodegradation, the GBF group began testing the compostability of a variety of synthetic plastics as well as cellulose-, starch- and polylactic acid-based compounds. The laboratory obtained samples from firms across Germany and lab members synthesized numerous additional propane-based compounds. In the mid-1990s, the research group started to publish a series of articles in peer-reviewed journals documenting methods and describing the synthesis and testing of novel biodegradable compounds.[3]

When a Ph.D. student from GBF presented findings at a polymers conference in Stockholm and at the large 'K-Messe' (*Kunststoffmesse*, an annual synthetic materials trade show) in Düsseldorf, the BASF and GBF groups became aware of one another. For the GBF group, this connection posed both a challenge and an opportunity. BASF could supply additional materials for testing, but with its greater laboratory and legal resources, the firm was moving rapidly to patent new molecules.[4] Following discussions, BASF and GBF began collaborating through regular visits, presentations and the exchange of materials for testing. In a significant move, BASF supplied the Braunschweig group with butane-based compounds, a traditional feedstock for the company. GBF then directed research to testing the molecules supplied by BASF and stopped synthesizing new propane-based plastics for biodegradation tests.[5]

3.3.2 From the Laboratory to Product Development

Before beginning the collaboration with GBF, the BASF group studied known molecular structures and the chemical literature on degradation. Team members could also call on experts from across BASF's diverse product portfolio. Insights were drawn, for example, from discussions with scientists who worked on soaps and detergents. Their familiarity with environmental regulations and the chemistry of environmental breakdown was new to polymer chemists. According to BASF product managers, the company put the molecular structure at the centre of its innovation planning. As a result, scientists at the firm were willing to look beyond the prevailing approach of building new polymers from materials like starch and cellulose.[6]

The chemical compound that would become Ecoflex started with the hypothesis that combining classic aromatic polyesters with novel biodegradable aliphatic polyesters could generate a stable but biodegradable plastic. Traditional aromatic polyesters have high melting points (above 200 °C), but typically are not biodegradable. While aliphatic polyesters are biodegradable, their physical properties, especially low melting points, preclude mass-market applications. BASF scientists synthesized compounds that combined the different polymer classes, finding a lead candidate in a butanediol co-polyester whose melting point made it suitable for packaging and plastic bags, among other applications.

Following extensive experimentation, BASF modified the crystalline structure of polybutylene terephthalate (PBT) by incorporating an aliphatic monomer in such a way that the material properties of the polymer remained stable but it was chemically attractive to microorganisms. By 1992, the promising though still unnamed compound had undergone laboratory testing and initial compost trials at the firm to characterize its breakdown components. BASF also sponsored field tests in Kassel and other locations to evaluate how the material performed in actual large-scale compost systems being built at the same time.[7]

In addition to biodegradation tests, BASF carried out a variety of other toxicology studies and environmental tests on Ecoflex, as the product was branded, and its degradation compounds. Following a set of testing protocols standardized across OECD countries in the early 1990s, termed the screening information data set (SIDS), the firm tested for toxicity to daphnia, algae and plants (Becker et al., 2007). Additional tests examined use of the final compost to grow barley compared to standard soil blends. Affirmative results from these tests were later published in product brochures (BASF, 2006, 2007a). While not formally mandated in order to begin selling Ecoflex, BASF used this mix of toxicology and plant tolerance testing to help advance a market for compost. Although BASF would not earn revenue from compost sales, the firm anticipated questions regarding compost materials and proactively developed marketing materials related to downstream uses of the new material.

3.4 STANDARDS AS TECHNOLOGY GOVERNANCE

Even as BASF and GBF developed and tested Ecoflex, a process of negotiating technical standards for biodegradation was initiated in Germany. Standards for biodegradable plastics ultimately distinguished them from other polymers based on their environmental fate rather than on their source in starch, cellulose, petroleum or natural gas. As companies selling a variety of green products have discovered, product authenticity can become a critical stumbling block in consumer purchasing decisions. One successful response has been to work with national or international standards agencies to define terms like 'organic' or 'biodegradation'; another is to develop voluntary certification schemes (Star and Lampland, 2009; Conroy, 2007). For BASF, involvement with technical standard setting was an opportunity to add value to Ecoflex, giving it external verification as biodegradable and serving to distinguish it from competing plastics.

Overlapping, even redundant standards and certification schemes emerged in the wake of criticisms in the early 1990s that manufacturers were making bogus claims of biodegradation (Iles and Martin, 2013). Notably, some firms added a small amount of starch to polyolefins, which resulted in their disintegration but not chemical conversion. Regulators in the United States and Europe even brought legal actions against several firms for making false claims (Narayan, 1994). These cases also prompted companies to seek a scientific definition for biodegradation that would stand up to legal or regulatory challenge.

An initiative begun in 1992 by the Deutsches Institut für Normung (DIN) ultimately served as the core site for defining global plastics degradation standards. The DIN standard came about in two discrete phases. First, an ad-hoc working group (*Arbeitskreis*) primarily made up of academic scientists from Germany, elsewhere in Europe, and a few members from the United States and Japan met between 1992 and 1995. Second, a more formal group of industry and select academic experts was convened between 1995 and 1997 to develop and issue the official standard (Deutsches Institut für Normung, 1999).

DIN, a private institution established in 1917 by the German Engineering Association (*Verein Deutscher Ingenieure*), is a world leader in setting standards and norms. In its publications, DIN differentiates between norms, which are consensus documents involving all interested parties for products already on the market, and standards, which are negotiated by experts from invited organizations, but not necessarily with full consensus (Hartlieb et al., 2009). The process of setting standards is itself subject to standardized procedures, notably a sequence that includes meetings among technical experts, publication of drafts for expert comment, revisions and adoption of the final standard (Jänchen, 2008).

In the initial three-year working group phase, a total of 12 meetings were held to advance test methods and develop an official working paper. From the start, the ad-hoc working group had to resolve whether the breakdown that occurs to plastics from sunlight would count as biodegradation. Did a specific chemical reaction have to occur, and if so, how should it be measured? The working group soon focused on laboratory outcomes, specifically the chemistry of compost and measuring CO_2 output, rather than using historical measures of compost volume or demanding specific properties from the final compost. A second challenge for the ad-hoc group concerned test replication, both between labs and within a given lab over time. The working group included numerous laboratories with different approaches to testing and measurement. Over the course of three years, the group reduced test methods to six groups of procedures and then narrowed these to four specific test protocols.

A shift from academic to industrial expertise took place as the polymer biodegradation discussions moved from the ad-hoc group to a formal committee with the power to write an official DIN standard. During the second phase that began in 1995, representatives from BASF, other German and international chemical companies and applied research institutes in Germany joined with DIN experts. In early 1997, the group issued a position paper that built a definition for biodegradable polymers around the four protocols laid out in the ad-hoc group's 1995 working paper. The first involved the contents of the polymer; for example, it could not contain heavy metals and be considered biodegradable. The second established the laboratory procedures to test for complete biodegradation, as well as for the evaluation of the materials that remained at the end of the test. The third component detailed outdoor tests to replicate composting in a controlled but accelerated manner. Finally, the fourth part described ecotoxicity tests for the breakdown components in the final compost (Krzan et al., 2006).

At that point, the proposed standard was available for expert comment and generated over 100 responses from industry, academics and government scientists, including from the German environmental ministry.[8] DIN experts then wrote an official reply to each comment and invited participants to meetings at which they could contribute to the committee's work. Minor revisions to the standard were completed in mid-1997 and the final revised norm was formally issued by DIN in early 1998 (Deutsches Institut für Normung, 1997, 1998).

The final DIN standard classified a compound as biodegradable if it converted to carbon dioxide, water and biomass via microbial action. The key metric for producers was the conversion of 90 percent of the organic carbon to CO_2 in less than 180 days. Providing an example of how technical standards can diverge from everyday experience, wood and most tree leaves would not be certifiable as biodegradable under the standard, since they compost too slowly. By working in a sequence of technical groups and in close collaboration with DIN over the course of five years, BASF succeeded in advancing a definition of biodegradation that aligned to the technical properties of the new Ecoflex molecule.[9]

As the DIN biodegradation standard gained traction, BASF and DIN worked together to broaden its reach. A first step was to develop a European Union standard, later termed EN 13432, which adhered closely to the DIN standard. Second, the DIN group influenced revisions to American Society for Testing and Materials (ASTM) standards. By 1998, international standards imposed the additional requirement that the resulting compost be able to support plant life. Specific standards for test methods and additional technical requirements for commercial composting followed (Krzan et al., 2006; Riggle, 1998). The shift from ASTM and DIN to negotiations on international standards was dominated by industry and involvement of the original academic community declined. Expertise with new materials was increasingly found in industry, not in academic centres, and firms including BASF sought standards for biodegradation that worked on an industrial scale.

3.5 MARKET ANTICIPATIONS AND MARKET REALITIES

From 1994 onwards, BASF filed patents on Ecoflex and began experimenting with larger-scale production in a pilot plant. Once product testing was complete and the biodegradation standards were in place, the firm began scaling up production. In 1997, the BASF project team initiated sales to companies that converted bulk Ecoflex to plastic bags and thin-film food wrappers. The compound had met internal demands that it could be manufactured using existing facilities, initially between larger-volume runs of polyethylene. Nevertheless, its status at BASF was precarious, with uncertainty over which uses to advertise and which market niche it would occupy.

At the time of Ecoflex's market launch, the company had an internal assessment underway about future strategic directions. Ultimately, BASF's leadership elected to continue a focus on supplying other manufacturers, rather than brand materials and become a more visible consumer products firm. BASF had experimented with direct consumer sales in the past, including branded photographic film, magnetic tape and audiocassettes. The new strategy oriented the company's identity to its role as a manufacturer of materials used by consumer-facing firms. A new advertising campaign emphasized the centrality of its products to a wide array of consumer goods: 'We don't make a lot of the products you buy. We make a lot of the products you buy better.' (Verboven, 2011, p. 428)

But with over 2000 distinct chemicals in BASF's portfolio, Ecoflex was at risk of being ignored. The Ecoflex project leader described tensions arising from the company's typical marketing approach: 'If we had used existing relationships, the BASF sales personnel would have had to make 10 customer visits to sell a single ton of Ecoflex when they could sell 10 000 tons of polyethylene with a single phone call. Ecoflex would have been dead. So we created a dedicated team.'[10] Customers, primarily companies that would buy Ecoflex in bulk and then make plastic bags and films, had to be convinced to take a chance on an unproven market. But the Ecoflex project team had confidence in its marketing plan built around consumer uses of biodegradable plastic bags to line waste cans for kitchen scraps as well as other uses for plastics that would end up in the new compost facilities being built in Germany and elsewhere.

A second dimension to the Ecoflex market introduction was for BASF to submit the compound to companies and associations that certify products as biodegradable. These included Japan's GreenPla system for testing and certification, the US-based Biodegradable Products Institute, the US Composting Council (USCC), the Belgian 'OK Compost' certification and labelling system, and others in Europe (BioCycle, 2006). For BASF, each of these certifications involved fees for external laboratory analysis, in most cases following protocols developed in the DIN standardization process. In exchange, the company could use certification logos in advertising and on product information brochures. In a development found more generally across contemporary materials innovation, helping customers and the general public to understand that distinguishing the category of 'green' products from other materials was as important as differentiating Ecoflex from its competitors.

By the 1997 market launch of Ecoflex, BASF appeared to have effectively co-produced its new polymer, technical standards for biodegradation, and an anticipatory market of consumers and compost processors. A network of supporting institutions was developing in the form of retailers eager to sell biodegradable trash bags, large-scale compost facilities with dedicated waste pickup, and certification organizations that tested and labelled plastic bags. Standards served as the central coordinating device bringing together technical and organizational dimensions. To act as a capable agent, BASF connected general scientific knowledge of biodegradation to specific polymer knowledge at the firm. Representatives of the company worked within the structural context of DIN

standardization procedures but shaped the outcome through a sophisticated reframing of the very concept of biodegradation.

3.5.1   Consumer Behaviour and Market Repositioning

BASF's anticipated market for Ecoflex was built around changing rules
for garbage collection and waste management across Europe. Under
German, Austrian and EU-wide mandates, cities and regions set up
systems to collect kitchen, restaurant and grocery store waste, compost it,
and then distribute the usable final soil product to farmers and consumers. With landfill space projections showing shortages within two
decades and public concerns with the environment translating into
behavioural changes, these systems offered efficiency gains over individual compost, especially for people with no yards or only small
gardens (Scheinberg and Smoler, 1990).

A critical component of this program was to turn the collection and
segregation of biodegradable materials into both a civic duty and a
functioning market. The system was planned to operate primarily through
mandates for waste haulers and trash processing centres funded by waste
fees and taxes. But it also involved the creation of norms for individuals
to separate trash before pickup and a secondary market in compost.
However, as the systems were put into place, compost engineers found
that many people did not separate their waste in as disciplined a way as
the experts envisioned. Even German consumers failed to adhere to waste
separation, running counter to expectations that standardized procedures
would induce predictable and routinized behaviours (Cohen, 2005). In
the framework developed by Borrás and Edler (2014), a vital linkage
between capable agents and 'everyday users' was missed. While the
biodegradation standards had a significant reach into the market, they
could not regulate consumer behaviour. Compost facilities then found it
necessary to separate a variety of unwanted materials from desired
streams, including metals, glass and diverse plastics.

The separation of compostable from other waste materials poses a
particular problem. Despite branding efforts, facilities find it difficult to
differentiate biodegradable plastics such as Ecoflex from other plastic
bags that will not decompose. Some operators then installed large fans to
blow lightweight materials, especially plastic bags, out of the waste
stream before it is assembled into compost windrows. Extracted materials
are sent to plastic recycling facilities or landfills. In landfills, biodegradable plastics do not decompose in the same way or at the same speed as
in large-scale compost systems. However, biodegradable plastics –
including those based on starch and polylactic acid – need to be removed

from recycling processes that convert other plastics into such products as carpeting, polyester fibres or drink containers (Royte, 2006). Rather than fitting the envisioned market niche with precision, Ecoflex thus faced a dilemma in downstream uses from unruly consumer behaviour and the mixing of different plastics in a single waste stream.

In the face of this challenge, BASF shifted its marketing of Ecoflex and Ecovio, a blend of Ecoflex with corn-based polymers, to two additional markets (BASF, 2012). First, BASF built sales among farmers using plastic sheeting to prevent weed growth and trap moisture in the soil. A second market emerged among organic food packagers who were willing to pay a premium to promote packaging along with the specialty produce. Farmers could plough the sheeting back into the field after harvest and allow it to decompose naturally over time. It would not break down in the short timeframe of a sophisticated compost facility, but studies revealed that it did decompose over four to six months, depending on temperature and moisture (Siegenthaler et al., 2012). Organic food stores willing to pay for biodegradable packaging invested additional effort in separating materials, labelling packaging and educating consumers on backyard compost.

After several years of experimentation with different market applications, Ecoflex is presently used in plastic bags for organic waste as originally envisioned, as wide plastic films used by farmers and others, transparent cling films for food wrapping and coatings for paper plates and other products. Although a minor product relative to overall BASF sales, Ecoflex and Ecovio feature heavily in the company's advertising campaigns. Ads depict plastic bags arranged as petals of an open flower with the caption: 'Environmentally friendly plastic bags are a beautiful thing. Ecoflex, one of the latest breakthroughs from BASF, is a biodegradable plastic that can be used in bags and packaging. It's shelf stable for one full year, then completely decomposes in compost within a few weeks.'[11]

The failure of Ecoflex to align neatly with industrial compost systems posed a challenge to BASF's anticipated market. But flexibility at the firm with regards to uses and users helped avoid failure for the product. Supporters of the product within BASF drove a process to broaden the marketing of Ecoflex and Ecovio to a more diverse range of applications. The firm was not monolithic, but lead sponsors within the company could invoke the investments in developing product standards and anticipations for additional future regulations on plastics to uphold BASF's role as the central capable agent driving the systemic changes necessary to the market success of biodegradable polymers. Standardization of biodegradation remained critical to this sequence since it enabled the firm to differentiate a product category of biodegradable plastics relative to other synthetics. Ecoflex can thus command a price premium that covers its greater manufacturing costs even as it is used in a variety of ways. The sequence of events also demonstrates a long-term strategy at BASF, laying the groundwork for a future market in which polyethylene plastic bags are restricted or banned more widely than at present.[12]

3.6 CONCLUSION

Standards require a significant investment of time and money to write, harmonize internationally and for firms to adopt. Their present growth comes in a period of rapid technology change, expanding global trade and sustained consumer demand for new products and new materials. The adoption of environmental standards by companies that research and manufacture new plastics is illustrative of a broader movement in technology governance. Even as the regulation of product safety and competition still takes place through government agencies, governance of new technology increasingly relies on voluntary collaborative standards (Loconto and Busch, 2010).

This chapter demonstrates the importance of standards and standard setting organizations for the governance of change in socio-technical systems. The capable agent, BASF, introduced a new technology – the biodegradable plastic bag – into a previously wasteful and environmentally damaging system of use and disposal of thin-film plastics. To envision a market for biodegradable plastics, manufacturers had to build a connection to new systems for collecting and disposing of organic waste. BASF positioned itself strategically in the co-production of key institutions, namely German and EU regulations on landfills, standards for biodegradation, and the new plastic Ecoflex. At the same time, the market showed greater interdependencies with everyday users than anticipated. Thanks to inherent flexibility in the use of standards as a tool of technology governance, the capable agent BASF was thereupon able to reposition its product and widen the user market.

The invention, development and marketing of Ecoflex offer insights on green product innovation and standard setting processes more generally. Without regulations that put a cost on previously free environmental externalities, such as discarding plastics into landfills, a critical market pull feature is absent from green product innovation. Likewise, without standards and certification schemes that verify to consumers that products meet the claims made by manufacturers, plastics with very different environmental lifecycle and consumer lifestyle features are compared solely on the basis of price. Plastics regulations drive additional testing and ensure the safety of individual products, but they cannot coordinate across an industry or between users and waste management systems. Standards, on the other hand, serve to differentiate the category of green plastics and to coordinate among industry, government and consumers.

Market anticipations are important to companies from the very start of product innovation. Firms like BASF are engaging in a significant form of economic modelling even as they synthesize molecules, test their properties and work to develop new technical standards. Standards are a particularly important site for firms to develop product distinctiveness within broader categories. They are then invoked by manufacturers when informing consumers about a product's origins, uses and environmental fate. Technical standards for biodegradation, including criteria for laboratory and field tests, are key to differentiating biopolymers from other plastics. Rather than generating homogeneity, the standards helped BASF market a specialty product to consumers seeking plastic bags for kitchen waste, seeking sheeting for fields, and grocery stores and restaurants seeking food packaging. Negotiations over seemingly technical aspects of standards are thus sites for constructing governance of the material world we inhabit, even as we believe we are making autonomous and sophisticated market- and environment-shaping choices in purchase decisions.

NOTES

1. Council of the European Union, Directive 99/31/EC, Article 5, 26 April 1999.
2. Interview of institute director, Gesellschaft für Biotechnologische Forschung (GBF), Braunschweig, 27 September 2006.
3. Among others, see Witt et al. (1995, 1997), Müller et al. (1997) and Witt et al. (1999).
4. GBF took out one German patent in 1995 and an international patent in 1997 on biodegradable polyesters; BASF took out numerous patents on Ecoflex, its manufacture, and applications starting in 1992. For the original patent, see: Deutsches Patentamt, Biologisch abbaubare Polyester, Werkstoffe aus dem Polyester und Herstellungsverfahren (DE 19532771A1).
5. Interview of institute director, GBF, Braunschweig, 27 September 2006; see also Müller and Deckwer (2000).
6. Interview of the senior vice president polymer research and the product manager for Ecoflex, BASF, Ludwigshafen, 4 October 2006.
7. Interview of the senior vice president polymer research and the product manager for Ecoflex, BASF, Ludwigshafen, 4 October 2006.
8. According to DIN officials, this was nearly 10-fold the typical number of comments on a proposed standard.

9. Jänchen (2008) offers additional analysis of corporate strategies for standardization, including a helpful categorization of types of standards and the effectiveness of standards under different industry structures.
10. Interview of the senior vice president polymer research, BASF, Ludwigshafen, 4 October 2006.
11. This advertisement was run in a variety of print and electronic magazines. See, for example, BASF (2007b).
12. Interview of the senior vice president polymer research and the product manager for Ecoflex, BASF, Ludwigshafen, 4 October 2006.

REFERENCES

Augusta, J., R. J. Mueller and H. Widdecke (1992), 'Biologisch abbaubare kunststoffe: Testverfahren und beurteilungskriterien', *Chemie Ingenieur Technik*, **64** (5), 410–415.
BASF (2004), 'Ecoflex' *BASF Research Verbund*, Ludwigshafen: BASF.
BASF (2006), *Ecoflex: Biodegradable Plastic*, Ludwigshafen: BASF.
BASF (2007a), *Totally Convincing: Ecoflex*, Ludwigshafen: BASF.
BASF (2007b), 'BASF: The Chemical Company', *Harvard Business Review*, October, 11.
BASF (2012), 'Ecovio biodegradable plastic overview', accessed 11 December 2013 at www.bioplastics.basf.com/ecovio.html.
Becker, R. A., L. M. Plunkett, J. F. Borzelleca and A. M. Kaplan (2007), 'Tiered toxicity testing: Evaluation of toxicity-based decision triggers for human health hazard characterization', *Food and Chemical Technology*, **45** (12), 2454–2469.
Bilitewski, B., G. Härdtle and K. Marek (1994), *Waste Management*, Berlin: Springer Verlag.
BioCycle (2006), 'Certifying bioplastics compostability', *BioCycle*, May, p. 44.
Blind, K. (2004), *The Economics of Standards: Theory, Evidence, Policy*, Cheltenham, UK and Northampton, MA, USA: Edward Elgar.
Borrás S. and J. Edler (2014), 'The governance of change in socio-technical systems: Three pillars for a conceptual framework', in S. Borrás and J. Edler (eds), *The Governance Socio-technical Systems: Explaining Change*, Cheltenham, UK and Northampton, MA, USA: Edward Elgar.
C&EN (2012), 'Facts and figures of the chemical industry', *Chemical & Engineering News* **90** (27), 37–71.
C&EN (2013), 'Facts and figures of the chemical industry', *Chemical & Engineering News*, **91** (26), 25–31.
Cohen, M. D., R. Burkhart, G. Dosi, M. Egidi, L. Marengo, M. Warglien and S. Winter (2005), 'Routines and other recurring action patterns of organizations: Contemporary research issues', in G. Dosi, D. Teece and J. Chytry (eds), *Understanding Industrial and Corporate Change*, New York: Oxford University Press, pp. 65–108.
Conroy, M. E. (2007), *Branded! How the 'Certification Revolution' is Transforming Global Corporations*, British Colombia: New Society Publishers.

Crease, R. (2011), *World in the Balance: The Historic Quest for an Absolute System of Measurement*, New York: Norton.

Day, R. H., D. G. Shaw and S. E. Ignell (1990), 'The quantitative distribution and characteristics of neuston plastic in the North Pacific Ocean, 1985–88', in R. Shomura and M. Godfrey (eds), *Proceedings of the Second International Conference on Marine Debris*, Washington, DC: National Oceanic and Atmospheric Association, pp. 247–266.

Deutsches Institut für Normung (1997), *DIN V54900: Entwurf. Prüfung der Kompostierbarkeit von Polymeren Werkstoffen*, Berlin: Beuth Verlag.

Deutsches Institut für Normung (1998), *DIN 54900: Testing of the Compostability of Plastics*, Berlin: Beuth Verlag.

Deutsches Institut für Normung (1999), *Jahresbericht NA Kunststoffe (FNK)*, Berlin: DIN.

Favoino E., A. Tornavacca and M. Ricci (2003), 'Recent optimization of schemes for source separation of biowaste taking into account local conditions', ECN/ORBIT Source Separation Workshop.

Giesecke, S. (2000), 'The contrasting roles of government in the development of biotechnology industry in the United States and Germany', *Research Policy*, **29** (2), 205–223.

Hartlieb B., P. Kiehl and N. Mueller (2009), *Normung und Standardisierung*, Berlin: Beuth Verlag.

Iles, A. and A. N. Martin (2013), 'Expanding bioplastics production: Sustainable business innovation in the chemical industry', *Journal of Cleaner Production*, **45**, 38–49.

International Organization of Standardization (2012), 'ISO in Figures for the Year 2011', Geneva, Switzerland: ISO, accessed 11 December 2013 at www.iso.org/iso/iso-in-figures_2011.pdf.

Jasanoff, S. (2004), 'Ordering knowledge, ordering society', in S. Jasanoff (ed.), *States of Knowledge: The Co-production of Science and the Social Order*, New York: Routledge, pp. 31–54.

Jänchen, I. (2008), *Normungsstrategien für Unternehmen: Eine ökonomische Analyse*, Berlin: Beuth Verlag.

Krzan A., S. Hemjinda, S. Miertus, A. Corti and E. Chiellini (2006), 'Standardization and certification in the area of environmentally degradable plastics', *Polymer Degradation and Stability*, **91**(12), 2819–2833.

Loconto, A. and L. Busch (2010), 'Standards, techno-economic networks, and playing fields: Performing the global market economy', *Review of International Political Economy*, **17** (3), 507–536.

Meilke, J. (1995), *American Plastic: A Cultural History*, New Brunswick, NJ: Rutgers University Press.

Morris, P. (1986), *Polymer Pioneers*, Philadelphia: Center for the History of Chemistry.

Müller, R. J., J. Augusta and M. Pantke (1992), 'An interlaboratory investigation into the biodeterioration of plastics, with special reference to polyurethanes; Part 1: A modified sturm test', *Material und Organismen*, **27** (3), 179–189.

Müller, R. J., J. Augusta, T. Walter and H. Widdecke (1994), 'The development and modification of some special test methods and the progress in standardisation of test methods in Germany', in Y. Doi and K. Fukuda (eds), *Biodegradable Plastics and Polymers,* Amsterdam: Elsevier, pp. 237–249.

Müller, R. J. and W. D. Deckwer (2000), 'Biologisch abbaubare Polymere', in *GBF Berichte aus der Forschung,* Braunschweig: Gesellschaft für Biotechnologische Forschung, pp. 35–54.

Müller, R. J., U. Witt and W. D. Deckwer (1997), 'Biologisch abbaubare Polyester-Copolymere aus petrochemischen und nachwachsenden Rohstoffen', *Fett/Lipid* **99** (2), 40–45.

Narayan, R. (1994), 'Impact of government policies, regulation, and standards activities on an emerging biodegradable plastics industry', in Y. Doi and K. Fukuda (eds), *Biodegradable Plastics and Polymers*, Amsterdam: Elsevier, pp. 261–270.

O'Rourke, D. (2005), 'Market movements: Nongovernmental organization strategies to influence global production and consumption', *Journal of Industrial Ecology*, **9** (1–2), 115–128.

Riggle, D. (1998), 'Moving towards consensus on degradable plastics', *BioCycle*, March, 64–70.

Royte, E. (2006), 'Corn Plastic to the Rescue?', *Smithsonian*, August, 84–88.

Russell, A. (2013), *An Open World: History, Ideology, and Network Standards*, Cambridge: Cambridge University Press.

Scheinberg, A. and D. Smoler (1990), 'European food waste collection and composting programs', *Resource Recycling*, December, 76–81.

Siegenthaler, S. O., A. Künkel, G. Skupin and M. Yamamoto (2012), 'Ecoflex and Ecovio: Biodegradable, performance-enabling plastics', in B. Reiger, A. Künkel, G. W. Coates, R. Reichardt, E. Dinjus and T. A. Zevaco (eds), *Synthetic Biodegradable Polymers*, Heidelberg: Springer.

Star, S. L. and M. Lampland (2009), 'Reckoning with standards', in M. Lampland and S. L. Star (eds), *Standards and their Stories*, Ithaca, NY: Cornell University Press, pp. 3–24.

Tremblay, J. F. (2007), 'The chemical company', *Chemical and Engineering News*, **85** (12), 20–23.

Urstadt, S., J. Augusta, R. J. Müller and W. D. Deckwer (1995), 'Calculation of carbon balances for evaluation of the biodegradability of polymers', *Journal of Environmental Polymer Degradation*, **3** (1), 121–131.

Van de Velde, K. and P. Kiekens (2002), 'Biopolymers: Overview of several properties and consequences on their applications', *Polymer Testing*, **21** (4), 433–442.

Verboven, H. (2011), 'Communicating CSR and business identity in the chemical industry through mission slogans', *Business Communication Quarterly*, **74** (4), 415–431.

Witt, U., R. J. Müller and W. D. Deckwer (1995), 'New biodegradable polyester-copolymers from commodity chemicals with favorable use properties', *Journal of Environmental Polymer Degradation*, **3** (2), 215–223.

Witt, U., R. J. Müller and W. D. Deckwer (1997), 'Biodegradation behavior and material properties of aliphatic/aromatic polyesters of commercial importance', *Journal of Environmental Polymer Degradation*, **5** (1), 81–89.

Witt, U., M. Yamamoto, U. Seeliger, R. J. Müller and V. Warzelhan (1999), 'Biodegradable polymeric materials: Not the origin, but the chemical structure determines biodegradability', *Angewandte Chemie International Edition*, **38** (10), 1438–1442.

Yamamoto, M., U. Witt, G. Skupin, D. Beimborn and R. J. Müller (2002), 'Biodegradable aliphatic-aromatic copolyesters: Ecoflex', in Y. Doi and A. Steinbüchel (eds), *Biopolymers*, (vol. 4), Weinheim: Wiley-VCH, pp. 299–305.

4. Transitioning sustainability: performing 'governing by standards'

Allison Loconto and Marc Barbier

4.1 INTRODUCTION

Sustainability is a multi-faceted and highly contested topic in many sectors. As a discourse, it simultaneously brings together competing regimes of knowledge around how sustainability should be defined and practiced. The articulation of the present and the anticipated future varies across sectors, meaning that a vast array of phenomena and complex situations need to be considered, studied, and compared. In the industrial agriculture sector, cutting-edge biological, chemical and mechanical technologies maintain a monopoly, although tenuous, on the current agri-food system. However, socio-technical regimes are in flux and the appearance of stability to the outside eye actually consists of significant work to reinforce the dominance of the current knowledge regime and to limit alternatives to niche innovations or novelties. This is particularly the case when landscape pressures introduce new imperatives that all social actors should work towards, such as sustainability (Levin et al., 2012). Temporally, we stand within this transition to sustainability. In this current space the vision of sustainability remains a fluid and contested concept and the knowledge needed to govern both the transition and the future is uncertain (cf. Elzen et al., 2011; Levin et al., 2012; Barbier, 2010).

Due to this uncertainty, we witness competing or co-existing socio-technical systems in agriculture. From our vantage point we can observe, in real time, how each group is constructing the knowledge base and socio-technical infrastructure necessary for transitioning to wide-spread adoption of their version of sustainable agriculture. On the one hand, there is the push by multinational agribusinesses like Monsanto and Syngenta to promote the intensification of agricultural research and experimentation into genetic engineering (GE) and innovations in synthetic inputs as a means to make industrial agriculture more sustainable (cf. Lyson, 2002). Here, scientific knowledge production, and thus the organization of the socio-technical system, is mainly driven by biotechnology based on molecular biology (Vanloqueren and Baret, 2009). On the other hand, alternative approaches to sustainable agriculture, often in response to the dominant socio-technical regime, emerge in niches (Elzen et al., 2012). However, these 'niche emergences' remain as static configurations that cannot hide the messiness of the prevailing situation. This situation is characterized by increasing 'landscape pressures' for sustainability alongside only modest changes in practices initiated largely by a rather fragmented group of social innovation pioneers (Barbier and Elzen, 2012). A number of these system innovations are based on the scientific principles of agro-ecology (Altieri, 1987; Kloppenburg, 1991) and the organization of the expansion of food production within global food provisioning systems built on the management science of process standards and audits using third-party certification (for example, Bain et al., 2005; Higgins et al., 2008; Mutersbaugh, 2005). Paradoxically, this expansion of sustainable niches within the global agri-food system is made possible by new global rules, regulations and institutions implemented by the World Trade Organization (WTO) and by the growing influence of oligopolistic food retailers (Busch and Bain, 2004). In this paper we explore this second pathway to sustainability, bearing in mind how sustainability standards are attached to system innovations at the level of the farm.

On this path, sustainability is achieved through the creation, implementation and evaluation of sustainability standards (Loconto and Fouilleux, 2014). The reliance upon standards as a means to regulate agri-food systems suggests that a socio-technical regime based on the concept of 'certified sustainability' is emerging. However, the observation of a regime of 'certified sustainability' does not tell us much about how this socio-technical change is occurring. Therefore, in Chapter 4 we ask *how this regime is constructed and how standards are used to govern the transition to sustainability.*

Given the path-dependent nature of programs for sustainable agriculture (for example, Lowe and Murdoch, 2003), it is important to be more precise about the sources of lock-in (cf. Vanloqueren and Baret, 2009) and the types of knowledge being mobilized in this transition. A clarification of techniques and knowledge can help to 'peel the layers' of contemporary agri-food system transitions. In so doing we can identify actors, techniques and knowledge that are important for directing this transition towards sustainable agriculture from a market regulation point of view. We use the case of the Assurance Code developed by the ISEAL Alliance (the global association for social and environmental standards) to illustrate how this organization, which is an organization comprised of the leading social and environmental standards development organizations (SDOs), is framing the knowledge and infrastructure needed to govern the transition toward a regime of 'certified sustainability'. We draw upon participatory observation in the Assurance Code technical and steering committees between 2010 and 2012. Since ISEAL conducted their internal meetings according to the Chatham House Rule,[1] we do not use direct quotations from these observations but rather quotations from interviews (nine) conducted outside of the meetings and publicly available documents (for example, meeting minutes, public consultations, and community news).

Chapter 4 proceeds as follows. First, we present our conceptual framework that discusses socio-technical transitions and introduces the role of standards as a means of governing a transition. Following Borrás and Edler (2014), we focus on the opportunity structures and capable agents that are part of this transition and show how we intend to explore how changes towards sustainability might be governed by standardization processes. Second, we tie these questions to the analytical technique that we use in this paper to explore this potential role of standards. We do this by exploring the ways in which knowledge is framed in the construction of instruments of governance. Third, we present our empirical data and analyse the negotiations that took place during the writing of ISEAL's Assurance Code, which is a meta-standard for SDOs. We shed light on the relationship between credibility and legitimacy, the embodiment of skills in auditors, and the attempts to establish sampling protocols in order to tame risk. Fourth, we reflect upon what this meta-standard means for governing the transition to sustainability. We conclude by relating this case study to questions about the governance of change in socio-technical and innovation systems, which is the purpose of this volume.

4.2   CERTIFIED SUSTAINABILITY: OPPORTUNITY STRUCTURES AND CAPABLE AGENTS

The multi-level perspectives (MLP) approach to technological innovation (Geels, 2010; Geels et al., 2008; Rip and Kemp, 1998; Geels, 2002) theorizes that it is the way niches, regimes and landscape processes interact that determines a specific transition among various pathways. This framework is helpful for conceptualizing shifts in socio-technical paradigms over long periods of time, particularly when one can examine data retrospectively, like the shift from sailing to steam ships (Geels,

2002). However, we find ourselves within the midst of a transition to sustainability where there are increasing pressures at a landscape level to change practices, and there is significant mobilization from the bottom-up to propose alternative means to govern and practice this transition (Grin, 2006; Elzen et al., 2012). This overwhelming uncertainty about what to do and how to do it suggests that we need a more nuanced understanding of how transitioning can be done so that we don't lose track of the value that sustainability is intended to bring. Grin et al. (2010) highlight two levels of analysis that are important for understanding transitions to sustainability: the relationship between market, state and civil society, and value systems that prioritize sustainability.

In the move from socially responsible consumption practices and claims (Antil, 1984) towards what we are calling 'certified sustainability', sustainability standards are one result of shifts in the relationships between market, state and civil society actors as they collaborate in multi-stakeholder initiatives and transnational alliances. Scholars have noted the increased use of accountability politics (Florini, 2000) where NGOs have focused their attention toward the corporate sector and international organizations, rather than the state, as both the source and the resolution of their concerns (Armstrong and Bernstein, 2008; Schurman, 2004). Accompanied by a significant withdrawal of the state in regulatory activities, it is clear that both civic activism and corporate strategy have contributed to the construction of governance structures by non-state actors (Cashore, 2002; Guay et al., 2004).

This reconfiguration of relationships between social actors opened opportunities for the emergence of agri-food niches that value sustainability differently than that of the dominant agricultural paradigm (Beus and Dunlap, 1990; Van Der Ploeg, 2010; Lyson and Welsh, 1993). Indeed, the ability to construct alternative ways to value agriculture is fundamental to current trends in agri-food activism (Wright and Middendorf, 2008), to the emergence of systems of private regulation in the agri-food system (Bartley, 2007), and to the ways of managing the local collective risks of agro-chemical based agriculture (Barbier, 2008). Specific tactics used by agri-food movements 'within and against the market' attempt to turn activists into 'citizen consumers' (Lockie, 2009). These include the rise of the fair trade movement and other social and environmental standards schemes (Raynolds et al., 2007), which provide the means by which 'citizen consumers' can consume the values of fair trade, social justice, organic and environmentalism, presumably produced by citizen producers (for example, Guthman, 2002; Evans, 2011).

In other words, what we describe above is a silent shift from the tactics of moral practices and discursive repertoires traditionally found in civic activism (Tarrow, 2005), to hybrid fora (Callon and Rip, 1991) composed of civic actors who set the goals of activism, the values they want to promote and the ways to measure those values through the development of standards systems. These systems have implications for socially responsible investing (Guay et al., 2004) and organizational buying and accounting. Therefore, 'certified sustainability' might be characterized as a socio-technical regime that spans nations and sectors where civic activism is mixed with corporate strategies not only to identify the problems of sustainability, but also to propose the solution. Finally, certified sustainability describes a component of an emergent socio-technical regime where producers produce sustainability and consumers consume sustainability, both in parallel and in cooperation with the agro-industrial food provisioning system via large oligopolistic food retailers.

4.3   TRANSITIONING AS PERFORMATION: INSTRUMENTS AND GOVERNANCE MECHANISMS

Fundamental to the transition towards this new regime is the social and organizational technology of standards, whose role in governing this transition is not explained by social movement theories alone. Transition management has emerged as an approach that attempts to resolve questions related to the governance of large-scale societal transformations (for example, Smith et al., 2005; Schot and Geels, 2008). This body of literature examines and reflects upon strategies by actors to understand how and why certain pathways are forged and become dominant. Yet transition management has also been criticized for glossing over politics, controversy and the practicalities of everyday practices that are necessarily part of the practice of managing transitions (Shove and Walker, 2007). The recent work on sustainability transitions note these shortcomings and propose that new research is conducted that can bridge these gaps (Grin et al., 2010). We argue that in order to understand both the management of pathways and the politics involved, we must recognize that these activities, like other forms of governance, are performative (cf. MacKenzie et al., 2007; Busch, 2007; Law, 2008; Loconto, 2010). That is, these activities must be put into action and what happens when they are enacted makes changes to the activities themselves. Therefore, to effectively perform the transition, actors must control the way that types of knowledge and corresponding activities are framed, and learn from it.

This is where standardizing projects come into play as a setting for performing standards.

Standards are values, rules, norms and conventions for action, but they also assemble the script of this moral dimension into a network of material objects (Akrich, 1992) such as checklists, testing samples and labels (cf. Loconto and Busch, 2010; Grewal, 2008). They are the measures against which performances are judged, the organizing infra-structures that determine which performances are possible, and the devices that standardize those practices (Busch, 2011). Standards are created by dedicated organizations or by less formal collectives and are defined by how they are enacted, tested and verified within and outside of these collectives. As such, they are socio-technical devices that entangle a variety of actors into networks so to reproduce standardized meanings and practices over time (Rip, 2010; Callon et al., 2002). Indeed, it is through the compounding effects of entanglement where scholars have found a role for standards by creating path-dependency for innovations (for example, Allen and Sriram, 2000; Egyedi and Spirco, 2011). This occurs as the standardization of practices is reenacted by multiple actors over time, thus reinforcing the meaning of the standard and governing its future enactments. Put simply, standards are enacted and performative but also purposefully transformative.

Standards therefore provide a means through which actors can control the transition towards sustainability (Hatanaka et al., 2012). They do this through a regime of governance comprising: (1) actors who set standards; (2) those who certify and (3) those who verify their compliance, and attest to (accredit) the capacity of the certifier to verify compliance (Loconto and Busch, 2010; Hatanaka et al., 2012). These three core competencies have been described as a 'tripartite standards regime' (TSR) of governance and their construction constitutes a techno-economic network, or infrastructure, for the exchange of goods and services in a market economy (cf. Callon, 1991). The TSR describes a complex and dynamic system of market-based oversight, which relies upon the tools of standards and audit, and is believed to ensure the objectivity, honesty and credibility of actors at all levels (Loconto and Busch, 2010; Power, 1997). The increased importance of the TSR in society is referred to elsewhere as the phenomenon of 'governing by standards' (Loconto and Fouilleux, 2014; Ponte et al., 2011; Thévenot, 2009). 'Governing by standards' refers to the use of standards to regulate agri-food systems and by so doing creates a specific interpretation of sustainability in agribusiness. As a result, we have a decent understanding of how standards are used. What we still don't know is why some techniques are promoted over others and what this means for the shape and direction of the transition.

We propose that by focusing on how matters of concern are framed in the development of standards, we can see the politics and practicalities of transitioning to sustainability and in the end describe the regime of knowledge that justifies 'certified sustainability'. Our analytical framework draws upon Callon's (1998) notion of framing, as opposed to other approaches (cf. Benford and Snow, 2000; Gamson and Modigliani, 1989), because it focuses on how the framing of a controversial situation is an attempt by actors involved in the negotiations to make the problem calculable by limiting the number overflows (that is, what the frame fails to explain). This process of making things calculable is often contested as it entails changing them through the process of measurement (cf. Crease, 2011) and thus becomes political, i.e., making things calculable makes things political using measurement techniques and figures. This approach takes the materiality and the calculability of the situation into account and allows us to focus on the knowledge regimes that are being drawn upon in the framing process. We use Callon's (1998) interpretation of 'hot' and 'cold' negotiations in the framing process. Hot negotiations are destabilized situations where there is no clear normative and factual basis established and all aspects of the matter of concern are open for debate. Here, the facts and the values that inform decision-making are indistinguishable. Cold negotiations are more stabilized debates where the facts are clearer and the values are kept separate. The frames are made explicit and actors can easily calculate a solution to the matter of concern.

4.4   MODELS OF ASSURANCE – THE CASE OF THE ISEAL ALLIANCE

The ISEAL Alliance is a membership-based organization officially registered as a non-profit organization in the UK in 2002, but created by four SDOs in the late 1990s. The founding SDOs were the Forest Stewardship Council (FSC), the International Forum of Organic Agriculture Movements (IFOAM), Fairtrade International (FLO) and the Marine Stewardship Council (MSC). As of 2013, there were thirteen full members, six associate members, and forty-six subscribers. The purpose of ISEAL is to increase communication and collaboration among SDOs and to increase the influence of sustainability standards in society (ISEAL, 2013). The ISEAL Alliance is considered to be an important, and legitimate, actor in sustainability politics (Bernstein, 2011; Dingwerth and Pattberg, 2009).

ISEAL acts as an institutional entrepreneur who institutionalizes meta-standards for sustainability and develops internal and external legitimation strategies that establish ISEAL as the key regulator for 'certified sustainability' (Loconto and Fouilleux, 2014). These meta-standards are called 'credibility tools' and consist of codes of good practice for standards-setting, assessing impacts and providing assurance. They contribute to framing the political and moral dimensions of what has to be inscripted in the standard. Taken together, they 'provide end users and other interested parties with confidence in the effectiveness of the standards system as a whole'. (ISEAL, 2012c, p. 3)

The Assurance Code, launched in 2012, is fundamental to the transition to sustainability as it formally establishes the necessity of setting up a TSR by each of its members. The purpose of the Assurance Code is to 'encourage conformity by clients and instil public confidence in the results of assurance, thereby increasing the use of the standard'. (ISEAL, 2012c, p. 3) Specifically, the Assurance Code sets the limits of how certification and accreditation should be conducted for sustainability standards and furthermore defines how these activities are linked to the other ISEAL codes. The 'essential values that encourage conformity and instil trust in an assurance system' (p. 7) are: consistency, rigour, competency, impartiality, transparency and accessibility. These values also provide the intent behind the requirements and are used to determine if a conformity assessment system is credible.

Given the importance of how this standard governs other standards, we focus on three core negotiations that took place during the standard-setting process. These are credibility, auditor competency and sampling. In our discussion we explore how each concept was stabilized based on specific ways of knowing.

4.4.1 Auditor Competence: A Cold Negotiation

The first negotiation revolved around framing auditor competence. This is characterized as a cold negotiation since ISEAL members identified auditor competence as the most important aspect of assurance that could be addressed in part by new requirements or guidance before starting the standard setting process (ISEAL, 2011a). Moreover, within the debates the facts (auditor incompetency renders non-credible audits) and values (good auditors embody the values of the standard) were quickly identified, agreed upon and calculated.

Providing proof by identifying who is responsible for overflows and who is affected by them is important for making them calculable. For example, auditor competence was explained as follows: 'Auditing is always an issue. We train two auditors; one is good and one isn't – why?' (ISEAL, 2011b) There was debate within the technical and steering committees on this topic, and the responsibility for ensuring that auditors are competent was shifted from certification bodies to SDOs to the auditors themselves in a rather continuous cycle. The certification bodies are responsible for hiring those auditors who have the proper qualifications. Auditors have the responsibility of not only obtaining proper qualifications, but of having the right personality traits and being able to use their auditing expertise to evaluate the situation at hand. ISEAL members promote the use of the ISO 17024 standard, which has an extensive list of ideal auditor traits and characteristics. Moreover, the SDOs are responsible for ensuring that both the certification bodies and the auditors are trained on the particularities of their standards and understand the intent of the standard. This last issue was an interesting point of debate as the first public draft of the Assurance Code had the following training requirement: 'Scheme-owners shall ensure that auditors are trained according to the requirements of their positions. NOTE – Extra effort should be expended to ensure auditors are trained to audit to the intent of the scheme.' (ISEAL 2011c, p. 18)

This requirement recommends that auditors should audit to the intent of the standard, rather than the criteria of the standard. This requires an auditor to have a specific type of knowledge about the standards system that cannot be learned by studying the standard. It is an embodied, subjective knowledge gained only through experience. Only three out of the 815 comments received during the first public consultation addressed this point and only one of them questioned the (desire) ability of auditing to the intent of the standard. The debate during the technical committee meeting in January 2012 proceeded as follows:

> The only thing that the auditor can do is audit to the criteria in the standard, they cannot audit on intent.

> The reason for having this was based on the idea that the standards are not well written and it is not clear what is needed. The auditors have the same interpretation of the content – that is what is important. The criterion says one thing, but the auditor needs to be able to understand it.

> If there is that much confusion about what the standards say then this is being in non-compliance with the ISEAL standards-setting code!

> This clause, this set of conditions being applied and this intent of the scheme – and you need to have common interpretations in order to be able to audit effectively.

Intent and interpretation are two different things – you are going one step higher, up one level higher. Interpretation is not a problem, but there will always be a level of interpretation (they are trying for less, but it will always be there).

Most of this goes back to the standards code. We can say – you must provide good guidance – this is in the standards code.

What we are saying specifically here is that we want auditors to understand the intent (training on the intent) not to audit according to the intent.

The intent here was to try to address the criticisms that audits had turned into check-box exercise.

…

Who is measuring the intent? The scheme owner is supposed to assess the impact according to the impacts code. All three are supposed to be linked together more.

…

Oversight section should be linked to the impacts code and standards setting code – creating feedback loops.

This framing negotiation illustrates that in this case, the overflows are easily identified and the frame is quickly drawn by agreement on a specific type of experiential knowledge that auditors should have 'embodied'. Auditors should be trained, they should have tangible and tacit knowledge of the areas that they work in, and they should embody the ethical concerns of the SDO. The calculation of auditor competency became an exercise in defining a good auditor, with a focus on the framing of skills and human conduct. The transfer of knowledge from an objective form to a subjective form allows closer ties to be made between the components of the TSR infrastructure. For example, if an auditor needs to interpret the intent of the standard because they don't understand it, then the standard should be made more comprehensible. In this way ISEAL reflexively reinforces the linkages between the three components of a TSR (standard-setting, certification and accreditation). This reinforces the network by creating feedback loops and encouraging reflexivity about the way that the standards and actors should work together to create a seamless web of governance. It is this type of reinforced responsibilities that illustrates how knowledge and governance are woven together to aid a socio-technical transition.

4.4.2   Sampling: A Hot Negotiation

Sampling in social and environmental audits inspired hot negotiations during the framing process because the compromise that the standard setters reached did not stabilize the facts or values at stake. Specifically, they did not agree that auditing only a sample of producers rather than the entire population was a good practice for social and environmental standards (*the values*), nor did they agree on how to select the sample (*the facts*).

ISEAL members propose introducing sampling techniques in order to reduce the certification costs, which is a constant complaint of producers. One way to do this is to audit a selected sample of farmers at different intervals of time, rather than every single farmer, every year as is currently the practice. ISEAL members have also requested guidance on or harmonization of sampling techniques, as there is currently no standard in the sector. The most commonly used formula for sampling in group certification is a derivation of the square root formula,[2] originally developed by the United States Department of Agriculture (USDA) to sample individual products from large lots in order to identify defects. While some members are perfectly content to continue using this formula, others have been pushing in two directions for more rigorous methods. One direction is towards statistical sampling, while the other is towards judgmental sampling.

These two sampling techniques are important to ISEAL's framing activities because they each seek to contain specific overflows in order to lock-in the type of knowledge that they seek to produce. As noted above, the current culture of auditing relies on many forms of non-probability sampling techniques – mostly exercises in stratification that rely upon the competency of auditors to efficiently judge the context that they are auditing. In the background report commissioned by ISEAL, judgmental sampling was declared to be an appropriate method for the following types of auditing activities:

- Investigating specific areas of concern – for example focusing on a limited number of standard clauses rather than all standard clauses.
- Sampling within an audit where the process has been validated, and the client is low risk so a decision on whether a full audit is needed or not can be made.
- Reviewing activities of particular interest or concern to determine whether more extensive testing is needed. For example a short unannounced audit of limited scope to see if the client conforms to requirements – and if not a full audit to be held.

- Closing non conformities during a verification audit. (Taruna Group Limited and R. Bradley, 2011, p. 40)

However, discussions showed that there is more of an appreciation for judgmental sampling as the main tool for calculation in social and environmental audits. This was justified based on the complexities (often geographical, cultural, political and economic) that require local knowledge of the situation. Therefore, the argument put forward by this group was that: 'we should not try to integrate the academic statistical sampling approach – the square root method was helpful, it built a base-line, [we should be] careful about seeking perfection.' (ISEAL, 2011d, p. 4) This argument painted statistical sampling within the light of an academic exercise that works only in statisticians' models and theories. This is very much an isomorphism of what is at stake in evidence-based policy and in the development of regulatory science for safety agencies (Demortain, 2008).

Despite this recognition, based on committee members' own experiences with audits, a very clear desire for the statistical credibility that is part of probability sampling was mentioned often. This stems from their lack of confidence in the credibility of the square-root method to produce representative samples. A famous critique of the square root formula was quoted in the ISEAL background report:

> Determination of sample size as the square root of the lot size may create a sense of false security. Lot size alone is shown to provide an incomplete basis for determining sample size, whether by 'square root' sampling or percentage sampling. Sampling plans based on quantitative statements of the risks involved are recommended. (Keith Borland, 1950, p. 373)

This critique is part of further discussions of risk-based sampling and the way in which discourses of risk and risk assessment have also been brought into the frame.

Analysis of the presence of risk-based sampling currently coded into member standards showed that the more 'sophisticated' standards provide different options for sampling based on different situations that the CB will encounter: Individual vs. Group vs. Supply Chain. There are different types of operations within groups and different risks for different entities. Moreover, most of the risk analysis that is being conducted is really centred around trying to figure out who and/or what should be checked – rather than other risks posed by compliance with standards (for example, environmental risks, social risks, business risks).

This experience with risk-based sampling was originally only part of the need for consistent guidance on sampling, but during the committee meetings this morphed into using risk management as an organizing framework for the entire standard. In this scenario the standard would be a decision matrix that could help members to determine which model of assurance was fit for their purpose. However, risk was then demoted again solely to the requirement that members conduct a risk assessment of their assurance system (ISEAL, 2011c). This dynamic reflects a degree of uncertainty where the tools of risk assessment are concerned (for example, HACCP or ISO 31000, 31010),[3] based both on the nature of the problem and the existing knowledge of the same. While most in the room felt comfortable using risk to assess who should be audited, they did not feel comfortable using risk to assess the credibility or appropriateness of the governance models they constructed. This reflects the 'heat' of these negotiations as certain aspects of risk and sampling are considered settled and need only consistency and guidance, while others challenge the basic certainty of the facts and values. For example, many ISEAL members have invested heavily in consumer-facing labels, which claim that all farmers in their system have been confirmed to be in compliance with the standards and their values. In these circumstances, sampling techniques should not be debated because their existence in the system would defy the claims that are being made.

In the end, the Code recommended that each member develop a transparent sampling plan. Little guidance specific to social and environmental standards is included in the standard; rather the technical terminology was adapted from an accounting standard for audit sampling.[4] This also means that a judgment on consistency was not provided. By leaving the frame open ISEAL accommodated both expert (statistical) and experiential (judgmental) knowledge. However, this was very much a political compromise, taken in the interest of furthering their efforts to establish an interdependent system of certification, accreditation and standards setting and evaluation.

4.4.3   Credibility: A Hot Negotiation

The final framing process that we examine links the politics of expert and experiential knowledge that were hinted at above. It is through the framing of credibility that we see the governance implications of establishing a TSR for social and environmental standards systems.

ISEAL members, the secretariat and other interested stakeholders are keen to frame 'credibility'. Their notion of credibility refers to the credibility of social and environmental standards as a means to deliver a more sustainable future. This vision of credibility also includes the credibility of the systems that SDOs put into place to ensure that the standards are credible. ISEAL (2010) claims that 'standards systems that are effective and accessible can bring about globally significant social, environmental, and economic impacts' (p. 1). ISEAL has thus proposed, for debate and public consultation, *Credibility Principles* that constitute the foundation of standards systems that are credible (ISEAL, 2010). Thirteen principles were defined and the following principles were identified as underlying the Assurance Code: Transparency, Multi-stakeholder, Impartiality and Independence of Verification, Consistency of Verification Results, Accessibility, Complaints and Appeals and Inter-operability. These principles were the starting points for the development of the Assurance Code, but initial surveys and dialogue at the ISEAL meetings established specific matters of concern about conformity assessment[5] that needed to be framed in light of credibility: (1) specificity of social and environmental standards and (2) balancing accessibility and growth of members' systems (ISEAL, 2012d).

The first concern is the inadequacy of traditional auditing approaches and third-party certification systems for the reality of social and environmental standards. The main point of agreement among all ISEAL members is that the 'traditional' auditing practices developed in the financial sector and represented by the 'credible' International Organization for Standardization (ISO) standards 17065, 17067, 17011, 17021, and 17024[6] are not sufficient for building credibility in 'certified sustainability'. ISEAL argues that these practices consist mostly of following document trails and are not only inadequate to achieve credibility in standards practices, but they are also inappropriate for capturing the values of social justice and environmental conservation. The second concern is that, as ISEAL and its members push forward their goal of mainstreaming standards throughout the agri-food system, there is a need to balance their desire for creating standards that are accessible to all and standards that are rigorous enough to maintain legitimacy in the market. According to ISEAL, the solution to these problems is found in the adequate framing of credible assurance.

ISEAL identified challenges that their members faced with the ISO approach as related to the sector-based auditor skills (for example interviewing techniques) or unique practices (for example group certification) and the insufficiency of the ISO definitions of effectiveness in terms of impartiality and replicability (Mallet, 2009). In other words, ISEAL had been relying heavily on the ISO standards and the calculations that they allow for the practice of their members' standards, but ISEAL considered its own systems to be unique and wanted to make special concessions for the local contexts where their members' standards are used. ISEAL argued that these specific circumstances, such as working with thousands of smallholders (many of whom are illiterate) and working in geographically dispersed and remote areas, meant that their certifiers and accreditors needed to develop separate protocols to deal with the many non-conformities to the ISO system. For example, Derkx (2011) noted that ISEAL's accreditation members performed poorly when subjected to ISO-based accreditation audits. ISEAL argued that this was not because of incompetence, but because of the realities of where these organizations work.

This is illustrative of the reality that entangled into the ISO network are not only the standards, but also certification and accreditation bodies, checklists, calibration of auditors, formulae, sampling techniques and other intermediary objects, which have been building a consistent enactment of the ISO network over time and through space. ISEAL's members are not fully integrated into this network and in fact set out to develop their own network specific to social and environmental standards. They use ISO compliance as a means for learning as much as possible. Thus, the two questions posed throughout the technical committee meeting in January 2012 (namely 'why is this issue specific for social and environmental standards?' and 'has it been done better somewhere else?') permitted the Assurance Code committees to begin a framing process that allowed credibility to become calculable.

The proposition of 'redefining a credible guarantee' (Mallet, 2009, p. 7) was taken up within the Assurance Code. This is based on the notion that a standard should be 'fit for purpose', which is based on expertise developed in quality management where the term refers to meeting the customer's requirements, needs or desires (Harvey and Green, 1993) and is based on Juran's (1951) original and rather classical notion of 'fit for use' in product development and quality management. In this sense, ISEAL is trying to understand what level of guarantee is required to be credible for each audience when there are different end uses of social and environmental standards (for example, self-assessment, peer evaluation – participatory guarantee systems, supply chain audits, NGO/Trade Union audits, certification, accreditation) (Mallet, 2009). The question that inspired hot debates in the meetings was 'what assurance models or combinations achieve that guarantee?'

The Assurance Code proposed four models of assurance based on the use of first, second and third party assurance. The third party assurance model refers to an ISO 17065 or 17022 compliant model, while the second model is a combination of second and third party assurance. The third model is a combination of first and third party and the fourth model a combination of first and second. A model based solely on first party assurance was not included because 'they are not deemed to offer sufficient credibility' (ISEAL, 2011c, p. 29), thus arriving at agreement on at least one fact. However, these models received a reasonable number of comments (41 out of 815) during the public consultation period. Some of these comments questioned the desirability of ISEAL to make this value judgment; others questioned the validity of all the different types of models, and numerous comments pushed ISEAL to judge the value of credibility that each model can provide. For example:

> If ISEAL is making it explicit that different approaches can legitimately provide different levels of assurance, then this should be spelled out (as above) and justified. I agree it is true, and it's a good insight. If people's lives depend on something, you would rightly demand a high level of assurance about it, even if it's quite expensive and excludes some groups from entering the market....it also implies that systems using lower levels of assurance should be up front that this is what they are doing. Also that ISEAL should be prepared to say that certain types (which ones?) of assurance systems can indeed provide a higher 'level' of assurance. (ISEAL, 2012a, p. 30)

The state of the debate was summarized as follows in the January Assurance Code Newsletter:

> Our objective for the Assurance Code is to encourage innovation whilst ensuring the credibility of those who comply with the Code. Clearly a line needs to be drawn that excludes unacceptable (not credible) practices but where that line should be drawn remains elusive. If we enshrine traditional practice we risk stifling innovation, but if we leave the door open for innovation we risk authorising assurance systems that are not credible. (ISEAL, 2012b)

We see that this negotiation remains hot and in a state of uncertainty. ISEAL members question the framing process of certified sustainability. They fear that such standardization will potentially close down diversity and innovation, as the ISO model has through the widespread adoption of third-party certification. They also fear that if they do not take a stand on limiting the diversity, their own legitimacy as an organization that defines credibility in standards is at risk.

Therefore, the final code contains the four models of assurance, which are labelled A through D so to avoid ranking them. In the online community, ISEAL members still debate these four models and question whether or not some of these models (particularly C and D) should be considered credible. The problem remains unresolved for ISEAL, in that they consistently look to the ISO 17065 system of conformity assessment (which requires third-party certification) as the gold standard of credibility for certification schemes, but are struggling within their network to frame credibility in such a way that they can legitimately stand on their own without relying upon ISO's claim to credibility.

These debates raise interesting questions about the governance of socio-technical systems. Legitimacy is typically a concern of politics and actors who seek to govern, yet ISEAL debates credibility and not legitimacy. In the scientific tradition, credibility ought to be a goal with a non-calculable ethical purpose, yet ISEAL tries to frame this and make it calculably ethical. In other words, ISEAL is caught in a double-bind. It hopes to be creative with their own compliance systems by accommodating the many difficulties and sometimes paradoxical aspects of consolidating certified sustainability, but ISEAL and its members are simultaneously concerned about the legitimacy or credibility of these actions by those who are not part of the system. As a result, the rationalization process of certified sustainability contains, rather explicitly, a framework of mistrust; since the calculability of credibility acknowledges – even through statistical evidence-based methods – the existence of non-appropriate actors, auditors or even members. This suggests the importance of how knowledge is used to govern socio-technical systems. We suggest that expert knowledge and its vocabulary are used by standard setters for political ends, despite their desire to promote values that are better achieved through experiential or subjective knowledge.

4.5 GOVERNING GOVERNANCE

In the previous sections we presented and analysed three framing exercises during the construction of the ISEAL Alliance Assurance Code. We found that the framing of the knowledge needed for certified sustainability opens up new issues like the relationship between credibility and legitimacy, the embodiment of skills in auditors or the call for evidence-based systems in order to tame risk. In this section, we reflect upon what this means for governing the transition to sustainability.

First, a large part of the actions that are involved in a transition to sustainability are not only attempts to expand the scope of certified sustainability, but also to prove that their approach is indeed credible and thus legitimate (Loconto and Fouilleux, 2014). Through our analysis, we see that ISEAL relies upon the framing of credibility as a way to differentiate between their interpretation of conventional tools (for example, ISO standards, risk assessment and sampling methods) and the interpretation of others. ISEAL is attempting to recreate the ISO system, which is a well-established TSR with very clear, independent roles for certifiers, accreditors and standards-setters. However, ISEAL's version is intended to be innovative with multiple ways to achieve the intent, or values, of the standard. Through the framing of knowledge during technical debates, ISEAL puts forward a vision of conformity assessment that is based on the idea of appropriateness, 'fit for purpose' rather than an ideal type of credible guarantee. This illustrates ISEAL's pragmatic and strategic objectives of expanding their influence and the influence of their members' standards. By making values such as credibility, competency and risk calculable, ISEAL enables strategic thinking and management of its 'scaling up' activities. Indeed, this is what transitioning looks like. Socio-technical change is simply constructed through activities, at times pragmatic and at other times strategic, that continue a forward movement from a niche towards a new socio-technical regime.

Second, what this case shows is that the 'hot' situation of sustainability is being cooled through the framing of certified sustainability. This cooling is also opening up new issues like shifting a paradox outsourced from the mobilization of the ISO system to the embodiment of skills in auditors and the need for evidence-based risk management. In fact, while ISEAL is introducing a significant amount of flexibility into what can be considered credible based on a mix of expert and experiential knowledge, it is simultaneously reinforcing the core source of its knowledge, which is found in the ideas of total quality management. These ideas remain the core organizing concepts of ISO. Therefore, in practice, ISEAL is reinforcing the importance of ISO standards and the need for a global system of oversight that provides a consistent and transparent set of checks and balances. This is finally institutionalized within the social and environmental standards movement through the adoption of the Assurance Code.

Third, ISEAL members are beginning to raise the question of who accredits the accreditors, which is currently being completed to a certain extent by ISEAL's peer-review process among members. Yet, they seem to be looking for a more legitimate authority. In fact, ISEAL's Accreditation Body members have been petitioning, to no avail, to join the International Accreditation Forum. Thus, the need to rely upon ISEAL's peer-review process as the highest authority in their TSR means that reflexivity and continuous improvement are fundamental parts of their system. For example, the position of ISEAL is that no member should be able to be fully compliant with ISEAL standards from the start, but should strive to be reflexive and improve their practices so that within one year they can become compliant. Thus, gaining credibility also means a *governmentality* of conduct (Foucault, 1991). The technology of gaining credibility is becoming an ethic that empowers auditors and enables managerial perspectives based on a technology of the self (Styhre, 2001), since being an auditor or becoming a member represents a reflexive effort to achieve compliance to the standard. This activity of raising the bar for themselves is something that ISEAL argues is fundamental to the credibility of their standards and their vision of sustainability.

Finally, given the above two discussions, we see two layers emerging in the transition to certified sustainability. The first is the practice of governing by standards, which has been documented to a large extent by a number of scholars studying sustainability standards (Bartley, 2007; Bernstein, 2011; Ponte et al., 2011; Hatanaka, 2010). The second layer is the *governmentalization* by standards of the organization itself, which entails the construction of a TSR, which remains an understudied topic. This case study clearly shows that the three interrelated activities of standards-setting, certification and accreditation are increasingly becoming the dominant means by which the practice of governing by standards is governed.

The framework proposed by Borrás and Edler (2014) is useful here to explore the relationship between types of governance, the roles of the capable agents, the instruments of change and the questions of legitimacy that we identified in our analysis. The on-going construction of a TSR finds its legacy in many forms of initial struggles, initiatives taking place in niches and in interactions between NGOs and institutions with the aim of promoting the moral values of sustainability. It has also grown within the current socio-technical system of product and quality management standards institutionalized through the ISO. In up-scaling, niche-focused movements towards broader systems change that connects farmers to consumers, capable agents of change like the ISEAL Alliance, have gone in the direction of more institutional centered governance. Our characterization of how this transitioning process from niche to regime is realized in practices and discourses showed that it is fundamentally a process of *performation* of both the valuation of sustainability and of governing by standards. This shift also means an exposure of their institutional position to the larger economic context of framing, retailing and distributing certified sustainability that is 'black-boxed' within commodities. As shown in this case study, a rationalization process is at stake that also carries a possible paradox in terms of the values that ground the sustainability movement in self-organization and engagements. Through the construction of a TSR, NGOs have gone deeper into the management of their own enrolments, showing reflexivity and learning processes that are fundamental to their ability to govern by standards. Yet this shift also has major consequences for the internal organizational consistency of those agents of change and their abilities to uphold the legitimacy of their vision for socio-technical change.

In summary, by focusing on how practices and knowledge contribute towards a transition to certified sustainability, this example of framing within the practices of setting a standard for assurance has shown us that centres of calculation (that is, certification, accreditation and standards development bodies) for certified sustainability are being connected in such a way to facilitate governance at a distance (Latour, 1987). However, establishing such a centre does not occur without struggles (Loconto and Fouilleux, 2014), since the overt political strategies of ISEAL as an institutional entrepreneur are apparent in both the hot and the cold negotiations. This governing at a distance is important for a continued performance of governing by standards and, we would argue, to transitioning niche agricultural practices to a techno-economic regime of certified sustainability. This regime is characterized not so much by a consistent value of sustainability as by the constant practices of standardization, certification and accreditation. Thus the construction of a TSR becomes a tool that is used to implement the multi-layered idea of 'governance of governing by standards at a distance'.

NOTES

1. 'When a meeting, or part thereof, is held under the Chatham House Rule, participants are free to use the information received, but neither the identity nor the affiliation of the speaker(s), nor that of any other participant, may be revealed.' http://www.chathamhouse.org/about-us/chathamhouserule, accessed 10 March 2013.
2. The sample size is usually derived by taking the square root of the entire population plus one and dividing it by two.
3. HACCP stands for Hazards and Critical Control Points, which is a food safety standard that requires users to identify these. ISO 31000 contains the principles and guidelines of risk assessment and ISO 31010 contains risk assessment techniques.
4. International Standard on Auditing 530.
5. Conformity assessment is the term used by practitioners to refer to the systems of audit, certification and accreditation.
6. These standards are part of a suite of standards developed by the Committee on Conformity Assessment. ISO 17065 contains requirements for bodies certifying products, processes and services. ISO 17067 contain the fundamentals of product certification. ISO 17011 has general requirements for accreditation bodies accrediting conformity assessment bodies. ISO 17021 is contains requirements for bodies providing audit and certification of management systems, and ISO 17024 specifies requirements for a body certifying persons against specific requirements, including the development and maintenance of a certification scheme for personnel.

REFERENCES

Akrich, M. (1992), 'The de-scription of technical objects', in W. E. Bijker and J. Law (eds), *Shaping Technology/Building Society: Studies in Sociotechnical Change,* Cambridge, MA: MIT Press, pp. 205–224.

Allen, R. H. and R. D. Sriram (2000), 'The role of standards in innovation', *Technological Forecasting and Social Change,* **64,** 171–181.

Altieri, M. A. (1987), *Agroecology: The Scientific Basis of Alternative Agriculture,* Boulder, CO: Westview Press.

Antil, J. H. (1984),'Socially responsible consumers: Profile and implications for public policy', *Journal of Macromarketing,* **4,** 18–39.

Armstrong, E.A. and M. Bernstein (2008), 'Culture, power, and institutions: A multi-institutional politics approach to social movements', *Sociological Theory,* **26, 74–99.**

Bain, C., B. J. Deaton and L. Busch (2005), 'Reshaping the agri-food system: The role of standards, standard makers and third-party certifiers', in V. Higgins and G. Lawrence (eds), *Agricultural Governance: Globalization and the New Politics of Regulation,* London and New York: Routledge.

Barbier, M. (2008), 'Bottling water, greening farmers: The socio-technical and managerial construction of a 'dispositif' for underground water quality protection', *International Journal of Agricultural Resources, Governance and Ecology,* **7,** 174–197.

Barbier, M. (2010), 'The ecologization of agricultural development and the treadmill of sustainable development: A critique in a state of transition', *Przegląd Socjologiczny (Sociological Review),* October issue.

Barbier, M and B. Elzen (2012), *System Innovations, Knowledge Regimes, and Design Practices towards Transitions for Sustainable Agriculture,* Thiverval-Grignon: INRA SAD.

Bartley, T. (2007), 'Institutional emergence in an era of globalization: The rise of transnational private regulation of labor and environmental conditions', *American Journal of Sociology,* **113,** 297–351.

Benford, R. D. and D. A. Snow (2000), 'Framing processes and social movements: An overview and assessment', *Annual Review of Sociology,* **26,** 611–639.

Bernstein, S. (2011), 'Legitimacy in intergovernmental and non-state global governance', *Review of International Political Economy,* **18,** 17–51.

Beus, C. E. and R. E. Dunlap (1990), 'Conventional versus alternative agriculture: The paradigmatic roots of the debate', *Rural Sociology,* **55,** 590–616.

Borrás, S. and J. Edler (2014), 'The governance of change in socio-technical systems: Three pillars for a conceptual framework', in S. Borrás and J. Edler (eds), *The Governance of Socio-technical Systems: Explaining Change*, Cheltenham, UK and Northampton, MA, USA: Edward Elgar.

Busch, L. (2007), 'Performing the economy, performing science: From neoclassical to supply chain models in the agrifood sector', *Economy and Society,* **36,** 437–466.

Busch, L. (2011), *Standards: Recipes for Reality,* Cambridge, MA: MIT Press.

Busch, L. and C. Bain (2004), 'New! Improved? The transformation of the global agrifood system', *Rural Sociology*, **69**: 321–346.

Callon, M. (1991), 'Techno-economic networks and irreversibility', in J. Law (ed.) *A Sociology of Monsters: Essays on Power, Technology and Domination*, London: Routledge, pp. 132–163.

Callon, M. (1998), 'An essay on framing and overflowing: economic externalities revisited by sociology', in M. Callon (ed.), *The Laws of the Markets*, Oxford: Blackwell, pp. 244–269.

Callon, M., C. Méadel and V. Rabeharisoa (2002), 'The economy of qualities', *Economy and Society*, **31**, 194–217.

Callon, M. and A. Rip (1991), 'Forums hybrides et négociations des normes sociotechniques dans le domaine de l'environnement. La fin des experts et l'irrésistible ascension de l'expertise', *Environnement, Science et Politique, Cahiers du GERMES*, **13**, 227–238.

Cashore, B. (2002), 'Legitimacy and the privatization of environmental governance: How Non-State Market-Driven (NSMD) governance systems gain rule-making authority', *Governance: An International Journal of Policy, Administration, and Institutions*, **15**, 503–529.

Crease, R. P. (2011), *World in the Balance: The Historic Quest for an Absolute System of Measurement*, New York: W.W. Norton.

Demortain, D. (2008), 'Standardising through concepts: The power of scientific experts in international standard-setting', *Science and Public Policy*, **35**, 391–402.

Derkx, B. (2011), 'Metagovernance in the realm of private sustainability standards setting', *Faculty of Geosciences: Utrecht-Nijmegen Programme on Partnerships (UNPOP)*, Utrecht: University of Utrecht.

Dingwerth, K. and P. Pattberg (2009), 'World politics and organizational fields: The case of transnational sustainability governance', *European Journal of International Relations*, **15**, 707–743.

Egyedi, T. and J. Spirco (2011), 'Standards in transitions: Catalyzing infrastructure change', *Futures*, **43**, 947–960.

Elzen, B., M. Barbier, M. Cerf and J. Grin (2012), 'Stimulating transitions towards sustainable farming systems', in I. Darnhofer, D. Gibbon and B. Dedieu (eds), *Farming System Research into the 21st Century: The New Dynamic*, Dordrecht: Springer, pp. 431–455.

Elzen, B., F. W. Geels, C. Leeuwis and van Mierlo, B. (2011), 'Normative contestation in transitions "in the making": Animal welfare concerns and system innovation in pig husbandry', *Research Policy*, **40**, 263–275.

Evans, D. (2011), 'Consuming conventions: Sustainable consumption, ecological citizenship and the worlds of worth', *Journal of Rural Studies*, **27**, 109–115.

Florini, A. M. (ed.) (2000), *The Third Force: The Rise of Transnational Civil Society*, Washington, DC: Carnegie Endowment for International Peace.

Foucault, M. (1991), 'Governmentality' in G. Burchell, C. Gordon and P. Miller (eds), *The Foucault Effect: Studies in Governmentality*, Hemel Hempstead: Harvester Wheatsheaf, pp. 87–104.

Gamson, W. A. and A. Modigliani (1989), 'Media discourse and public opinion on nuclear power: A constructionist approach', *The American Journal of Sociology*, **95**, 1–37.

Geels, F. W. (2002), 'Technological transitions as evolutionary reconfiguration processes: A multi-level perspective and a case-study', *Research Policy*, **31**, 1257–1274.

Geels, F. W. (2010), 'Ontologies, socio-technical transitions (to sustainability), and the multi-level perspective', *Research Policy*, **39**, 495–510.

Geels, F. W., M. P. Hekkert and S. Jacobsson (2008), 'The dynamics of sustainable innovation journeys', *Technology Analysis & Strategic Management*, **20**, 521–536.

Grewal, D. S. (2008), *Network Power: The Social Dynamics of Globalization*, New Haven: Yale University Press.

Grin, J. (2006), 'Reflexive modernization as a governance issue – Or: Designing and shaping re-structuration', in J.-P. Voß, D. Bauknect and R. Kemp (eds), *Reflexive Governance for Sustainable Development*, Cheltenham, UK and Northampton, MA, USA: Edward Elgar, pp. 54–81.

Grin, J., J. Rotmans and J. W. Schot (2010), *Transitions to Sustainable Development: New Directions in the Study of Long-Term Transformative Change*, New York: Routledge.

Guay, T., J. P. Doh and G. Sinclair (2004), 'Non-governmental organizations, shareholder activism and socially responsible investments: Ethical, strategic, and governance implications', *Journal of Business Ethics*, **52**, 125–139.

Guthman, J. (2002), 'Commodified meanings, meaningful commodities: Re-thinking production-consumption links through the organic system of provision', *Sociologia Ruralis*, **42**, 295–311.

Harvey, L. and D. Green (1993), 'Defining quality', *Assessment and Evaluation in Higher Education*, **18**, 9–34.

Hatanaka, M. (2010), 'Governing sustainability: Examining audits and compliance in a third-party-certified organic shrimp farming project in rural Indonesia', *Local Environment*, **15**, 233–244.

Hatanaka, M., J. Konefal and D. Constance (2012), 'A tripartite standards regime analysis of the contested development of a sustainable agriculture standard', *Agriculture and Human Values*, **29**, 65–78.

Higgins, V., J. Dibden and C. Cocklin (2008), 'Building alternative agri-food networks: Certification, embeddedness and agri-environmental governance', *Journal of Rural Studies*, **24**, 15–27.

ISEAL (2010), 'ISEAL credibility principles: Public draft for comment 0.1 – May 2010', ISEAL Alliance, accessed 22 November 2013 at www.iseal alliance.org/sites/default/files/ISEAL%20Credibility%20Principles%200.1%20 May10.pdf.

ISEAL (2011a), 'Assurance Code critical issues survey summary', ISEAL Alliance, accessed 22 November 2013 at www.isealalliance.org/online-community/resources/assurance-code-critical-issues-survey-summary.

ISEAL (2011b), 'Assurance Code newsletter – April 2011', ISEAL Alliance, accessed 22 November 2013 at www.isealalliance.org/online-community/resources/assurance-code-newsletter-april-2011.

ISEAL (2011c), 'Code of good practice for assuring compliance with social and envrionmental standards: Public draft for consultation, version 0.1-31 October 2011', ISEAL Alliance, accessed 22 November 2013 at www.isealalliance.org/sites/default/files/Assurance%20Code_v01_comment-version.pdf .

ISEAL (2011d), 'Notes – ISEAL Assurance Code meeting, 17 October 2011', London: ISEAL Alliance.

ISEAL (2012a), 'Assurance Code comments – First consultation 1 November 2011 – 31 December 2011', ISEAL Alliance, accessed 22 November 2013 at www.isealalliance.org/sites/default/files/Assurance_Code_1st_Consultation_comments_&_responses.pdf.

ISEAL (2012b), 'Assurance Code newsletter – January 2012', ISEAL Alliance, accessed 22 November 2013 at www.isealalliance.org/online-community/resources/assurance-code-newsletter-january-2012.

ISEAL (2012c), Assuring compliance with social and envrionmental standards: Code of good practice, version 1.0, accessed 2 February 2012 at www.isealalliance.org/code.

ISEAL (2012d), 'ISEAL codes of good practice', accessed 2 February 2012 at www.isealalliance.org/code.

ISEAL (2013), 'Our vision, mission and values', accessed 22 November 2013 at www.isealalliance.org/about-us/our-vision.

Juran, J. M. (1951), *Quality-Control Handbook*, New York: McGraw-Hill.

Keith Borland, J. (1950), 'The fallacy of the square root sampling rule', *Journal of the American Pharmaceutical Association*, **39**, 373–377.

Kloppenburg, J. (1991), 'Social theory and the de/reconstruction of agricultural science: Local knowledge for an alternative agriculture', *Rural Sociology*, **56**, 519-548.

Latour, B. (1987), *Science in Action: How to Follow Scientists and Engineers through Society*, Milton Keynes, England: Open University Press.

Law, J. (2008), 'On sociology and STS', *Sociological Review*, **56**, 623–649.

Levin, K., B. Cashore, S. Bernstein and G. Auld (2012), 'Overcoming the tragedy of super wicked problems: Constraining our future selves to ameliorate global climate change', *Policy Sciences*, **45**, 123–152.

Lockie, S. (2009), 'Responsibility and agency within alternative food networks: assembling the "citizen consumer"', *Agriculture and Human Values*, **26**, 193–201.

Loconto, A. (2010), 'Sustainably performed: Reconciling global value chain governance and performativity', *Journal of Rural Social Science*, **25**, 193–225.

Loconto, A. and L. Busch (2010), 'Standards, techno-economic networks and playing fields: Performing the global market economy', *Review of International Political Economy*, **17**, 507–536.

Loconto, A. and E. Fouilleux (2014), Politics of private regulation: ISEAL and the shaping of transnational sustainability governance, *Regulation & Governance,* **8**, 166–185.

Lowe, P. and J. Murdoch (2003), 'Mediating the "national" and the "local" in the environmental policy process: A case study of the CPRE', *Environment and Planning C – Government and Policy*, **21**, 761–778.

Lyson, T. A. (2002), 'Advanced agricultural biotechnologies and sustainable agriculture', *Trends in Biotechnology*, **20**, 193–196.

Lyson, T. A. and R. Welsh (1993), 'The production function, crop diversity, and the debate between conventional and sustainable agriculture', *Rural Sociology*, **58**, 424–439.

MacKenzie, D. A., F. Muniesa and L. Siu (2007), *Do Economists Make Markets?: On the Performativity of Economics*, Princeton, NJ: Princeton University Press.

Mallet, P. (2009), 'Assurance as a tool for scaling up social and environmental impact', PowerPoint presentation, ISEAL Webinar Series, 29 April 2009, ISEAL Alliance, accessed 22 November 2013 at www.isealalliance.org/sites/default/files/ISEAL_Assurance_Code_Presentation.ppt.

Mutersbaugh, T. (2005), 'Fighting standards with standards: Harmonization, rents, and social accountability in certified agrofood networks', *Environment and Planning A*, **37**, 2033–2051.

Ponte, S., P. Gibbon and J. Vestergaard (2011), *Governing Through Standards: Origins, Drivers and Limitations*, Houndmills, Basingstoke, Hampshire and New York: Palgrave Macmillan.

Power, M. (1997), *The Audit Society: Rituals of Verification*, Oxford, UK: Oxford University Press.

Raynolds L., D. Murray and J. Wilkinson (2007), *Fair Trade: The Challenges of Transforming Globalization*, London and New York: Routledge.

Rip, A. (2010), 'Processes of entanglement', in M. Akrich, Y. Barthe, F. Muniesa and P. Mustar (eds), *Débordements: Mélanges offerts à Michel Callon*, Paris: Transvalor – Presses des MINES.

Rip, A. and R. Kemp (1998), 'Technological change', in S. Rayner and E. L. Malone (eds), *Human Choice and Climate Change*, Columbus: Battelle Press, pp. 327–399.

Schot, J. and F. W. Geels (2008), 'Strategic niche management and sustainable innovation journeys: theory, findings, research agenda and policy', *Technology Analysis & Strategic Management*, **20**, 537–554.

Schurman, R. (2004), 'Fighting "frankenfoods": Industry opportunity structures and the efficacy of the anti-biotech movement in Western Europe', *Social Problems*, **51**, 243–268.

Shove, E. and G. Walker (2007), 'CAUTION! Transitions ahead: politics, practice, and sustainable transition management', *Environment and Planning A*, **39**, 763–770.

Smith, A., A. Stirling and F. Berkhout (2005), 'The governance of sustainable socio-technical transitions', *Research Policy*, **34**, 1491–1510.

Styhre, A. (2001), 'Kaizen, ethics, and care of the operations: Management after empowerment', *Journal of Management Studies*, **38**, 795–810.

Tarrow, S. G. (2005), *The New Transnational Activism,* New York: Cambridge University Press.

Taruna Group Limited and R. Bradley (2011), 'Background research for the ISEAL Alliance Assurance Code Project', version: final 13 June, accessed 22 November 2013 at http://www.isealalliance.org/sites/default/files/Assurance_Code_Background_Research1.pdf.

Thévenot, L. (2009), 'Governing life by standards: A view from engagements', *Social Studies of Sciences*, **39**, 793–813.

Van Der Ploeg, J. D. (2010), 'The food crisis, industrialized farming and the imperial regime', *Journal of Agrarian Change*, **10**, 98–106.

Vanloqueren, G. and P. V. Baret (2009), 'How agricultural research systems shape a technological regime that develops genetic engineering but locks out agroecological innovations', *Research Policy*, **38**, 971–983.

Wright, W. and G. Middendorf (2008), *The Fight over Food: Producers, Consumers, and Activists Challenge the Global Food System*, University Park, PA: Pennsylvania State University Press.

5. Governance and technological change: the effects of regulation in medical devices

David Barberá-Tomás and Jordi Molas-Gallart

5.1 INTRODUCTION

Any process of technical change carries with it an element of uncertainty: market responses are unpredictable, technologies may not work as expected and they may have unforeseen consequences. Such uncertainty occurs both when changes relate to a specific technology operating within a given innovation or socio-technical system, or when the changes are more profound and affect the whole system. Managing such uncertainty becomes one of the functions of a governance system, and in particular of the governance of processes of technological change. One of the instruments of such systems of governance is the development and implementation of regulatory frameworks. By focusing on regulatory frameworks, this paper addresses one of the three pillars of the analysis of the governance of change in innovation systems identified by Borrás and Edler (2014): the 'instrumentation of the governance of change'. We see regulation as a form of governance instrument, shaping the ways in which actors involved in the innovation process develop, implement and use innovations. We understand regulatory frameworks as arrangements of 'legally binding formal regulations which constrain and regulate interaction' in innovation systems (Borrás and Edler, 2014). In other words, regulatory frameworks affect the way in which actors involved in innovation processes coordinate their activities: they 'guide the search' of innovation systems (Hekkert et al., 2007),[1] and shape the direction of technological change and the evolution of innovation systems.

One of the main problems with the extant studies of the role of regulatory frameworks in innovation systems is that they typically assume a static framework (Kemp, 1998; Blind, 2004, 2010), overlooking the dynamic nature of the interaction between regulation and innovation.[2] Hekkert et al. (2007) argued that this dynamic deficit is shared by the broader research on innovation systems: the analysis of the structural complexity of national, regional, sectoral, or large-technological system levels leaves little space for the detailed account of dynamic change.

> Even though [the innovation system] framework is based on theories such as interactive learning and evolutionary economics, most analyses of innovation systems are quasi-static in character. There is a focus on comparing the social structure of different innovation systems (actors, their relations and institutions) and, thereby, explaining the differences in performance. Less emphasis is put on the analysis of the dynamics of innovation systems. (Hekkert et al., 2007, p. 414)

Instead, the 'micro' level of analysis facilitates the study of innovation dynamics, overcoming these static frameworks by directing the analysis to specific technological fields or product technologies. Further, the study of the dynamics of technological knowledge at the product level can benefit from the insights offered by one of the most important research traditions in Innovation Studies in the last three decades (Martin, 2012): Product Life-Cycle Theory (PLT).

In this work we draw on insights from PLT to help us analyse the dynamic interaction between US regulation in medical devices and innovation in a medical product (hip prosthesis) developed originally in the late 1960s. We will argue that US regulation is based on a crucial distinction that assumes that the risks of implementing incremental innovations are lower than those associated with radical innovations, but does not consider that throughout the life-cycle of a product such difference does not remain fixed. We will suggest that in the hip prosthesis case this static regulatory division between radical and incremental innovation has led to recent attempts to engage in riskier, albeit incremental solutions, which ultimately failed. This outcome is somewhat paradoxical. Regulatory frameworks in medical devices were developed mainly to reduce the potential risks to patients of new technologies; they emerge as a governance tool to manage the uncertainties associated to new developments. Yet, we will show how the regulatory approach taken in the US has led to a specific form of technological change: incremental and, from a certain point on, increasingly risky.

The next section provides a theoretical grounding for our proposition that riskier incremental innovations could in fact characterize late stages in the life-cycle of a specific product technology. Our argument will be anchored in recent complexity thinking about Product Life-Cycle, and it will consider the regulatory framework as a crucial variable in the later stages of the cycle. Section three will try to flesh out these ideas in the context of the technological history of hip prosthesis, which in our interpretation have been influenced decisively by the current US Medical Device Regulation. In the light of the hip prosthesis case, the last section proposes avenues for further theoretical and empirical research.

5.2   INNOVATION DYNAMICS AND PRODUCT LIFE-CYCLE THEORY (PLT)

Although the roots of PLT are based on research on market entry barriers (Mueller and Tilton, 1969) and international trade theory (Vernon, 1970), the canonical formulation of the theory is anchored in Innovation Management, as the seminal works of Abernathy and Utterback (1975, 1978) were originally concerned about which kind of innovation (radical or incremental) would have more possibilities of success during the market life of a particular industrial product. In its most popular form, heavily influenced by evolutionary thinking, the theory essentially distinguishes two innovative stages in a product life-cycle. In the early phases of the development of a product most innovations are radical and generate great product variety, as there is a high uncertainty about the characteristics of the new technology. As the cycle advances, a 'dominant design' is selected from this variety and improved incrementally until a new cycle of radical innovation begins (Figure 5.1 shows a representation adapted from a classic article by Anderson and Tushman, 1990). The most commonly used example to illustrate the PLT is the early history of the automobile (Clarck, 1985): while in 1900, at the beginning of its development, three radically different solutions were present in the market with a comparable share (electric, gasoline and steam engines), in 1920 the gasoline engine had been selected as the 'dominant design'; since then, incremental innovations have been improving this dominant design.

Murmann and Frenken (2006, p. 944) warned that when analysing product life-cycles we must distinguish between the nature (incremental or radical) of technological change and the magnitude of the social impact that such technological changes trigger. Probably due to their intellectual sources, anchored in Business Management, PLT studies have typically equated social impact with the competitive implications of technological change (radical or incremental)[3] for firms. Yet the social implications of product life-cycles go beyond firm dynamics and market exit and entry rates: importantly for the role of regulation in innovation,

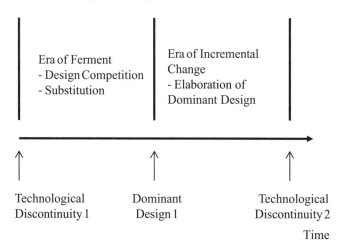

Source: Adapted from Anderson and Tushman, 1990.

Figure 5.1 Innovation in product life-cycle

the changing relationship between radical and incremental innovation through a product life-cycle affects the risk in the adoption of new products.

The relationship between the type of technological change and the increase in risk is not direct and linear. First, in complex systems catastrophic events can be triggered by small changes in one specific component – as in the O-ring failure of the Challenger shuttle catastrophe (Perrow, 1999; Reason, 1990). Similarly, literature on medical innovation (see Consoli and Mina, 2009, for a review) has showed that the relationship between body and technology is so complex[4] that improvements in technology cannot be linearly related with risk reductions.

Complexity theory has also used evolutionary arguments to build a dynamic understanding of the relationship between innovation and risk. Borrowing the notion of 'landscape' from evolutionary biology, some authors (Dennet, 1996; Frenken, 2006; Kaufmann, 1993) have proposed that incremental innovations can be conceived as local evolutionary searches[5] in a landscape where the neighbourhood topology is determined by the similarities of the related technologies and the heights of the landscape are the performance values of each technology; performance values can be very different –creating a *rugged* landscape (Kaufmann, 1993) – even in the same technological neighbourhood, as the interaction of different elements of the artefact could have huge effects in performance with even an incremental change in one of its elements

(Frenken and Nuvolari, 2004). Following this logic, if we consider safety as one 'service' dimension of technological performance (Lancaster, 1966; Frenken, 2006), an incremental search on a local but rugged 'safety' landscape can lead to a severe technological failure.

This already gives us some clues about the possible dynamic relationships between innovation and risk regulation through a product life-cycle. If a regulation is based on the assumption that the magnitude of technological change is directly and linearly related with increases in risk, it will place more burdensome regulatory requirements on radical innovations and less demanding ones on incremental innovations. This would create incentives for innovators to explore the local landscape of technological possibilities (focus on incremental innovation), although, if this landscape is 'rugged', small changes can generate considerable and negative effects on safety. Furthermore, as 'leapfrogging' in the landscape in search of radical innovations (Frenken, 2006) is penalized by regulation, technological discontinuities will become rarer and product life-cycles will tend to be longer (Figure 5.1). The implication here is that innovators will continue their incremental search in the same local neighbourhood, even in the most rugged and risky terrains. Thus, regulation can lead to 'exhaustion' in the search for safe incremental innovations in late stages of the life-cycle: that incremental search will continue even if it is around a 'peak' of risk in the landscape. This has interesting implications for the issue of regulation and the governance of change in socio-technical systems. Usually, the discussion about assumptions embodied in institutional instruments related with scientific and technological change has been focused on societal values, as in the case of genetics and obesity (Korthals, 2011). In medical regulation, the societal values involved often referred to patient safety and wellbeing (Foote, 1992). However, the assumptions we are analysing here refer to the very nature of innovation (incremental or radical) and its relationship with risk. As we will see, an incorrect assumption in this respect may result in undesirable and unexpected outcomes which damage those societal values embodied originally in the institutional instruments.

5.3   THE HIP PROSTHESIS CASE

We will begin with a broad review of the regulatory environment for hip prosthesis in US.

5.3.1 The US Medical Device Regulatory System

The 1976 Medical Device Act was the first comprehensive regulation of medical technologies (Foote, 1992). Before 1976, US medical devices were not subjected to any premarket review (Anderson et al., 2006). The Act introduces two different sets of regulatory requirements for innovations. When a device is classified as a radical innovation (that is, not 'substantially equivalent' to any pre-1976 device or to any post-1976 device already approved for market use), it has to pass premarket clinical testing. Such testing can cost millions of dollars and take an average of four years to complete (Foote, 1992). However, if the device is considered an incremental innovation ('substantially equivalent' to already approved devices or to pre-1976 devices), it can be introduced into regular use without premarket clinical testing through the so-called 510k process, where only laboratory trials with synthetic models are required. Manufacturers claim the similarity of their products to a specific 'predicate device' and the Center for Devices and Radiological Health of the Food and Drug Administration (FDA) decides whether to classify the new device as 'substantially equivalent' to its predicate (Institute of Medicine, 2011). It has been claimed that this regulatory environment notably reduced the innovativeness of US medical devices industry and delayed the introduction of radical improvements in the US market (Miller, 2002) by making it more costly to achieve radical improvements. An early study on 62 medical products and 26 firms in the sector seemed to confirm this claim (Hauptman and Roberts, 1987).

The history of hip prosthesis development since the 1970s also seems to confirm this assertion. In this field, the introduction of bioceramics has been one of the most important innovations: the friction of ceramic artificial articulations creates less wear debris than the materials traditionally used, like metals and plastics (Anderson et al., 2006). Since the 1980s, several ceramic prosthesis have been introduced into clinical use in Europe. In the US, however, these prosthesis were not eligible to be approved without premarket testing (contrary to incremental innovations in metal and plastic prosthesis, considered as 'substantially equivalent' to hip designs commercialized before 1976). It was not until 2005 that the first ceramic prosthesis was commercialized in the US, after fulfilling the premarket clinical testing requirements (Kurtz and Ong, 2009).

5.3.2   Regulation and Exhaustion of Innovation

Now we can come back to the argument developed in section 2, where we have argued that a burdensome regulatory framework imposed on radical innovations can exhaust the search of safe incremental innovations in late stages of a product life-cycle. As radical changes are discouraged by onerous regulatory obligations, the technological discontinuity that could start a new cycle of 'fresh' search of safe incremental innovations is delayed; instead, there is a continued search for incremental innovations in the late stages of the product cycle, exhausting all possible avenues for safe incremental innovation, and thus leading to the pursuit of riskier incremental changes.

We argue that a recent failure in incremental innovation in hip prosthesis, that has attracted media (Meier, 2011a,b,c; Meier, 2010) and institutional (Institute of Medicine, 2011) attention, could be interpreted as an expression of this safety exhaustion in incremental search. In 2005, a new prosthesis with *bigger* prosthetic femoral heads was classified as 'substantially equivalent' to prior (smaller) standard femoral heads. The small head standard size was established in the 1970s as a trade-off between the anatomical head size and the problems caused by wear debris in the artificial articulation; wear debris originating from the friction of the articulating components can migrate to the implant-bone interface and can cause an allergic reaction and implant loosening. This mechanism is the most common mode of failure of hip prosthesis. The chosen standard size was smaller than the anatomical femoral head, and thus had a higher risk of dislocation, as dislocation distance increases with the reduction of head size; at the same time, however, a smaller head size causes fewer loosening failures since the head's size is inversely correlated with the amount of debris generated by friction (Figure 5.2). Until the early 1990s, when wear debris was identified as the underlying mechanism behind many implant failures, the nature of the allergic mechanisms that cause implant loosening was not known (Kurtz, 2009; Anderson et al., 2006).

In 2005 (about 35 years after the introduction of hip prosthesis in the market), a US company developed a new design with bigger prosthetic femoral heads. The rationale for the new bigger head design was based on improvements in manufacturing of existing metallic materials, which allegedly reduced wear debris in the artificial hip articulation even with larger head diameters (which have less risk of dislocation than the smaller standard head). The device was classified by the FDA as 'substantially equivalent' to the prior smaller heads design (Food and Drug Administration, 2005).

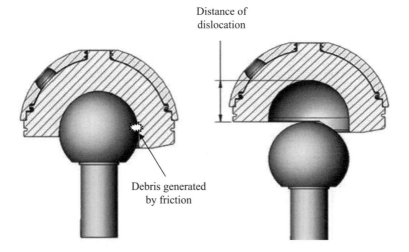

Note: The diameter of the femoral head is related both with the risk of dislocation (right) and with the amount of debris generated by friction (left).

Source: Authors' elaboration.

Figure 5.2   The diameter of the femoral head

Apparently, this incremental improvement solved the trade-off between wear debris and dislocation risk. However, in 2010 (after five years of regular use), an important amount of early failures of the prosthesis caused by allergic reaction to debris were identified and the prosthesis was retired from the market in 2011 (Langton et al., 2010; Graves, 2011). It is estimated that the failure of the prosthesis will affect 30 000 patients, who will have to be re-operated on (Meier, 2011a).

The bigger head design was a step towards a solution to a persistently ill-understood problem – the allergic reaction provoked by wear debris – by means of an incremental innovation in the manufacturing of existing materials. The unintended and ill-understood interaction between two presumably independent elements of the hip prosthesis system (the artificial articulation where the wear debris is generated by friction and the bone-implant interface where the debris migrates and provokes the allergic reaction responsible for the loosening of the implant, Figure 5.2) meant that even an incremental change in the diameter of the head could have dramatic consequences in safety. Moreover, this risky incremental change happened in 2005, more than 35 years after the product cycle started with the original designs of hip prosthesis. Although we have seen that the US medical device regulation has probably influenced the delayed introduction in US of radical innovations like the use of ceramic materials (which also arrived in 2005 to the US market), this does not mean that research efforts were absent. A keyword search in PatStat database give us 683 US patents related to hip prosthesis technology for the 1976-2005 period (from the approval of the Medical Device Act to the failure of 'bigger heads' incremental innovation). As the radical or incremental character of patents cannot be derived from available patent databases, we do not know the innovative degree of these patents. In any case, they confirm a continuous inventive activity during that period which may have led to an 'exhaustion' of incremental innovation.

5.4 DISCUSSION

Our brief account of the regulatory and technological history of hip prosthesis suggests that an incremental search in a highly uncertain and risky terrain could be an outcome of a search exhaustion at the late stage of product life-cycles. Supported by theoretical work on the nature of product life-cycles, we interpret the failure of the 'bigger heads' incremental innovation, after 35 years of extensive use of and continued research on hip prosthesis, as a case of search exhaustion. Our story also suggests that search exhaustion has been intensified by the US regulation in medical devices, which incentivizes incremental innovation regardless of the dynamic character of the product life-cycle.

More generally, Chapter 5 has highlighted the need for a dynamic perspective in the understanding of innovation knowledge when dealing with regulatory instruments of governance. In the hip prosthesis case, this regulatory instrument seemed to 'guide the search' within the US hip prosthesis industry towards incremental improvements, under the implicit assumption that incremental rates of innovation linearly induce incremental growth in risk. If incremental search exhaustion is a general property of the late stages of product life-cycles, governance of change in these late stages (Stegmaier et al., 2012) could benefit from the lessons of the hip prosthesis case. To fulfil their risk-reduction function, regulatory instruments need to acknowledge the dynamic character of technological change, and be adaptable to the different implications of incremental search strategies in different stages of a product life-cycle.

This opens a new set of research challenges. As Blind (2010, p. 238) put it: 'a systematic analysis of the timing of regulation in the context of a whole innovation cycle is missing. Especially, the co-evolution of innovation and the regulatory framework has so far not been addressed.' Our interpretation of the relationship between the US medical device regulation and the innovation dynamics of hip prosthesis is a first step towards addressing this gap. Our research suggests that regulation, as a form of instrumentation of the governance of change, needs to adapt to the technological characteristics of such change. That the product life-cycles have a bearing on the adequacy of some governance instruments to steer technological change towards some pre-specific goals (here the reduction of risks for patients) implies that the evolution and outcomes of a governance system for technological change do not depend solely on socio-political factors (structure and capability of the agents, and legitimacy issues), but also on the technological characteristics of the product families subjected to regulation.

Our analysis has focused on the 'instrumental pillar' of governance. The case we have presented also has implications for the other 'pillars' in the governance of change identified by Borrás and Edler (2012). Yet, the problems with prosthetic hip designs we have presented here are relatively recent and it is too early yet to assess the roles that the other pillars in the governance of change will come to play. For instance, the technological failures we have referred to are likely to have an effect on the legitimacy of governance structure; patients and institutions as the Institute of Medicine (a part of the US National Academy of Science) are questioning the regulatory systems that have so clearly failed to fulfil the objective of increasing safety and reducing risk. Yet, the way in which this legitimacy crisis will play up remains uncertain, since from the beginning of the crisis the industry has waged an aggressive campaign to discredit the report of the Institute of Medicine, which asked for stricter regulation (Meier, 2011a). The way the regulatory framework will be able to acquire legitimacy depends on the learning processes, but the lessons that the public will draw from the events we have described and analysed are not predetermined. There will be arguments and debate, and the regulatory policy that will emerge as being more legitimate is not predetermined by the technological developments and the ensuing legitimacy crisis we are presenting here. The different pillars have their own dynamics and it is too early, in our case, to identify how the interactions among them will develop. We are still in the early phases of what we expect will be a crisis of legitimacy and an uncertain process of 'learning', triggered by a problem generated by the way in which technological change occurs under a particular regulatory instrument. It is important to note, however, that an important element that emerges in the process of the technological change we have described occurs because of a 'given logic, which is not culturally or socially determined' (Bimber, 1994, p. 84), that is, the critical relationship between the size of the artificial hip prosthesis head and wear debris production. This is a purely technological relationship which is crucial to explain late failures of hip prosthesis. The way in which society will steer technological change to respond to this challenge will depend on the forms of learning and the types of regulation that will acquire legitimacy in the aftermath of a regulatory crisis. In our account, organizations and individuals create regulations using dubious assumptions about the relationship between innovation, risk, and time; yet these assumptions may be persistent. Other kinds of organizations and individuals have creatively followed the incentives posed by those regulations, discovering new incremental innovations until this form of search has become exhausted because of the technological characteristics of the landscape we have described. It is in the analysis of the social response to this crisis that the remaining 'pillars' of technological change governance will come to play a role, which is so far unpredictable.

We have shown how such unpredictability has so far been rooted in scientific uncertainty about the mechanisms underlying the deleterious effect of wear debris. In our interpretation, this uncertainty meant innovators were unable to predict how riskily 'rugged' the technological landscape was that they were exploring. Notably, the risky explorations of the size-wear debris relationships happened late in the product life-cycle: it was only after various decades of prolonged search in other locations (and apparently characterized by less intense uncertainty) when innovators decided to also explore new designs with bigger heads. Although this exploration only implied size variation, this incremental change drove the innovative agents to uncertain terrains which ultimately resulted in being intolerably risky. How public policy and, with it, technological change will respond to this problem is also unpredictable; not because of technological uncertainty, but because of the uncertain outcome of complex policy processes in which different policy stake-holders may draw different lessons from their experiences and propose different regulatory and technological solutions.

From our point of view, and from a more normative perspective, we would argue that our research suggests that safety regulations for incremental innovation may need to become more restrictive towards the end of a product life cycle. This recommendation is, of course, exceedingly difficult to implement in practice and is unlikely to be universally shared. In medical devices regulation terms, it could mean that the premarket clinical trials should be applied to every innovation (incremental or radical) and lighter regulatory frameworks – without premarket trials – should only be applicable, if at all, to incremental innovations in the mid-part of the product life-cycle, when local search has not yet exhausted safer incremental improvements. Normatively, such decisions call for a highly reflective system of governance: there is a need for continuous monitoring and learning, as the implications of technological change for the governance systems of such change are constantly changing with the levels of product maturity.

ACKNOWLEDGEMENTS

We especially thank Enrique Palmí, Carlos Montrós, Francesc Más, Rafael Albert, Carolina Ávila, Stefano Deotti and Iñigo Morales for technical advice about hip-prosthesis history. Usual caveat applies. We also thank Diana Rojas, Richard Woolley, Adriana Nilsson, Davide Consoli and Pablo D'Este for fruitful comments and discussion.

NOTES

1. An example of the 'guide of search' function in innovation systems is environmental regulation, which sets goals for many areas of industrial innovation (Blind, 2010). Regulation performs this function together with other institutional structures derived from softer norms or values (Bergek et al., 2008).
2. Until now, the literature on the relationship between regulation and innovation has mostly stressed the impact of regulation on innovation intensity, measured typically through R&D expenditure and patent counts (Vernon, 2005; Gerard and Lave, 2005; Golec and Vernon, 2010).
3. These competitive consequences usually refer to the exit and entry rates of firms during the life-cycle: in the initial stages, new opportunities are reflected in a growing rate of entries, a small rate of exits and thus a rapid growth in the population of firms. When the dominant design appears, only a small number of firms can achieve economies of scale, setting high entry barriers, thus inducing a high number of exits and a small rate of entries, triggering an 'industry shake-out' (Gort and Klepper, 1982). Again, the classic example is the automobile industry: in the 1920s, two decades after the beginning of the cycle, more than 250 companies competed in the market; after the industry shake-out created by the emergence of the Ford T as 'dominant design' and the economies of scale achieved by Fordist manufacturing techniques, less than 20 companies remained (Klepper, 1997).
4. Typical complex phenomena in this field are, for example, side effects emerging suddenly several years after the therapeutic act (Gelijins and Rosenberg, 1994).
5. Which are evolutionary in the sense that uncertainty is so pervasive in innovation that searches are partially 'blind' (Campbell, 1960; Nelson and Winter, 1982).

REFERENCES

Abernathy, W. J., and J. M. Utterback (1978), 'Patterns of industrial innovation', *Technology Review*, **64**, 254–28.

Anderson, J., F. Neary and J. V. Pickstone (2006), *Surgeons, Manufacturers and Patients: A Transatlantic History of Total Hip Replacement*, Basingstoke, UK and New York, NY: Palgrave Macmillan.

Anderson, P. and M. L. Tushman (1990), 'Technical discontinuities and dominant designs: a cyclical model of technological change', *Administrative Science Quarterly*, **35**, 604–633.

Bergek, A., S. Jacobsson, B. Carlsson, S. Lindmark and A. Rickne (2008), 'Analyzing the functional dynamics of technological innovation systems: A scheme of analysis', *Research Policy*, **37** (3), 407–429.

Bimber, B. (1994), 'Three faces of technological determinism', in M. R. Smith and L. Marx (eds), *Does Technology Drive History?*, Cambridge, MA: MIT Press, pp. 79–100.

Blind, K. (2004), *The Economics of Standards: Theory, Evidence, Policy*, Cheltenham, UK and Northampton, MA, USA: Edward Elgar.

Blind, K. (2010), 'The use of the regulatory framework for innovation policy', in R. Smits, S. Kuhlmann and P. Shapira (eds), *The Theory and Practice of Innovation Policy*, Cheltenham, UK and Northampton, MA, USA: Edward Elgar, pp. 217–246.

Borrás, S. and J. Edler (2014), 'The governance of change in socio-technical systems: Three pillars for a conceptual framework', in S. Borrás and J. Edler (eds), *The Governance of Socio-Technical Systems: Explaining Change*, Cheltenham, UK and Northampton, MA, USA: Edward Elgar.

Campbell, D. T. (1960), 'Blind variation and selective retention in creative thought as in other knowledge processes', *Psychol. Rev.*, **67**, 380–400.

Clarck, K. (1985), 'The interaction of design hierarchies and market concepts in technological evolution', *Research Policy*, **14**, 235–251.

Consoli, D. and A. Mina (2009), 'An evolutionary perspective on health innovation systems', *Journal of Evolutionary Economics*, **19** (2), 297–319.

Dennett, D. (1996), '*Darwin's Dangerous Idea: Evolution and the Meanings of Life*', New York: Simon & Schuster.

Food and Drug Administration (2005), '510(K) summary on safety and effectiveness conserve femoral head', accessed 10 November 2011 at www.fda.gov.

Foote, S. B. (1992), *Managing the Medical Arms Race: Innovation and Public Policy in the Medical Device Industry*, Berkeley: University of California Press.

Frenken, K. (2006), *Innovation, Evolution and Complexity Theory*, Cheltenham, UK and Northampton, MA, USA: Edward Elgar.

Frenken, K. and A. Nuvolari, (2004), 'The early development of the steam engine: An evolutionary interpretation using complexity theory', *Industrial and Corporate Change*, **13** (2), 419–450.

Gelijns, A.C. and N. Rosenberg (1994), 'The dynamics of technological change in medicine', *Health Affairs*, **13** (3), 28–46.

Gerard, D. and L. B. Lave (2005), 'Implementing technology-forcing policies: The 1970 Clean Air Act Amendments and the introduction of advanced automotive emissions controls in the United States', *Technological Forecasting and Social Change*, **72** (7), 761–778.

Golec, J. and J. A. Vernon (2010), 'Financial effects of pharmaceutical price regulation on R&D spending by EU versus US firms', *Pharmacoeconomics* **28** (8), 615–628.

Gort, M. and S. Klepper (1982), 'Time paths in the diffusion of product innovations', *Economic Journal*, **92** (367), 630–653.

Graves, S. (2011), 'What is happening with hip replacement?', *The Medical Journal of Australia*, **194** (12), 620–621.

Hauptman, O. and E. Roberts (1987), 'FDA regulation of product risk and its impact upon young biomedical firms', *Journal of Product Innovation Management*, **4** (2), 138–148.

Hekkert, M. P., R. A. Suurs, S. O. Negro, S. Kuhlmann and R. E. H. M. Smits (2007), 'Functions of innovation systems: A new approach for analysing technological change', *Technological Forecasting and Social Change*, **74** (4), 413–432.

Institute of Medicine (2011), 'Medical devices and the public's health: The FDA 510(k) clearance process at 35 years', accessed 15 December 2011 at www.nap.edu/catalog.php?record_id=13150.

Kauffman, S.A. (1993), *The Origins of Order. Self-Organization and Selection in Evolution*, Oxford: Oxford University Press.

Kemp, R. (1998), 'Environmental regulation and innovation: Key issues and questions for research', in Leone, F. and J. Hemmelskamp (eds), *The Impact of EU-Regulation on Innovation of European Industry*, Seville: IPTS, pp. 12–39.

Klepper, S. (1997), 'Industry life cycles', *Industrial and Corporate Change*, **6**, 145–181.

Korthals, M. (2011), 'Coevolution of nutrigenomics and society: ethical considerations', *The American Journal of Clinical Nutrition*, **94** (6 Suppl), 2025S-2029S, Kurtz, S. (ed.) (2009), *UHMWPE Biomaterials Handbook*, Elsevier Inc.

Kurtz, S. M. and K. Ong (2009), 'Contemporary total hip arthroplasty: Hard-on-hard bearings and highly crosslinked UHMWPE', in Kurtz, S. (ed.) (2009), *UHMWPE Biomaterials Handbook*, Elsevier Inc., pp. 55–79.

Lancaster, K. J. (1966), 'A new approach to consumer theory', *Journal of Political Economy*, **14**, 133–156.

Langton, D. J., S. S. Jameson, T. J. Joyce, N. J. Hallab, S. Natu and A. V. F. Nargol (2010), 'Early failure of metal-on-metal bearings in hip resurfacing and large-diameter total hip replacement: A consequence of excess wear', *The Journal of Bone and Joint Surgery (British Volume)*, **92** (1), 38–46.

Martin, B. (2012), 'The evolution of science policy and innovation studies', *Research Policy*, **41** (7), 1219–1239.

Meier, B. (2010), 'The implants loophole', *New York Times*, 16 December 2010, available at www.nytimes.com/2010/12/17/business/17hip.html?ref=barrymeier.

Meier, B. (2011a), 'Metal hips failing fast, report says', *New York Times*, 15 September 2011, available at www.nytimes.com/2011/09/16/health/16hip.html?_r=1&ref=barrymeier.

Meier, B. (2011b), 'Medical device approval process is called flawed', *New York Times*, 30 July 2011, available at query.nytimes.com/gst/fullpage.html? res=9804E0DA143EF933A05754C0A9679D8B63&ref=barrymeier.

Meier, B. (2011c), 'New study faults approval process for medical devices, *New York Times*, 29 July 2011, available at www.nytimes.com/2011/07/30/business/ study-calls-approval-process-for-medical-devices-flawed.html?_r=1.

Miller, D. (2002), 'Orthopaedic product technology during the second part of the twentieth century', in L. Klenerman (ed.), *The Evolution of Orthopaedic Surgery*', London: Royal Society of Medicine Press.

Mueller, D. and T. Tilton (1969), 'Research and development costs as a barrier to entry', *Canadian Journal of Economics*, 2 (4), 570–579.

Murmann, J. P. and K. Frenken (2006), 'Toward a systematic framework for research on dominant designs, technological innovations, and industrial change', *Research Policy*, 35 (7), 925–52.

Nelson, R. R. and S. G. Winter (1982), *An Evolutionary Theory of Economic Change*, Cambridge: Belknap Press of Harvard University Press.

Perrow, C. (1999), *Normal Accidents: Living with High-Risk Technologies*, Princeton, NJ: Princeton University Press.

Reason J. T. (1990), *Human Error*, Cambridge University Press.

Stegmaier, P., S. Kuhlmann and V. Visser (2012), *Governance of the Discontinuation of Socio-Technical Systems*, paper presented at 'The Governance of Innovation and Socio-Technical Systems in Europe: New Trends, New Challenges' International Workshop, Copenhagen Business School, Denmark, 1–2 March.

Utterback, J. M. and W. J. Abernathy (1975), 'A dynamic model of process and product innovation', *Omega*, 3 (6), 639–656.

Vernon, J. A. (2005), 'Examining the link between price regulation and pharmaceutical R&D investment', *Health Economics*, 14 (1), 1–16.

Vernon, R. (ed.) (1970), *The Technological Factor in International Trade*, National Bureau of Economic Research.

6. The discontinuation of socio-technical systems as a governance problem

Peter Stegmaier, Stefan Kuhlmann and Vincent R. Visser

6.1 INTRODUCTION

Abandonment of socio-technical systems occurs more often than one would expect. Companies cancel the development, production or support/ service of devices, technologies and even established systems. For example, in 2011, Siemens exited from building nuclear power plants; and even a state agency like NASA has a long track of stopping systems before or after start-up.[1] Yet, we know little about how socio-technical systems cease to exist and what it means to discontinue incumbent socio-technical systems actively.[2] As purposeful transitional change is hard to achieve (Markard et al., 2012), how difficult is it then to abandon existing systems purposefully? Bringing a system to an end might be taken for granted as just a side aspect of change – if one is interested in the entire transition trajectory including the fading out of old and the rise of new systems or their parts. Purposeful discontinuation could none the less turn out to be an essential element of creating a basis for change in general and for implementing it in particular. A better understanding of the conditions, forms, roles, effects and limits of the governance of abandoning longstanding socio-technical systems is a relevant question sui generis, and it can also contribute to a better insight into the governance of systems change in general.

Our point of departure is the observation that the governance of socio-technical systems (Hekkert et al., 2007; Bergek et al., 2007[3]) has preferentially been perceived and associated with advancement and innovation. This may have to do with a bias for progress and continuity in innovation policy and the study of it (cf. Smits et al., 2010; Giddens, 1991, p. 5) or with trust in the often experienced durability of social institutions (Simmel, 1897, pp. 667-8; Berger and Luckmann, 1966, pp. 77-8). On the other hand, purposeful abandonment, dismantling, decrease, termination or exit strategies have been the subject of some policy/governance studies so far (Bardach, 1976; de Leon, 1978; Behn, 1978; Brewer, 1978; van de Graaf and Hoppe, 1996, pp. 211-7; Sato, 2002; Sato and Frantz, 2005; Streeck and Thelen, 2005; Bauer, 2009). However they are not dealt with in most of the handbooks on policy-making and governance. The same is true for the limited interest in 'de-institutionalization' in general sociology and organization studies (Berger and Luckmann, 1966, p. 81; Zucker, 1991, p. 105; Hasse and Krücken, 2005, pp. 64-67; Maguire and Hardy, 2009; Stegmaier, 2009, p. 50-1). In Chapter 6, we use the term 'discontinuation' to include all these aspects and dimensions with regards to governance studies.

The governance of the discontinuation of socio-technical systems appears on the political agenda whenever an actor or group of actors (a government, parliament, company or industry association, or group of countries) make a sharp reversal of direction and actively disengage from an on-going policy or governance commitment. In Chapter 6, we first conceptualize the governance aspect of discontinuation processes as a twofold issue: the governance of a 'problem' and a 'problem for governance action' (section 6.2). This leads us to a programmatic list of heuristic views on 'discontinuation governance' (section 6.3). Next, we offer a first empirical sketch, concentrating on one example of discontinuation, the deliberate, purposeful exit from the production or/and usage of incandescent light bulbs (ILB) in the EU within the framework of the European Commission's eco-design directive (European Commission, 2009)[4] (section 6.4). Chapter 6 closes with a preliminary set of governance problem dimensions (section 6.5) and a discussion of the overall understanding of 'governance of systems change' (section 6.6).

6.2   FROM SOLUTIONS TO PROBLEMS: GRASPING THE GOVERNANCE ASPECT OF 'DOING DISCONTINUATION'

In Section 6.2, we discuss elements of governance theory that are needed for the empirical study of 'discontinuation governance' phenomena. First, we turn to the basic conception of governance processes. Second, we review theory broaching the issue of what we call 'discontinuation governance'.

6.2.1 Governance as Process and Practice

Governance-makers claim to find 'solutions' to 'problems'. Yet, if we want to understand how these solutions come about and materialize, the conflicts and negotiations about and around them, and most importantly how problem-related questions arise, we need to study carefully the questions and problems governance-makers pose themselves in situated interaction (Lerner and Lasswell, 1951; Hisschemöller and Hoppe, 2001, p. 51; Dunn, 2007, pp. 6, 83; Colebatch, 2009, p. 30).[5] When studying governance and change, we must keep in mind that experienced governance-makers know that what appears as a 'solution' will in turn provoke new practical questions and problems.[6] We have to understand governance as a process of interpreting and defining problems in such a way that coordination and cooperation is stimulated in a desired manner. Forming a policy and constituting a governance framework 'rests on problematization: ... interpreting the world in a way that makes particular forms of organized response appropriate' (Colebatch, 2009, p. 30). By 'coordination' we mean social action that takes effect aiming at a durable social order, or working together in a well-tuned manner to sustain social order, which can take place in contexts of competition, market, hierarchy, state, network, community, or else, in a variety of forms of activities and interactions and with a variety of mechanisms (cf. Benz, 2006; Schimank, 2002).

Discontinuation, not just as epiphenomenon of broader transitions, needs to be seen as such an interpretive governance process, in the course of which problems (of defining questions and answers, difficulties and – possible – solutions) are negotiated and enacted in politicized interactions (cf. Hall, 1986, p. 19; Strauss, 1993, pp. 245-62). 'Governance' is our conceptual perspective for addressing those efforts that aim to initialize or end, align or de-align, with a binding character, concerted action across multiple, competing modes of making, maintaining, and destabilising social order for public or private purposes (drawing on Hoppe, 2010, p. 14 and O'Toole, 2000, p. 278). This conceptual perspective is used as 'a heuristic, borrowed from political science, denoting the dynamic interrelation of involved (mostly organized) actors, their resources, interests and power, fora for debate and arenas for negotiation between actors, rules of the game, and policy instruments applied' (Kuhlmann, 2007, p. 6; cf. Kuhlmann, 2001; Benz, 2006; Braun, 2006).[7] Whether and how a given governance context is constituted by a more hierarchical or heterarchical structure, within or in-between which arenas (Delemarle and Larédo, 2014, in this book; Strauss, 1993), and, in addition, whether state actors or non-state actors drive change (Borrás and Edler, 2014, in this book) has to be answered empirically.

6.2.2   The Governance of the Discontinuation of a Governance

The patterns of development of socio-technical systems have been studied broadly (cf. for example, Mayntz and Hughes, 1988), in particular concerning the growth and the governance of large technical systems (Coutard, 1999; Schneider and Bauer, 2009), issues of path dependence (Garud and Karnøe, 2012; Meyer and Schubert, 2007), the transformation of established systems, for example, by regime change (Geels, 2007; Geels and Schot, 2007; Markard and Truffer, 2006; Markard et al., 2012; Konrad et al., 2012), or the change stimulated by new technology (Dolata, 2013). However, the success of a new technology goes hand in hand with the hybridization, fading out, marginalization or failure of existing technologies. The number of studies addressing this kind of development is rather small. Newer conceptualizations of sociotechnical system or regime transitions take 'destabilization' into account (Freeman, 1997; Turnheim and Geels, 2012), but there is no literature to look in-depth at what happens in terms of active, purposeful destabilization. Deters is among, if not *the* first to analyse the phase-out of the ILB in a case study (Deters 2012), but he has no intrinsic interest in the phase-out governance-making as such, but only as an example for depoliticized EU decision-making.

It is worthwhile to explore the theoretical efforts made to understand *termination* as a governance problem and process. One area in which we have quite some literature is the 'policy termination' as a side issue in policy studies (van de Graaf and Hoppe, 1996, pp. 221-227; cf. Bauer, 2009, for a detailed overview).[8] Policy termination may both result from a changed formulation or perception of a policy problem or from a changed formulation or perception of a policy solution (van de Graaf and Hoppe, 1996, pp. 221-227; Hogwood and Gunn, 1984, pp. 250-254). We are interested in the dynamics and underlying processes that lead actors to make a sharp reversal of direction and actively disengage from an on-going policy or governance commitment, as stated before. Action is always linked to prior, on-going and follow-up perceptions of the social reality in which it is (will be or was) conducted (Berger and Luckmann, 1966, pp. 20-46). Termination in this sense means observing an environment in which discontinuity is, for policymakers, the obvious thing to happen or to make happen, or at least a possible option.

Drawing upon the latter terminology, 'policy dismantling' has recently been introduced by Bauer et al. as an analytical notion for 'a distinctive form of policy change, which involves the cutting, reduction, diminution or complete removal of existing policies' (Bauer and Knill, 2012, p. 31). The authors see their analytical framework as a contribution to the analysis of policy change. They focus on politicians' preferences and dismantling strategy choices in the context of external factors, institutional constraints and opportunities, and situational factors in light of outcomes and effects (Bauer and Knill, 2012, p. 32). Yet, when it comes to the discontinuation of complex socio-technical systems it is not enough to observe politicians as central actors, we have to take a broader spectrum of actors into account. Also one has to trace the development of a discontinuation *trajectory* rather than limiting the view to pre-defined sets of 'factors' and 'variables' in a rather static framework. The understanding of a specific combination of actions, structures, situations and circumstances are, in our view, the result of the investigation rather than pre-defined categories.

Our research leads us to expand on the 'termination' or 'dismantling' concept further in terms of a 'governance *of* termination'. In paraphrasing van de Graaf's and Hoppe's notion of 'policy termination' (1996, pp. 21-7), we see 'discontinuation' as a particular way of solving a governance problem which is the result of a changed perception and formulation of a governance problem. This is a twist missed in other literature (Bauer et al., 2012; Ferry and Bachtler, 2013): the governance efforts that are necessary to end the governance structures and processes underpinning the old system are of equal importance in order to see the full picture of system's discontinuation. This does not necessarily mean the termination of a policy/governance only, but also the governance and policies that accompany the ending and the aftercare of what cannot be fully dismantled (like nuclear waste, or DDT for vector control which is still allowed to be used after the worldwide ban of DDT for agricultural use under the Stockholm convention in 2004; cf. Stockholm Convention 2009). The analysis shows that to terminate a governance means, most often, to start a new one dedicated to discontinuation. The governance efforts to end a socio-technical system may even last longer than the governance of the socio-technical system that has been terminated.

6.3 TOWARDS A TENTATIVE HEURISTIC FOR THE STUDY OF DISCONTINUATION GOVERNANCE

The key question of Chapter 6 is: 'How to discontinue incumbent socio-technical systems?' We will now turn to the case of incandescent light bulbs (ILB) as a first illustration, working with a tentative research heuristic that will be revised and improved in the course of progressing empirical case research. The heuristic starts from a number of *key orientations* on how socio-technical systems are brought to a halt:

1.   We turn away from the normal focus of studies of socio-technical systems that emphasize progress and innovation, institutionalization and continuity, and *turn to ending phenomena*: processes and acts of destabilization, deinstitutionalization, deconstruction, dismantling, termination and related strategies and structures in socio-technical contexts.
2.   Analytically and empirically, we focus on *the patterns of discontinuity in the governance* of socio-technical systems. From this point of view, innovation, replacing technologies and progress may appear in a new light.
3.   We *focus on discontinuation as a purposeful action sui generis* (in socio-technical contexts), be it setting change in motion (enacted discontinuation) or seizing on prevailing developments of change (emergent discontinuation); be it active governance or the broader regime context.
4.   We analyse discontinuation as a *problem of interpretation and action* for governance makers. We assume that discontinuation achievements are both a result of a changed formulation or perception of a governance problem as well as of a governance solution. This means that those making 'discontinuation governance' work always need to grasp the problem personally and collectively (intersubjectively) – understand, communicate and negotiate the problem structure individually and together. This encompasses both the perception of facts and of values, of what is the case and what ought to be the case.
5.   We take into consideration both *the discontinuing of a governance* (of a socio-technical system) and *the governance of the discontinuing* (of a socio-technical system). Both might refer to existing, or lead to new forms of, institutionalizing and legitimizing governance. Both might lead to the dismantling and/or expansion of governance (cf. Bauer and Knill, 2012, p. 33).

6.4   THE CASE OF THE INCANDESCENT LIGHT BULB

Several policy initiatives for the phasing-out of the energy-inefficient incandescent light bulb (ILB) have been introduced recently around the globe (Edge and McKeen-Edwards, 2008, pp. 2–7). In 2009, after years of discussion in EU member states, in the European Parliament and the European Commission, an EU directive was presented for the gradual phasing-out of traditional (or so-called 'energy inefficient') household lighting (European Commission, 2009). This process is described in some detail below: drawing on a pilot study by Visser (2012), in which the agenda setting for governance changes ('establishing the problem') was reconstructed from policy documents available online. These documents were analysed with regard to the communications on all sorts of problems faced by the proponents of the ILB ban.

The phase-out of the ILB technology through EU regulation 244/2009, based on the Eco-Design of Energy-Using Products Directive 2009/125/ EC, started in 2009. Immediate discontinuation applied only to general-purpose, non-directional 100 watt incandescent bulbs. For the rest, the permitted watt limit was gradually reduced while the efficiency levels were raised step-by-step until September 2012. Although many new types of energy-efficient light bulbs had already entered the market, the ILB was the one most often used for domestic lighting until it came into disrepute because of the energy waste attributed to its technology. This negative attribution occurred in the context of redefining political and technical criteria for lighting technology. This was a process of mutual adoption that was part of a 'governance dispositif' in which both public actors (for example EU commission, European Parliament, member state parliaments) and private actors (for example lobby organizations of the lighting industries, NGOs) played a role. The formation of such a dispositif requires the cognitive and political-strategic alignment of actors in terms of problem perception ('making sense together') and coordinated action (forming an advocacy coalition).

In the case of domestic lighting, the governance trajectory of the eco-design regulation for the discontinuation of the ILB started with an omnipresent push for the phasing-out of the ILB in order to stimulate the use of energy-efficient light bulbs. The agenda-setting process of this discontinuation had a long history and involved many different actors, such as the lighting industry, NGOs and political parties on multiple levels. Ultimately, the proposed ban of ILBs was pushed bottom-up by different interest groups and was part of a global policy diffusion. Important driving factors for this policy diffusion were the low costs of the discontinuation governance and the relative ease of its implementation due to the widespread support from industry and environmentalists (Edge and McKeen-Edwards, 2008, pp. 2–7). The main argument for a policy to ban the use of ILB, at least in publicly available documentation, was based on the notion of sustainability, which mobilized a wide public consensus. As a consequence, the European Lamps Companies Federation (ELC) considered proposing to phase out the ILB before there even was any regulation (ELC, 2007). At the same time, several member states introduced or discussed first governance initiatives to phase out ILBs (European Parliament, 2007).

The governance process for a final regulation on the discontinuation of the ILB was mainly facilitated and structured by the European Commission by embedding it in the eco-design directive (Visser, 2012). The eco-design directive (European Union, 2005, 2009) is a framework regulation for improving the environmental performance of energy-using products through eco-design requirements. Eco-design requirements aim to set new standards for the design of a product to improve its environmental performances, or to improve the supply of information on its environmental aspects. This eco-design framework operates on the supranational level to overcome separate national legislation and to preserve the free movement of goods. For domestic lighting, an eco-design regulation was proposed with the emphasis on improving the energy-efficiency performance of lamps and their environmental performances.

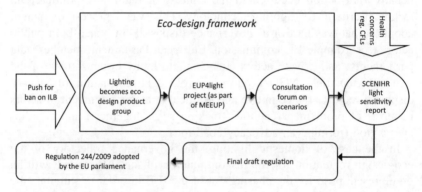

Source: Based on Visser (2012, p. 17).

Figure 6.1   The EU governance trajectory of the ILB discontinuation

Within the eco-design framework, the governance-making process of eco-design requirements was facilitated and pre-structured by the European Commission with the help of fixed approaches, such as MEEuP[9], and additional formats of combined expertise and governance during the policy-making trajectory, such as the so-called SCENHIR report. After domestic lighting was recognized as a product group, the second step within the eco-design framework included an open stakeholder project

(Vito, 2009b). This project facilitated stakeholders' participation in the development of scenarios for the phasing out of inefficient lighting and set eco-design requirements. To be able to formulate eco-design requirements for domestic lighting, the European Commission installed the EUP4light project to carry out a technical, environmental and improvement analysis of domestic lighting in a fixed format (Vito, 2009a). In the aftermath of the study, the Commission proposed different scenarios for the phasing-out of inefficient domestic lighting (European Commission, 2009). During the third phase of the eco-design trajectory, a closed stakeholder participation project was set up that included experts and representatives of member states to discuss the formulated scenarios. This was called the Consultation Forum and enabled the representatives of member states and invited experts to discuss possible eco-design requirements and propose a final discontinuation scenario (Consultation Forum, 2008). After these scenarios were discussed in the Consultation Forum, the Commission proposed a draft regulation to the European Parliament. Before this draft regulation could be amended, however, pressure from societal actors who were concerned about the consequences of the use of energy-efficient lighting led to an additional step in the governance-making trajectory, namely the preparation of a 'light sensitivity report' (SCENIHR, 2008). This report in turn concluded that the proposed health concerns were mostly ungrounded. This paved the way for the Commission to draft the regulation. After some amendments by the European Parliament, the discontinuation of the ILB was introduced and implemented in the member states (European Commission, 2009). Figure 6.1 provides a graphical model of the governance-making trajectory of the discontinuation of the ILB.

6.5 PRELIMINARY SET OF GOVERNANCE PROBLEMS IN THE ILB BAN CASE

Against the background of this illustration and our earlier conceptualization, we can now further distinguish six procedural dimensions of dedicated discontinuation governance (not to be understood as subsequent steps) and related core governance problems[10]:

6.5.1 Aligning Problem Perceptions through Increasingly Structured Interaction

The increasingly structured interaction of a variety of actors (the lighting industry, their associations, NGOs, EU commission, EU parliament, parties, member countries, and so on) became the driving forces for changing or establishing the problem perception. Their task was to raise the issue in the first place and to find common ground for understanding the policy problem. 'Making sense together' (Hoppe, 2010, pp. 167–8) was essential in this phase for politically and technically redefining the lighting technology and attributing energy waste to the old type of bulbs. Hence, while governance-makers mainly looked at the amount of energy wasted through the usage of the old bulbs, many critics also pointed at the energy waste during the production of the new bulbs. Meanwhile, other ambiguities had to be managed (Choo, 2006, pp. 5–8, 75–125), for example over concerns such as the mercury contained in energy saving bulbs. Representatives from various pools of expertise with different kinds of knowledge had to be mobilized: technical and legal experts, policy experts in national, EU, NGO and corporate realms, and so on. Still, this phase was rather diffuse, as various global and regional interest groups contributed more or less explicitly to the formation of the ILB ban and energy saver introduction dispositif.

6.5.2   Setting and Keeping the Problem on the Political Agenda…

The task throughout the whole trajectory was to set the new problem perception and keep it on the political agenda, whereby getting domestic lighting recognized as a product group within the eco-design framework proved to be the main problem. The actual political plan that had to be carried through in collaboration with and against others was described as a 'continuing, contested and ambiguous process' of 'agenda construction' (Colebatch, 2009, p. 91). Nonetheless, one could argue that this process provided the platform for a debate about the policy level to which the problem would have to be attributed; and at the end of the day, the initiators reached their aim when the European Commission decided to approach the ILB via the Eco-design directive. Interestingly, only after the decision was taken citizens mobilized against the ban by way of petitions to the European Parliament in 2009 and 2010, as well as with pop-cultural means of information, protest, and polemization (with web sites and even a documentary film called 'Bulb Fiction').

6.5.3   … In Combination with Building, Maintaining and Changing Advocacy Coalitions

Simultaneously, advocacy coalitions had to be established and maintained. Only through a broader alliance of actors, which were partially changing over time, could the waste of energy be attributed to the old type of bulbs. Because the ILB policy-making was referring to the eco-design directive, it was possible to make use of the existing policy-making-infrastructure for setting up new eco-design-rules.

6.5.4 Mobilising Existing/New Governance Instruments

Overall, the entire eco-design framework is, in a sense, a tool for managing and processing governance projects as, in our case, is the replacement of an old lighting technology with various new ones. Several specific existing and new governance instruments were mobilized in this process: initially the MEEuP (Methodology for the Ecodesign of Energy-using Products) was followed as the standard procedure. Later, and in accordance to the SCENIHR scheme, the so-called 'Light sensitivity report' by the 'Scientific Committee on Emerging and Newly Identified Health Risks' was added. For the assessment, another specific instrument called the EU4light project was used.

6.5.5 Politically Binding and Legitimate Decision-making

The phase-out of ILBs and the introduction of CFLs (compact fluorescent lamps, commonly called 'energy saving lamps') is an example of politically binding and legitimate decision-making through which a regulation project was adapted within the existing legal framework, which in turn was further developed with a new specific regulation. This way, using the eco-design framework, the general eco-design directive for all sorts of energy using products could be developed into a specific eco-design regulation for domestic lighting products for all EU member states.

6.5.6 Governing Socio-technical Aftercare

In general, abandoned socio-technical systems do not vanish completely and some continued governance effort is necessary long after their exit (for example nuclear waste and DDT for vector control). In case of the ILBs, lamps that are used for special purposes in medical or design settings are still allowed, which means that an ongoing dedicated governance structure is required. As the ILB is concerned, one could interpret the phase-out stage as an initial aftercare effort. The step-by-step reduction of wattage was necessary in order to allow time for the new, not yet fully functioning and marketable replacement products to mature, and to make users aware of the advantages of efficient lighting. The gradual production ban is a form of managing the end-of-life period after the exit decision has been taken. Having reached the last step, the aftercare currently consists of two main elements. First, it deals legally, politically and technically with the remaining kinds of old bulbs that are still permitted and, often enough, piled up for sale after the implementation of the production ban; second, it manages the soon-to-be implemented exit from some of the replacement products, for example the CFLs, which contain mercury and therefore will have to be banned until 2020, according to the 2013 Minamata Convention.

The above set of dimensions will be further developed on the basis of a number of further case studies of different socio-technical systems.

In Chapter 6, we were able to identify two conceptual innovations for the study of discontinuation governance, (1) the sense-making and problem construction before the actual agenda work, as well as (2) the relevance of aftercare:

- A new problem perception is a necessary prerequisite for change, because if the problem perception remains unchanged, any call for action is perceived as futile and remains without consequence (other than unnoticed shifts).
- Aftercare is a necessary prerequisite for change in so far as it allows unsolved issues of a governance process to be dealt with. It helps to avoid fraying and to control the loose ends of 'undead' regime and system parts.

6.6 CONCLUSIONS: ANALYSING THE GOVERNANCE OF DISCONTINUATION

The presented research approach towards the governance of the discontinuation of socio-technical systems is still under construction, as has been repeatedly emphasized in this paper. Yet, with a serious note of caution, we can assume that:

(1) discontinuation indeed takes place, and it does so in a highly complex context – technically as well as socially – (the DDT ban, e.g., seems to be situated within a rather unchanged framework of continuity of crop protection in general[11]) and;

(2) in most cases, discontinuation has to cope with quite some resistance to dedicated, forceful change (think of the exit from nuclear energy production with all the many backward and forward movements in countries like Germany and Japan);

(3)　the ILB phase-out is an exceptional case in which resistance was relatively small and coalitions among actors broad.

Unsurprisingly, in spite of some strong political will, institutional inertia and vested interests are prevalent. We suggest that discontinuation achievements are both a result of a changed formulation or perception of a governance problem as well as of a governance solution: discontinuation agents, if successful, have to manage the unbundling of forces and the dismantling of existing structures in order to overcome inertia of current systems and networks. They have to find and use instruments and resources (Frantz, 2002), as well as interpret and try to affect on-going processes (Rein and Schön, 1993).

In contrast to, for example, 'discontinuity' as a market phenomenon (Utterback, 2003) and 'destabilization' as a regime transition phenomenon (Turnheim and Geels, 2012), our attention is firmly focused on dedicated governance for the discontinuation of established systems – in other words, on 'discontinu*ation*' as purposeful governance action *sui generis* in socio-technical contexts. By coining the notion 'discontinuation' we indicate the process orientation of our research focus. Smith et al. also started looking into this direction when they developed their typology of transition contexts including highly coordinated forms: committed processes driven internally (endogenous renewal) or externally (purposive transition, quite similar to the idea of a transition management project) (Smith et al., 2005, pp. 1498–1502). A key question is what discontinuation means as a *problem of interpretation and action* for policy-makers (cf. Hoppe, 2010; Colebatch, 2009).

The phase-out of the incandescent light bulb technology through the EU regulation 244/2009, based on the Eco-Design of Energy-Using Products Directive 2009/125/EC, started in the EU in 2009 (Visser, 2012; Stegmaier et al., 2012; Edge and McKeen-Edwards, 2008). Looking at the governance process, it can be noted that the ILB governance problem is fully under control or 'structured' in the sense that currently there is no open process, but the knowledge and value questions have been settled. Governance actors treat the case as unproblematic. Thus the European Union, follows three years after Cuba and two years after Australia and the U.S. who were among the first two OECD countries to start phasing ILB out or to pass phase-out legislation. Japan and Canada are planning phase-outs in 2012, China gradually bans ILB imports and sales starting in 2012. The phase-out appears disruptive in several countries. After some pioneers went ahead, increasingly coordinated action was organized, most formally designed within a regulatory framework, partially dedicated to the ILB ban, partially a general one for diverse products. We would like to emphasize the interplay of internal and external drives. In the ILB case, the discontinuation is mainly legitimized by pointing at the inefficiency of the 'old technology' (internal driver), although finally an external driver was needed to realise the transition (the eco-design directive); all promised new technology was not yet available at the begin of the ban in 2009, such as LED lamps, which were not yet ready for the market up until 2011.[12]

The crosscutting basic assessment of what the problem of 'discontinuation governance' is and how the structures of knowledge and agreement are developed, both under change conditions and under changing conditions, also helps to concretize the following three pillars developed by Borrás and Edler (2014), because for each pillar we have to reveal the practical and fundamental *movens*, the tensions and ways of dealing with an issue from a governance perspective.

First, Borrás and Edler ask what and who drives or inhibits change. They subscribe to the idea that agents (individual and collective actors) navigate in more or less complex environments and struggle for aligning positions and resources for change, while institutions might provide opportunity structures or thresholds for change activity (Borrás and Edler, 2014). Indeed, is it a core question for our investigation into 'discontinuation governance' which framings institutions and which reframing actors suggest; how much room for manoeuvre in terms of political bargaining and negotiation is available; how structures and acts of power and interest are mobilized; and which role normal actors, on the one hand, and particularly visionary or entrepreneurial governance activists, on the other hand, may play (Smith et al., 2005; Smith and Stirling, 2010). Our dimensions 'dynamics' and 'actors' echo such a focus on opportunity structures and capable agents. Crucially, we are able to show empirically how both *actors observing institutions*, on the one hand, *and institutions observing actors*, on the other hand, actually interpret and frame opportunities, reasons, utility and meaningfulness of fostering (or hindering) change, and which often ambiguous patterns of relevance, motives, interests and experiences they associate with change, or with discontinuation in particular.

This is linked, second, to 'policy instruments', our dimension that covers the enquiry into how governance is executed. More specifically, we need to further investigate how instruments are constructed and designed, how they work or do not work, and how they interact with other, non-instrumental governance (Borrás and Edler, 2014). There are certainly economic and regulatory instruments used for discontinuation governance, and further research will show what they are supposed to do and what they can do – instruments between nudging and forcing change of behaviour. The question for further investigation is how far they combine economic and legal aspects. Besides, one should ask, who does actually instrumentalize whom, when domestic lighting producers push ILBs into the eco-design framework, while the European Commission takes this as an opportunity to set an example for active EU level environmentalism, by putting pressure on the lighting industries to innovate their ILB-replacing products more quickly than planned, and on the consumer public to change their household lighting habits towards more efficient technology (while there are still some groups denying the need for using efficient lighting because they focus on the burdens of using new lamps and their electronic waste). Furthermore, it needs to be investigated which instruments (and other governance aspects) are part of which broader strategy or governance style (mode). Our case study indicates so far that governance instruments and strategies embrace far more than state actors.

Third, why is change accepted (or not) and how is legitimacy created? This is the third dimension on which Borrás and Edler put emphasis (2014). We differentiate between the aspects of regulation and justification and focus explicitly on the social process and practice character of seeking, finding or loosing legitimacy at the input and/or output stage. This way, we direct a clear empirical focus, not a normative one, on governance and legitimacy. We ask how legitimacy is claimed, criticized, lost and won, and how it explains the institutional order (Berger and Luckmann, 1966, p. 93), how the 'legitimate order' (Weber, 1978) is empirically constituted, in which arenas and in which frame of reference. When discontinuation takes time, it is only logical that governance practitioners and we observers have to check for throughput legitimacy, too – this is for procedures on which enduring legitimacy is built (cf. Luhmann, 1969) and for the ups and downs of legitimacy. The crisis moments in the preparation of the ILB ban, when health issues about the replacing CFLs were brought up, in a striking way show how legitimation needs to be maintained especially during the process.

Change and discontinuation require actors to learn to adapt to altering or altered states of what they know and value. Governance is not only coordination, negotiation and (perhaps, to some extent) collaboration in a technical manner – it builds on actors' understanding of their world and how they get socialized into it. If the perceived world is changing, 'problems' arise and institutions that are taken for granted get destabilized or are actively dismantled by those who have defended them up to now, entire frameworks of reference have to be readjusted, new routines in dealing with the conditions of political, economic and technical behaviour have to be found, and prior decisions and beliefs reconsidered.

In short, the governance of change in socio-technical and innovation systems both has to cope with and is an object of discontinuation.

ACKNOWLEDGEMENTS

Chapter 6 has benefited appreciably from comments by Jakob Edler and Susana Borrás.

NOTES

1. For instance, the Space Shuttle system programme 1972–2011 or the Project Apollo 1961–72 that were stopped after years of usage, whereas the permanent moon base, aka 'Lunar outpost', was halted in 2010 after four years of development. Considering how difficult it turns out to be for Microsoft to discontinue Windows XP (by making it impossible to use it safely, for instance), it seems that sometimes discontinuation precedes change.
2. However, the governance of the discontinuation of socio-technical systems has only recently been put on the agenda of social scientific research in an explicit manner (Stegmaier et al., 2012; Turnheim and Geels, 2012). Chapter 6 results from the research project 'Governance of Discontinuation of Sociotechnical Systems' (Disc-Go), carried out by a consortium consisting of four research groups at SPRU Brighton, TU Dortmund University, IFRIS Paris and University of Twente, funded from 2012–2015 through an Open Research Area (ORA) scheme grant by NWO, DFG, ESRC and ANR.
3. This has some overlap with the body of literature on the 'regime' notion (cf. Geels and Schot, 2007; Nelson and Winter, 1982).
4. The Ecodesign Directive 2009/125/EC (extension to energy related products) followed the Amending Directive (2008/28/EC) and the initial version of the Ecodesign Directive (2005/32/EC).
5. In policy studies, this has led to coining the notions of 'wicked problems' and 'problem structuring' (Rittel and Webber, 1973; Dunn, 2007; Hoppe, 2010).
6. This does not imply that our problem-oriented approach sees social science as a problem *solver*.
7. Besides policy-makers we include all kinds of actors as governance-makers, such as industry, NGOs, distributors, dealers, as well as simple users and organized user-groups. In the case of the ILB, the industry itself had already organized some plans and strategies to fade out the ILB before the European commission actively pursued the ban.
8. The issue at stake here – the submergence (as the opposite of emergence) and abandonment (actively exiting) of a governance or an object of governance – has also been referred to as 'retrenchment' elsewhere (Pierson, 1994).
9. MEEuP stands for 'Methodology Study for Ecodesign of Energy-using Products' (see http://ec.europa.eu/enterprise/policies/sustainable-business/ecodesign/method ology/index_en.htm).
10. In Visser (2012) and Visser and Stegmaier (2014) we also look at the socio-technical problems of the phasing out (challenges for industry and burdens for users, burdens for infrastructure) and the way these challenges also had to be tackled by the choice of governance instruments. We call this the 'socio-technical regime' side of the coin.

11. This observation is currently developed by Pierre-Benoît Joly and colleagues in one of the discontinuation governance projects.
12. Besides, we also observe that sometimes 'old technologies' (for example LPs, that is 'long play' records) are reintroduced – not only by the public and in for a niche market, but also by some technology start-ups that use an old technology or technological idea, solve the old technical problems and reintroduce the technology in a new form. But this is worth another investigation of its own right.

REFERENCES

Bardach, E. (1976), 'Policy termination as a political process', *Policy Sciences*, **7** (2), 123–131.

Bauer, M. W., A. Jordan, C. Green-Pedersen and A. Héritier (eds) (2012), *Dismantling Public Policy: Preferences, Strategies, and Effects*, Oxford: Oxford University Press.

Bauer, M. W. and C. Knill (2012), 'Understanding policy dismantling: An analytical framework', in M. W. Bauer, A. Jordan, C. Green-Pedersen and A. Héritier (eds) (2012), *Dismantling Public Policy, Preferences, Strategies, and Effects*, Oxford: Oxford University Press, pp. 30–51.

Bauer, M. W. (2009), 'The policy termination approach: Critique and conceptual perspectives', *Lehrstuhl für Politik und Verwaltung Working Paper Series* (WP #1/2009), Berlin: Lehrstuhl für Politik und Verwaltung, accessed 22 July 2011 at www.sowi.hu-berlin.de/lehrbereiche/politikundverwaltung/wps/working-paper-1.

Behn, R. D. (1978), 'How to terminate a public policy: A dozen hints for the would-be policy terminator', *Policy Analysis*, **4** (3), 393–414.

Benz, A. (2006), 'Governance in connected arenas – Political science analysis of coordination and control in complex control systems', in D. Jansen (ed), *New Forms of Governance in Research Organizations. From Disciplinary Theories towards Interfaces and Integration*, Heidelberg and New York: Springer, pp. 3–22.

Bergek, A., S. Jacobsson, B. Carlsson, S. Lindmark and A. Rickne (2007), 'Analyzing the functional dynamics of technological innovation systems: A scheme of analysis', *Research Policy*, **37**, 407–429.

Berger, P. L. and T. Luckmann (1966), *The Social Construction of Reality. A Treatise in the Sociology of Knowledge*, Garden City, New York: Doubleday.

Borrás, S. and J. Edler (2014), 'The governance of change in socio-technical systems: Three pillars for a conceptual framework', in S. Borrás and J. Edler (eds), *The Governance of Socio-technical Systems: Explaining Change*, Cheltenham, UK and Northampton, MA, US: Edward Elgar.

Braun, D. (2006), 'Delegation in the distributive policy arena: The case of research policy', in F. Gilardi and D. Braun (eds), *Delegation in Contemporary Democracies*, London: Routledge, pp. 146–170.

Brewer, G. D. (1978), 'Termination: Hard choices, harder questions', *Public Administration Review*, **38** (4), 338–344.

Choo, C. W. (2006), *The Knowing Organization: How Organizations Use Information to Construct Meaning, Create Knowledge, and Make Decisions*, Oxford: Oxford University Press.

Colebatch, H. (2009), *Policy*, Berkshire: Open University Press.

Consultation Forum (2008), 'Annex 2: Working document on possible ecodesign requirements for general lighting equipment', accessed 21 April 2012 at http://ec.europa.eu/energy/efficiency/ecodesign/doc/forum/2008-03-28.zip.

Coutard, O. (2002), *The Governance of Large Technical Systems*, London: Routledge.

Delemarle, A. and Ph. Larédo (2014), 'Governing radical change through the emergence of a governance arrangement', in S. Borrás and J. Edler (eds), *The Governance of Systems Change*, Cheltenham, UK and Northampton, MA, US: Edward Elgar.

Deters, H (2012), 'Arenas and Bargaining Dynamics in EU Efficiency Policy-Making', paper presented at the 42nd UACES Annual Conference in Passau, 5 September 2012.

Dolata, U. (2013), *The Transformative Capacity of New Technologies. A Theory of Sociotechnical Change*, London and New York: Routledge.

Dunn, W. N. (2007), *Public Policy Analysis: An Introduction*, New Jersey: Pearson/Prentice Hall.

Edge, J. and H. McKeen-Edwards (2008), 'Light bulbs and bright ideas? The global diffusion of a ban on incandescent light bulbs', paper presented at the 80th Annual Conference of the Canadian Political Science Association, University of British Colombia, 5 June 2008, accessed 15 June 2013 at www.cpsa-acsp.ca/papers-2008/Edge-McKeen-Edwards.pdf.

European Commission (2009), 'Regulation 244/2009: Implementing Directive 2005/32/EC of the European Parliament and of the Council with regard to ecodesign requirements for non-directional household lamps', accessed 14 February 2012 at http://eur-lex.europa.eu/LexUriServ/LexUriServ.do?uri=OJ:L:2009:076:0003:0016:EN:PDF.

European Lamp Companies Federation (ELC) (2007), 'The ELCs proposal for domestic lighting', accessed 23 April 2012 at http://www.elcfed.org/documents/2.%20Phase-out%20proposal.pdf.

European Parliament (2007), 'E-1184/07: Written question', accessed 24 April 2012 at www.europarl.europa.eu/sides/getDoc.do?pubRef=-//EP//TEXT+WQ+E-2007-1184+0+DOC+XML+V0//EN.

European Union (2009), 'Directive 2009/125/EC for establishing a framework for the setting of ecodesign requirements for energy-related products (recast)', accessed 14 February 2012 at http://eur-lex.europa.eu/LexUriServ/LexUriServ.do?uri=OJ:L:2009:285:0010:0035:en:PDF.

European Union (2005), 'Directive 2005/32/EC for establishing a framework for the setting of ecodesign requirements for energy-using products', accessed 14 February 2012 at http://eur-lex.europa.eu/LexUriServ/LexUriServ.do?uri=OJ:L:2005:191:0029:0029:EN:PDF.

Ferry, M. and J. Bachtler (2013), 'Reassessing the concept of policy termination: The case of regional policy in England', *Policy Studies*, **34** (3), 255–273.

Frantz, J. E. (2002), 'Political resources for policy terminators', *Policy Studies Journal*, 30, 1, pp. 11–28.

Freeman, C. (1997), 'The diversity of national research systems', in R. Barré, M. Gibbons, J. Maddox, B. Martin, P. Papon (eds), *Science in Tomorrow's Europe*, Paris: Economica International, pp. 183–194.

Garud, R. and P. Karnøe (2012), *Path Dependence and Creation*, Hove: Psychology Press.

Geels, F. W. (2007), 'Transformations of large technical systems: A multilevel analysis of the Dutch highway system (1950–2000)', *Science, Technology & Human Values*, **32** (2), 123–149.

Geels, F. W. and J. Schot (2007), 'Typology of sociotechnical transition pathways', *Research Policy*, **36** (3), 399–417.

Giddens, A. (1991), *The Consequences of Modernity*, Cambridge: Polity.

Graaf, H. v. d. and R. Hoppe (1996), *Beleid en Politiek. Een Inleiding tot de Beleidswetenschap en de Beleidskunde*, Bussum: Coutinho.

Hall, P. (1986), *Governing the Economy: The Politics of State Intervention in Britain and France*, New York: Oxford University Press.

Hasse, R. and G. Krücken (2005), *Neo-Institutionalismus*, Bielefeld: transcript.

Hekkert, M. P., R. A. A. Suurs, S. O. Negro and S. Kuhlmann (2007), 'Functions of innovation systems: A new approach for analyzing technological change', *Technological Forecasting and Social Change*, **74** (4), 413–432.

Hisschemöller, M. and R. Hoppe (2001), 'Coping with the intractable controversies: The case for problem structuring in policy design and analysis', in M. Hisschemöller, R. Hoppe, W. N. Dunn and J. R. Ravetz (eds), *Knoweldge, Power, and Participation in Environmental Policy Analysis*, New Brunswick: Transaction, pp. 47–72.

Hogwood, B. W. and L. A. Gunn (1984), *Policy Analysis for the Real World*, Oxford: Oxford University Press.

Hoppe, R. (2010*), The Governance of Problems: Puzzling, Powering and Participation*, Bristol: Policy.

Konrad, K., J. Markard, A. Ruef and B. Truffer (2012), 'Strategic responses to fuel cell hype and disappointment', *Technological Forecasting & Social Change*, **79** (6), 1084–1098.

Kuhlmann, S. (2007), 'Governance of research – Nine comments on Arthur Benz', in D. Jansen (ed), *New Forms of Governance in Research Organizations: From Disciplinary Theories towards Interfaces and Integration*, Heidelberg and New York: Springer, pp. 23–25.

Kuhlmann, S. (2001), 'Future governance of innovation policy in Europe – Three scenarios', *Research Policy*, **30**, 953–976.

de Leon, P. (1978), 'A theory of policy termination', in J. V. May and A. B. Wildavky (eds), *The Policy Cycle*, Beverly Hills: Sage, pp. 279–300.

Lerner, D. and H. D. Lasswell (1951), *The Policy Sciences: Recent Developments in Scope and Methods*, Stanford: Stanford University Press.

Luhmann, N. (1969), *Legitimation durch Verfahren*, Neuwied and Berlin: Luchterhand.

Maguire, S. and C. Hardy (2009), 'Discourse and deinstitutionalization: The decline of DDT', *Academy of Management Journal*, **52** (1), 148–178.

Markard, J. and B. Truffer (2006), 'Innovation processes in large technical systems: Market liberalization as a driver for radical change', *Research Policy*, **35** (5), 609–625.

Markard, J., R. Raven and B. Truffer (2012), Sustainability transitions: An emerging field of research and its prospects, *Research Policy*, **41**, 955–967.
Mayntz, R. and T. P. Hughes (1988), *The Development of Large Technical Systems*, Frankfurt/M.: Campus.
Meyer, U. and C. Schubert (2007), 'Integrating path dependency and path creation in a general understanding of path constitution: The role of agency and institutions in the stabilisation of technological innovations', *Science, Technology & Innovation Studies*, **3**, 23–44.
Nelson, R. and S. G. Winter (1982), *An Evolutionary Theory of Economic Change*, Cambridge, MA: Harvard University Press.
O'Toole, L. J. (2000), 'Research and policy implementation: Assessments and prospects', *Journal of Public Administration Research and Theory*, **10** (2), 263–288.
Pierson, P. (1994), *Dismantling the Welfare State?*, Cambridge: Cambridge University Press.
Rein, M. & Schön, D. A. (1993), 'Reframing policy discourse', in: F. Fischer & J. Forrester (eds), *The argumentative turn in policy analysis and planning*, Durham/London: Duke UP, pp. 145–166.
Rittel, H. W. J. and M. M. Webber (1973), 'Dilemmas in a general theory of planning', *Policy Sciences*, **4** (2), 155–169.
Sato, H. (2002), 'Abolition of leprosy isolation policy in Japan: Policy termination through leadership', *Policy Studies Journal*, **30** (1), 29–46.
Sato, H. and J. E. Frantz (2005), 'Termination of the leprosy isolation policy in the US and Japan : Science, policy changes, and the garbage can model', *BMC International Health and Human Rights*, **5** (3), 1–16.
Stockholm Convention (2009), 'Stockholm convention on Persistent organic pollutants', Stockholm: The Secretariat of the Stockholm Convention, accessed 26 June 2013 at http://chm.pops.int/Convention/ConventionText/ tabid/2232/Default.aspx.
Schimank, U. (2002), *Handeln und Strukturen. Einführung in die akteurstheoretische Soziologie*, Weinheim and München: Juventa.
Schneider, V. and J. M. Bauer (2009), 'Von der Governance – zur Komplexitätstheorie. Entwicklungen der Theorie gesellschaftlicher Ordnung', in J. Weyer and I. Schulze-Schaeffer (eds), *Management Komplexer Systeme. Konzepte für die Bewältigung von Intransparenz, Unsicherheit und Chaos*, München: Oldenbourg, pp. 31–53.
Scientific Committee on Emerging and Newly Identified Health Risks (SCENIHR) (2008), 'Light sensitivity', Brussels: Health & Consumers DG, Directorate C: Public Health and Risk Assessment, Unit C7 – Risk Assessment, Brussels, European Commission, accessed 19 July 2013 at http://ec. europa.eu/health/archive/ph_risk/committees/04_scenihr/docs/scenihr_o_019. pdf.
Simmel, G. (1897), 'The persistence of social groups: I', *American Journal of Sociology*, **3**, 662–698.
Smith, A. and A. Stirling (2010), 'The politics of social-ecological resilience and sustainable socio-technical transitions', *Ecology and Society*, **15** (1), 11.
Smith, A., A. Stirling and F. Berkhout (2005), 'The governance of sustainable socio-technical transitions', *Research Policy*, **34**, 1491–1510.

Smits, R. E., S. Kuhlmann and P. Shapira (eds) (2010), *The Theory and Practice of Innovation Policy. An International Handbook*, Cheltenham, UK and Northampton, MA, US: Edward Elgar.

Stegmaier, P., S. Kuhlmann and V. R. Visser (2012), 'Governance of the discontinuation of socio-technical systems', paper presented at the Jean Monnet Conference: The Governance of Innovation and Socio-Technical Systems in Europe: New Trends, New Challenges, International Workshop, Copenhagen Business School, Denmark, 1–2 March 2012.

Stegmaier, P. (2009), *Wissen, was Recht ist. Richterliche Rechtspraxis aus wissenssoziologisch-ethnografischer Sicht*, Wiesbaden: VS.

Strauss, A. (1993), *Continual permutations of action*, New York: Aldine de Gruyter.

Streeck, W. and K. Thelen (eds) (2005), *Beyond Continuity: Institutional Change in Advanced Political Economies*, Oxford: Oxford University Press.

Turnheim, B. and F. W. Geels (2012), 'Regime destabilisation as the flipside of energy transitions: Lessons from the history of the British coal industry (1913–1997)', *Energy Policy*, **50**, 35–49.

Utterback, J. (2003), 'The dynamics of innovation in the internet and the university', Aspen Institute Forum 2002, Educause, 81-103, accessed 27 February 2012 at http://net.educause.edu/ir/library/pdf/FFPIU024.pdf.

Visser, V. R. and P. Stegmaier (2014), 'The discontinuation of the incandescent light bulb in the EU', (in preparation).

Visser, V. R. (2012), 'The purposeful governance of technology discontinuation: An explorative study on the discontinuation of the incandescent light bulb in the EU', Enschede, available at Master thesis, http://essay.utwente.nl/61736/.

Vito (2009a), 'Preparatory studies for eco-design requirements of EuPs: Final report Lot 19: Domestic lighting', accessed 22 February 2012 at www.eup4light.net/assets/pdffiles/Final_part1_2/EuP_Domestic_Part1en2_V11.pdf.

Vito (2009b), 'Preparatory Studies for Eco-design Requirements of EuPs: Project Report Lot 19: Domestic lighting', accessed 6 March 2012 at www.eup4light.net/assets/pdffiles/Final_part1_2/EuP_Domestic_Project_report_V10.pdf.

Weber, M. (1978), *Economy and Society. An Outline of Interpretive Sociology*, Berkley: University of California Press.

Zucker, L. G. (1991), 'The role of institutionalization in cultural persistence', in W. W. Powell and P. J. DiMaggio (eds), *The New Institutionalism in Organization Analysis*, Chicago: Chicago University Press, pp. 83–107.

7. Translational research: entrepreneurship, advocacy and programmatic work in the governance of biomedical innovation

Etienne Vignola-Gagné, Peter Biegelbauer and Daniel Lehner

7.1 INTRODUCTION

A number of conceptual and disciplinary splits reduce the analytical power of STI policy and systems analyses. Most notably, STI policy analyses have tended to frame these processes as out of their boundaries, despite the recognition that debate or bargaining as processes shape policy instruments and their targets in a world of constrained resources (Holzinger, 2004; Saretzki, 2009), making the formulation and implementation of policy instruments an inherently political matter (Meadowcroft, 2009; Biegelbauer and Hansen, 2011; Geels and Verhees, 2011). Yet, several decades of policy analysis provide ample proof that only in the rarest of cases do policy interventions come out of the blue. Normally they are the result of struggles for power, the ambition to be represented, to have one's interests included, to learn from experience, to win an argument, to see a set of ideas vested with the power to explain, and the like (for example Truman, 1956; Lasswell, 1970; Hall, 1993; Sabatier and Jenkins-Smith, 1993; Gottweis, 1998; Parsons, 2003).

Therefore power struggles are not the only highly political element in policy-making. Bargaining, entrepreneurship and advocacy may be required even for the continued maintenance and performance of innovation systems. Complementarities need to be activated and reactivated. Interdependencies between areas of expertise and between organizations often 'fall out' and become dysfunctional. Here, we will show that governance is not only about the creation of legitimacy towards a broad public for the 'reception of technology', but also the building of legitimacy within a network to build support for the 'reception' of an organizational form. Indeed, governance does not end at the doorstep of an organization; rather, the term has an inside and an outside quality. We are interested in both, the governance of change on the level of policies, and on the level of organizations, their structures, norms and values (Hall and Taylor, 1996; Peters, 1999; Hollingsworth, 2000).

Initiative, entrepreneurship and advocacy are constantly required at the organizational level to ensure collaboration and coordination. In these contexts of high ambivalence, entrepreneurial activity is also required to negotiate which policy instruments will be marshalled in the specific context, and how. An important condition to achieve successful advocacy by entrepreneurs are sets of policy rationales and/or programmatic statements that clarify targets and tactics for collective action. STI policies in implementation are confronted with a policy field in which varying sets of skilled actors are making them part of their opportunity structures when they try, for example, to raise funds for new projects or institutions. This is the case for 'hard', that is, regulatory and distributive, and 'soft', that is, information delivery and community formation measures, both of which are subject to interpretation by various actors. In the process, new rationales, scientific concepts and programmatic frameworks are utilized as framings: opportunistically, in order to gain funding; as sense-making tools, in order to interpret social problems and environments; but also instrumentally, as mechanisms to coordinate and channel the efforts of the range of actors brought together by advocacy efforts.

In short, Chapter 7 focuses on change in some of the experimental and organizational practices that are central components of socio-technical systems. It uses novel observations drawn from case studies of biomedical innovation systems reform to trace the role of selected parameters in this process of transforming existing practices. Specifically, we look at the role of (1) programmatic statements; (2) their advocacy by entrepreneurs and (3) their interplay with existing and new policy instruments, in explaining the governance of socio-technical change. This analytical strategy could have explanatory power in other cases of socio-technical change where policy design and implementation define parameters of the process.

The three case studies each revolve around efforts in the implementation of translational research (TR) programmes in biomedical RTD sites located in Austria and Germany. TR can be defined as a policy rationale (Braun, 2005) that first problematizes current practices in biomedical practices, offering a distinct diagnostic of well-discussed 'crisis situations' in biomedical innovation systems. These innovation crises include:

(1) public disappointment with the outcomes for patients of big science projects such as the Human Genome Project;
(2) a perceived widening gap between the practice of academic medicine and the advances of molecular biology;
(3) decreased RTD productivity in the pharmaceutical industry which has led to the loss of thousands of RTD jobs (Kraft, 2013; Vignola-Gagné, 2014).

TR advocates championing a specific set of scientific approaches, organizational arrangements and policy packages as the way out of these problems. The most prominent interventions on biomedical innovation systems and attendant policies that are advocated through TR include:

- closer integration of clinical experience with cutting-edge laboratory experimentation (including sequencing technologies and biomarker discovery experiments), notably through forms of 'patient-oriented research' and the development of experimental routines within clinical trials;
- investment of research monies and scientific work capacity in 'gap areas', such as clinical pharmacology and drug development as a scientific/engineering problem;
- redistributed and new professional roles across the continuum of labour in biomedical innovation, including greater leadership from clinician-scientists;
- greater coordination and orientation of innovation projects, to increase efficiency and reduce trial-and-error in intervention development.

As the dimensions above make clear, much of the TR rationale is aimed explicitly at change in the governance of biomedical innovation systems rather than techno–scientific change alone. Nevertheless, the TR rationale is entangled with broad developments brought on by genomic sequencing technologies, continuing reform of clinical research, past achievements and desired futures. Prior to the establishment of the initiatives studied in Chapter 7, TR had been used since the 1990s, in the US most notably, to justify and orient policy-driven efforts targeting the dimensions mentioned above. The TR rationale attempts to harness and orient change in biomedical innovation systems brought on by advances in genomics towards a specific set of outcomes, both techno-scientific and governmental.

The three cases of implementation of TR rationales into regional STI policies that will be studied below highlight the importance of the interplay between scientific entrepreneurs and explicit programmes of change in reforming experimental and organizational practices in biomedical innovation. Entrepreneurs and advocates of TR negotiate the formulation and implementation of pre-existing policy instruments to build their networks, draw on higher-level debates about the legitimacy of biomedical innovation to frame their action and shape the role of other actors. These findings are relevant for the pillars of theory building introduced by Borrás and Edler (2014), highlighting how advocacy, entrepreneurship and governance processes around the design and implementation of policy instruments (pillar 2) are themselves entangled with structures of opportunity (pillar 1) and in processes of legitimacy building (pillar 3).

Detailing our understanding of how: (1) policy rationales and programmes of socio-technical change; (2) advocacy works to enrol allies for these programmes and (3) entrepreneurs interact to produce change in experimental and organizational practices through TR initiatives studied here, raises the following research questions:

- How is a global rationale such as TR made use of in locales far removed from its origins in Austria and Germany?
- How are programmatic statements, concepts and assumptions about current crises and benefits of the TR-model used to shape or drive socio-technical change, and to shape or drive change in related governance arrangements?
- How do entrepreneurs engage in advocacy activities and deploy programmatic statements in their innovation practices, and how do these interact with policy instruments already deployed in the field?

The rest of Chapter 7 will be structured as follows: Section 7.2 reviews previous efforts to use policy rationales, programmatic statements and the role of entrepreneurs as analytical units in order to explain change in socio-technical systems and their governance. It highlights especially the potential contribution of the two categories 'entrepreneur' and 'advocacy work' to this research agenda. Section 7.3 provides a brief overview of our data collection and analytical strategies. Section 7.4 presents and analyses our empirical material, starting with a review of the emergence and evolution of TR rationales in the USA, and later internationally (section 7.4.1). This step is essential for understanding the interventions advocated by the entrepreneurs in our case studies. Subsection 7.4.2 details case study material, with observations structured along the three pillars by Edler and Borrás (2014). The presentation of the policy instruments deployed in each initiative is successively contextualized with a view to the entrepreneurial (section 7.4.2.3 – pillar opportunity structures and capable agents) and advocacy work (section 7.4.2.4 – pillar legitimacy) that has aligned and framed them. Section 7.5 concludes with a discussion of the findings, detailing the crucial role of entrepreneurs and their advocacy of TR programmes in producing change in socio-technical systems and their governance mechanisms.

7.2 LITERATURE REVIEW: RATIONALES, PROGRAMMATIC STATEMENTS AND ENTREPRENEURS

To understand the role of policy rationales and programmes in managing change in socio-technical systems, one can follow along the lines of work that aims to combine traditions of analysis in the economics of innovation and in the politics of policy (to use the terms of Jacobsson and Lauber, 2006). One approach employed in this strand of works has been to identify 'technology-specific coalitions' that 'engage in wider political debates in order to gain influence over institutions and secure institutional alignment' (Jacobsson and Lauber, 2006, p. 259). While Geels and Verhees (2011) have also studied the role of coalitions, cognitive frames and discourses in innovation systems and policy, they have yet to look in detail at how these processes reorganize systems of knowledge production, for example at the level of mundane experimental and institutional practice. Hillman et al. (2011) have provided STI policy and systems analysts with typologies of parameters for modelling the steering action of governance arrangements on innovation systems. Governance in innovation systems may include regulatory, market, cognitive and normative mechanisms. These authors rightly point out the unique role of public or governmental policy-makers in shaping and performing the governance of innovation systems. Nevertheless, the current chapter should make it clear that while governmental actors may be obligatory passage points in governance processes, they are not the critical source of agency for change.

Elsewhere, scholars have combined the analysis of 'traditional STI' policy instruments and of 'modes/strategies of governance' by deploying a more dynamic approach to system building and resource utilization. They have looked at the formation of networks to establish shared resources, including reputational capital, standardization authorities or financial resources (Musiolik et al., 2012). An important finding has been that the system building process is partly determined by the type of networks that lead these efforts and the resources they have access to. This opens a path to further analyses of how policy instruments are actively elaborated and operationalized within the mundane practices of innovation, notably by highly entrepreneurial local actors.

Entrepreneurs have been the subject of a long-standing line of work in economics. These studies have emphasized the role of individuals in organizing or catalysing institutional change, taking risks and building alliances for achieving their aims (Bergeron et al., 2013). The concept has now been integrated across the social sciences, and the policy entrepreneur or change entrepreneur has emerged as a useful analytical unit to understand policy change. Interesting findings from the attendant literature have highlighted how entrepreneurs realize their interests by transforming the social space and institutional arrangements they evolve in, rather than reproducing them; how they create and frame collective crises and direct attention towards specific resources to solve them; and how they play on the fragmentation of social systems and boundaries or differences between groups and institutions to generate innovation and/or benefit (Bergeron et al., 2013; Castel and Friedberg, 2010).

Authors have also highlighted the interaction between entrepreneurs and policy rationales or programmes in pushing governance change. Hassenteufel et al emphasize the determination of 'programmatic actors' on the content of policy change, on the legitimization of some programmatic statements and the marginalizing of others. 'By selecting, translating, recombining, and, most important, imposing ideas, they fulfil a genuinely creative and constructive role' (Hassenteufel et al., 2008, p. 529). Programmatic statements are an essential component of policy change, since crises and external destabilizations on policy processes do not alone determine solutions.

These findings are in line with the original formulation of the advocacy-coalition framework (ACF), formulated by Paul Sabatier and Hank Jenkins-Smith, who state that policy change is mainly induced by external effects such as economic crises or natural disasters, rather than by policy entrepreneurs. Indeed, the ACF has been less interested in the role of entrepreneurs, but more focused on the level of a policy subsystem and the advocacy coalitions, which are seen as the main constituent of policy fields. In the ACF, policy advocates are the prime movers of advocacy coalitions, being linked by shared policy beliefs and interests (Sabatier and Jenkins-Smith, 1993; Sabatier, 1998).

Hassenteufel and colleagues oppose programmatic actors compared to policy entrepreneurs in that the latter are seen mostly as brokers and packagers but not creators. Such a strict delineation between the two categories is questionable, however. Indeed, transfer and brokering rarely leaves policy content intact. Clavier (2010) has shown the importance of the self-initiative of local entrepreneurs in diffusing and implementing public health and health care policies elaborated by the World Health Organization. Much like TR rationales and other scientific programmes, WHO policies are proposed interventions that are not intrinsically backed with financial or regulatory obligation. Their careers rest on persuasion, marketing and advocacy. Clavier's examples provide a clear view of the crucial role played by the combination of broadly circulated programmes and policy rationale, as well as appropriation by local entrepreneurs for enacting local change of practices and institutional arrangements.

Similarly, Peter Biegelbauer finds that in Austrian RTD policy-making, major programmes usually are the result of policy entrepreneurs' actions with entrepreneurs in most cases (also) playing an important part in the creation and (re)combination of policy ideas (2007, 2013b).

In the science, technology and society (STS) literature, forms of advocacy have been captured in actor-network theory analyses of the construction of innovation networks. Especially, a recent iteration of the theory has drawn attention to the future-oriented work that is performed to justify and, indeed, advocate for certain technological options rather than others (van Lente and Rip, 1998; Hedgecoe and Martin, 2003). Advocacy through raising technological expectations is here considered a crucial strategy for building new networks of actors and artefacts, and thus conducting socio-technical change. Arguments and rationales about preferred courses for collective action have also been shown to be an important component of the implementation and effectiveness of policy formulated by governmental agencies (Borrás and Radaelli, 2011).

7.3   RESEARCH STRATEGY

A critical mass of attention has recently been afforded to TR rationales within the biomedical innovation community, with a number of initiatives being put into place internationally (Shahzad et al., 2011; von Roth et al., 2011). Here, we mobilize case studies of TR-related entrepreneurship in three initiatives established in Austria and Germany. The selected initiatives have been launched in the last ten years and have been explicitly construed by their promoters as being focused on TR. The initiatives offer a degree of diversity and contrasting experiences to allow for in-depth comparison. Taken as an ensemble, the initiatives should constitute a broadly typical panel of cases. In a first case study TRAIN (Translational Research Alliance In Lower-Saxony), a core group of entrepreneurs very actively advocate for the TR model to reform regional innovation practices. Based on their work, new mechanisms of coordination, for what were previously dispersed and discrete experimental projects, are being put into place and renewed legitimacy is offered to RTD activities. In a second case study ASC (Anna-Spiegel Center), technological change is emphasized, with the other dimensions only marginally present. The absence of a core single or group of entrepreneurs is noticeable here, and both advocacy activities and uptake of the rationale appear to be low. Use of TR was of a highly instrumental character. The third initiative (OncoTyrol) offers a middle case in that it is characterized by a strong group of entrepreneurs, but with less pronounced advocacy work. Financial resources are used as driver of change, more so than programmatic statements, although change is aimed in part at the implementation of the TR model presented above. TR rationales thus have more of a guiding role, but are also crucial to legitimize the strongly centralized and top-down mode of coordination encountered in this consortium.

For each case study, semi-directed interviews were conducted with coordinators, administrators, research leaders and policy-makers, who had been identified as playing a central role in the establishment and maintenance of the respective initiative (six interviews for the TRAIN case study; seven for the OncoTyrol case study; 11 for the ASC case study). Interviews and relevant documents were coded and analysed following an analytical grid that aimed to capture the diachronic development of the initiatives, who was involved and how, the relations to the international policy discussion, coordination issues, governmental support and the features of the experimental practices deployed locally.

Lastly, this discrete investigation into TR initiatives was part of a broader research programme concerned with understanding the origins and implications of TR as a 'reform movement' in contemporary biomedical innovation. Even if they do not form the focus of analysis here, our reflections on this topic have also drawn from 39 further interviews conducted in Germany, EU-networks and the USA, as well as a document analysis of governmental white papers and approximately 200 editorials, commentaries and reviews about TR, that are published in peer-reviewed biomedical journals.

7.4 RESULTS

TR is a policy rationale that appeared in the early 1990s. More specifically, it advocates for certain institutional and experimental reforms as privileged means to solve a number of crises that have shaken biomedical innovation systems since the 1970s (Vignola-Gagné and Biegelbauer, 2013).

7.4.1 Translational Research: Scope and Novelty

Section 7.4.1 looks at these constitutive crises and the kind of structural changes in biomedical innovation that TR advocates aim for.

In the 1970s, the character of biomedical research was irrevocably changed by the steady expansion of molecular biology approaches in the field. Whereas the period immediately after World War II until the 1960s saw a 'golden-age' of research performed by medical doctors in close proximity to clinical contexts and practices, a paradigm retrospectively dubbed 'patient-oriented research' (Swazey and Fox, 2004), the new approach emphasized the control and replicability of laboratory systems and modelling. Molecular biologists were slowly filling an increasing number of research positions at academic medical centres and university clinics, and also started to systematically outperform medical doctors in obtaining National Institutes of Health research funding. Starting in the late 1970s, but lasting up to now, a number of biomedical policy actors and academic medicine leaders started to problematize the situation of these clinician-scientists (for primary literature see: Wyngaarden, 1979; Nathan, 2002; for secondary analysis see: Wilson-Kovacs and Hauskeller, 2012; Vignola-Gagné, 2014). They argued that these professionals possessed a unique dual expertise in both clinical care and clinical or laboratory research, and were thus privileged drivers of biomedical innovation with relevance to patients. Yet, the increasing sophistication of molecular biology made them experience an increasing 'gap' between both areas of practice, and increased public support was necessary to enable these clinician-scientists to be competitive again in funding calls. In 1991, with the establishment of a number of specialized centres for clinical oncology research by the National Cancer Institute in the USA, the notion of TR was first introduced and was immediately associated with ongoing policy discussions about the future of clinician-scientists (Cancer Letter, 1991). Major TR initiatives that came later also planned support for clinician-scientists (for primary literature see: Zerhouni, 2005; Borstein and Licinio, 2011; for secondary analysis see: Vignola-Gagné, 2014).

The perception of a gap or disconnection between molecular biology-driven biomedical research and clinical application gained much broader currency in the early 2000s, in the immediate aftermath of the international Human Genome Project. This big science project of unprecedented scope in biology and medicine raised high expectations of short- and mid-term contributions to clinical innovation, which were however followed by a cycle of disappointment (for primary literature see: Anonymous, 2012; Lander, 2011; for secondary analysis see: Martin et al., 2009; Hogarth et al., 2012). Advocates have positioned TR as the approach that would make genomics and related technological platforms relevant to the clinic (Collins, 2011). This involves, most notably, modernising clinical research networks so as to make genetic sequencing an integral part of clinical testing and the development of new interventions, or expanding experimental platforms such as biobanks, which can generate therapeutic hypotheses by directly using human tissues instead of model systems.

The latest, but possibly the most urgent, series of developments to have shaped the trajectory of TR concepts has been the increased perception of a situation crisis in the pharmaceutical industry. With its 2004 report *Innovation/Stagnation,* the US Food and Drug Administration brought the existence of data indicating stagnating productivity in the pharmaceutical industry in terms of new innovative drugs, despite increasing investments, to the attention of a broad audience (Food and Drug Administration, 2004). Although the data and interpretations have been subjected to discussion, by the late 2000s, events seemed to confirm the diagnosis. Large pharmaceutical companies have recently slashed thousands of RTD jobs as their recently off-patent portfolio 'blockbuster' drugs, selling for billions annually, had failed to be replaced by new ones (Milne, 2009). In prevision or in reaction to this situation, a number of biomedical leaders and academic administrations had advocated the establishment of 'academic drug pipelines', hence providing for unprecedented forms of development research, divisions of labour and industrial RTD equipment within the public research systems (Tralau-Stewart et al., 2009; Becker and van Dongen, 2011).

TR as policy rationale thus emerged as a response to these three interconnected series of developments. Although the TR rationale repeats many themes and proposals commonly voiced by reformers of biomedical innovation since the 1970s (Vignola-Gagné, 2014), the programme has received unprecedented levels of commitment. It is now backed by major research funds, training programmes and institutes (Zerhouni, 2005; Collins, 2011; Shahzad et al., 2011; von Roth et al., 2011).

7.4.2   Case Study Results

Section 7.4.2 presents the results of our case studies of TR initiatives. For each case, the relevant policy instruments are described. It is then shown how these instruments were introduced and put into operation by local entrepreneurs, simultaneously, as they advocated for the adoption of the TR model.

Based on interviews and literature studies described above, Table 7.1 below uses the four dimensions of socio-technical change advocated by TR programmes (see section 7.1) to summarize the technological and organizational changes that have taken place at the sites of each of our three case studies.

Table 7.1   Forms and depth of socio-technical change brought by TR initiatives in three regional biomedical innovation systems

	ASC	OncoTyrol	TRAIN
Lab – clinic integration	+ +	+	+
Investment in gap areas	+ +	+ +	+ +
New division of labour	–	+	+ +
Enhanced coordination	–	+ +	+

7.4.2.1   Description of cases

The three case studies from the ASC, OncoTyrol and the Translational Research Alliance in Lower-Saxony are described below.

7.4.2.1.1   Anna Spiegel Center for Translational Research   The ASC is a research building situated at the Medical University of Vienna (MUV), as part of the General Hospital of Vienna (AKH). It has specifically been labelled as a translational centre and was built with the intention to create more lab-space and to centralize 'Core Facilities' – high-tech to support basic research at the AKH/MUV. Opened in 2010, the centre is an example of a highly modern research institute composed of relatively independent teams that were previously situated in a more clinical environment at the main buildings of the MUV.

The ASC consists of six research departments (surgery, dermatology, cardiology, paediatrics, oncology and haematology), which comprise a varying number of research and/or lab-groups. The official mission of the centre is to conduct clinically-driven research using the latest techniques biomedical research has to offer. The chemists and biologists at the ASC work closely together with the physicians at the clinic located at the main building of the AKH/MUV. Their research projects are based on clinical considerations/observations, and they try to translate their new findings (new diagnostics, bio-markers) immediately to the clinic. Accordingly, the scientific practices are translational in a bi-directional manner since both areas – the lab and the clinic – need each other's expertise and knowledge. Moreover, this close relationship is based on 'material exchange', as the basic researchers need, for example, tissue samples from patients or bio-banks.

The ASC does not have a director or management team of its own. The ASC staff have a very heterodox understanding of TR notions, ranging from an economic conception to a more clinically oriented definition.

7.4.2.1.2 OncoTyrol OncoTyrol comprises a regional cluster of 22 research groups located in universities, research institutes and companies, specialising in applied research in the growing field of personalized cancer medicine in the area of Innsbruck. OncoTyrol operates as a GmbH (limited liability company). The consortium is led by the board of shareholders (56 per cent universities; 21 per cent Hospital Holding; 23 per cent Province of the Tyrol), and decisions are implemented by the management in Innsbruck. Currently, OncoTyrol is employing about 90 scientists and providing facilities for the research teams (for example, offices for HTA-research, lab-space in a special building, facilities for bio-informatics).

The research teams are expected to produce patents, licences or products in cooperation with industrial partners. Part of the IPR from the funded projects is retained by the OncoTyrol management – a situation which prompts the consortium administrators' hope that it will become self–sufficient in the future, without a need for additional public funding. In terms of the sheer amount of industrial partners involved, OncoTyrol is an atypical TR initiative. Although some industrial members act more as *mécènes*, providing funding in the background in the hope of the development of eventual products, other projects have called for joint and sustained collaborations.

As a consortium with its own dedicated project funding mechanism, OncoTyrol features a unique structure within the networks and initiatives we have studied. Whereas in TRAIN funding is mostly provided for building and equipment infrastructure, in OncoTyrol funding is given to projects directly (including personnel costs). The OncoTyrol administration can decide (and has been known) to withdraw membership and funding from project teams that are not committed enough towards clinical and/or commercial aims.

7.4.2.1.3   Translational Research Alliance in Lower Saxony   TRAIN, a state in the Centre–North of Germany, is an initiative explicitly dedicated to developing new drug compounds that are typically brought forward by pharmaceutical corporations. TRAIN regroups seven main institutional partners, all of which directly take part in various tasks and work packages of the collaboration's projects. The institutes are located in relative proximity in the two largest cities of the region. Their founding members include universities, public research institutes and a medical school. A number of joint ventures between partner institutes have significantly extended the local expertise in drug development. Further, the consortium includes a firm specialized in managing life science projects (VPM).

Based on the capacities that are being regrouped, the TRAIN management claims that within the TRAIN partnership it is possible to go from pathophysiological hypothesis to lead compound to early phase II clinical trials (that is, clinical development with tests on human subjects to measure safety and administration modalities, thus requiring a comparatively complex infrastructure). This claim positions the consortium as a structure of unique breadth and complexity in Germany and at the European level.

7.4.2.2   Pillar 1: policy instruments

As discussed in Section 7.1, a number of different policy instruments have been advocated in the literature to realize the TR programme (Vignola-Gagné and Biegelbauer, 2013; Vignola-Gagné et al., 2013). Reformulated in the language of STI policy analysis, these instruments most importantly include:

- measures of organization building in the sense of creating the infrastructure for TR;
- funding programmes fostering TR, but also general research funding programmes;
- the professionalization of education such as support for clinician-scientists with degrees in both medicine and natural sciences;
- efforts of governance coordination in which either various governance initiatives are coordinated and/or in which actors are brought together in order to exchange information.

In all three case studies, measures of organization building and general funding programmes proved to be most central. In the case of the ASC, the funds that had been earmarked for the completion of the General Hospital (AKH) were used for a building for two research institutions, the ASC and the Research Center for Molecular Medicine (CeMM). The cost of 41 million Euro for the building was shared between the city of Vienna and the Austrian Ministry for Science and Research. Research at the ASC is supported by standard principal investigator grants or project funding from thematic programmes (from the Austrian Science Fund (FWF)'s general competitions, 'Translational Research' and 'Clinical Research' (both FWF), 'Patients in Focus' (Centre for Innovation and Technology of Vienna, ZIT) and the life science programmes of the Vienna Science and Technology Fund (WWTF)).

OncoTyrol was mostly funded by the Austrian COMET programme (Competence Centres for Excellent Technologies; Biegelbauer, 2007), a multi-actor, multi-purpose competence centre programme, aiming at linking actors in science and industry by realising cooperative research initiatives co-funded by federal and state (Länder) levels, companies and research institutions. When its predecessor Kplus was set up in 1998, it was arguably the most complex RTI policy instrument in Austria and in 2013 it remains to be one of the most important RTI funding instruments in the country (Biegelbauer, 2013b). In addition to COMET funding (from 2008–2012, approximately 18 million Euro came from the federal level, 6 million from the state of Tyrol, 23 million from industry and 1 million from academia), additional support stems from a variety of research funding programmes. Broadly, the OncoTyrol consortium can be said to have been assembled by the combination of policy instruments commonly used in the last 20 years to foster commercially-oriented STI activities: centres of excellence with a high level of participation from industrial partners; the availability of venture or seed capital; and high interdisciplinarity. Nonetheless, the specific configuration of expertise and disciplines present within the consortium, especially its emphasis on fostering clinically-informed laboratory research, is aligned with TR rationales.

TRAIN institutionalizes previously dispersed regional expertise in drug development in a clear model, through regional coordination and cooperation, and a consensual division of labour between local actors. This policy plan was jointly developed by local leaders of relevant institutions and the Lower Saxony Ministry of Science and Culture. The model makes direct reference to the rationale of academic pipelines (see section 7.4.1), thus providing 'blueprints' for local TR projects, including model collaborations. The central office of the initiative (staffed by one part-time administrator), together with the life sciences project management firm VPM, encouraged active participation of research teams that are affiliated with consortium member institutions. The business managers and coordinators were central agents for transforming research projects of autonomous teams into complex TR projects with centralized coordination and strategic commercial planning. The consortium model also assigned specific tasks to different expert groups within the consortium. The infrastructure building activities that have taken place there since 2007, especially multiple joint ventures, have helped to establish the consortium collaboration blueprint more readily. A first wave of such joint ventures was initially funded by the local Lower Saxony Ministry of Science and Culture (at the level of slightly under 30 million Euro). With this initial funding secured and the overarching concept established, members of the consortium have also been able to secure infrastructure funding for other joint institutions from the German federal programme for university infrastructure building, the *Forschungsbau* programme.

Despite the focus on infrastructure funding up to now, business managers and coordinators at the consortium central office can also assist member teams with obtaining grants or venture capital to finance actual experimental work. A drug development project related to the consortium benefitted, for example, from funding from the German federal Bio-Profile programme, which offers proof-of-concept funding for exploratory development work in the life sciences conducted in biotechnology firms or academic settings. Drawing on this funding, and directed by principle of the 'academic pipeline', the TRAIN consortium has thus focused on the development of the large-scale equipment used in industrial drug development, including natural substance libraries and a chemical screening facility.

OncoTyrol is an interesting case here as the COMET funding programme allows funding of research groups and facilities alike and thus offers OncoTyrol's management some flexibility. Yet COMET funding is tied to a number of conditions, most importantly science-industry cooperation. In order to provide the management with the structures necessary for coordinating competence centres with a large number of actors with diverse multi-disciplinary commercial and non-commercial background, COMET centres are set up with a clear hierarchical structure (Biegelbauer, 2007). OncoTyrol features a network structure combined with a strong hierarchical component, while ASC and TRAIN are less hierarchical. Leadership in ASC is externalized in the form of the management of the AKH/MUV. TRAIN's strongest management structure is the cluster formed by a steering committee in which representatives of the six founding partner institutions are co-located with the consortium administration office.

7.4.2.3 Pillar 2: opportunity structures and capable agents

The cases of TR collaborations we studied have highlighted the central role of a few academic leaders in implementing local iterations of the proposals made in the international policy discussion. They show how the emerging policy rationale, and its specific repertoire of problems and solutions, was used by these entrepreneurs to reframe collective interpretations of the biomedical innovation process shared by local actors, and of their preferred policy instruments.

Within TRAIN, understandings of TR have been most thoroughly shaped by the sub-rationale of crisis in innovation productivity in the pharmaceutical industry. The consortium leaders are also very clear about the origins of this initiative as a response to the pharmaceutical innovation crisis. The uptake of the consortium model has been actively advocated among the member institutions by information sessions or 'internal PR'. In their presentations, consortium coordinators directly refer to the models recently expounded by Francis Collins, the current director of the US National Institutes of Health (NIH), who has called for universities and public institutions to take on some of the scientific risk associated with drug development and increase collaboration with the pharmaceutical industry. The explicit goal of these information activities is to promote the TR model of biomedical innovation locally among research teams and other relevant actors, some of them being core funders at the regional and federal level. Establishing the TRAIN consortium has thus called for action on local work programmes, problematizing capacities for biomedical innovation and presenting the TR model as the preferred solution. Nonetheless, consortium leaders also worked at the level of resources and incentives, offering expertise to potential partners with regard to business management, patent portfolio development or networking with venture capital. The TRAIN entrepreneurs aligned governmental funding schemes and other policy instruments with the demands of local projects to realize a coherent TR network that is in accordance with current rationales about biomedical innovation.

OncoTyrol's origins lie in the strong departments for clinical oncology at the Medical University Innsbruck and related biological research centres. In 2002, this collective of excellent scientists already present in Innsbruck was consolidated into a more closely knit network by a prime mover with a background both in science and industry. Notably problematic at that point was a perceived financing gap for proof-of-concept studies, which meant that promising therapeutic intervention candidates, who had been developed locally, were 'lost' to industry instead of being led through early clinical development within Medical School.

The opportunity to establish an excellence centre for oncology arose when COMET calls for application were issued. Similar to TRAIN, the founders of OncoTyrol seized the increasing difficulties within the pharmaceutical industry as an opportunity to elaborate a centre of excellence model around 'open innovation' (they made an explicit reference to the work of Henry Chesbrough), with strong networks of collaboration between the Medical University and industry partners. This way, tentative TR projects would obtain proof-of-concept funding and access to industry-specific competences and infrastructures while retaining more control over product development than was previously possible.

With the excellence centre approved and in place, the coordination of participating TR projects changed dramatically. The consortium directly employs more than 80 administrative and technical staff, and participating research teams obtain most of their project funding and even salaries through the OncoTyrol administration. Continued availability of this funding is subject to successful progress in TR terms, and in terms of clinical and commercial relevance. COMET funding, which itself was marshalled by a few entrepreneurs that identified a unique support opportunity and made use of the international rationale of TR to advocate their vision, thus durably altered the structures of opportunity for regional biomedical actors as well as their understanding of TR. While the compliance of participating research teams with the TR model does not rest on its advocacy by the entrepreneurs alone (as it does in TRAIN), the OncoTyrol leadership nonetheless has made use of its programmatic statements in preparing future expansions of the consortium (including a move towards financial self-sufficiency).

In the case of ASC, several scientific entrepreneurs came to the conclusion that lab space was too limited in the Medical University Vienna and therefore infrastructure building was the only possible solution to the problem. In lengthy negotiations with the City of Vienna and the Austrian Ministry for Science it became clear that a new building would become more feasible when sharing space with a second institution. This turned out to be CEMM, which was at this time rapidly expanding and therefore also looking for a new building.

Labelling the building with TR coincided with the fact that different elements of the TR metaphor had already taken root in Austrian RTI policy discussions, leading to the first TR funding programmes at the time. Policymakers therefore were receptive to the programme of TR, with its affinities for their own commitment towards the renewal of medical schools. However, once they had successfully marshalled funds for their infrastructure and equipment project, the entrepreneurs did not push through with the organizational interventions advocated in international TR programmes.

7.4.2.4 Pillar 3: questions of legitimacy

To a certain extent, we can reduce the question of opportunity structures surrounding TR to the issue of legitimacy in biomedical innovation systems. The opportunity for TR consortium building appears to have been thoroughly shaped by global policy discussions about how best to conduct biomedical innovation so as to ensure its continued relevance in the eyes of a broad civil constituency, as well as its 'value for money' (in the sense of Braun, 2005; see also Leonelli and Sunder Rajan, 2013; Maienschein et al., 2008).

Despite this potential for making TR a vehicle for extended civil participation in RTD systems, our results show that this has not been the case in Austria and Germany. The consortia we studied had no mechanism to ensure patient or citizen input into decision-making. Interview respondents sometimes considered the market's demand for given health products, or that clinicians' experiences with patients provided the best means to capture patient or end user preferences, with even patient representatives being sceptical about the possibility of co-decision making regarding TR on grounds of the involved issues' complexity.

This does not mean that legitimacy is not an important dimension in order to make sense of the changes brought about by TR in biomedical innovation systems. Indeed, 'internal' or intra-network legitimacy, as a resource that can be deployed to ensure coordination and collaboration within the narrowly defined communities of innovation studied here was a central concern of the consortia. This can be most clearly witnessed in the case of TRAIN, where, as discussed above, the actual realization and performance of the consortium model depended on well-coordinated collaboration of a number of research teams with broadly different disciplinary and organizational missions and demands to answer to. Establishing participation in TRAIN as a new and distinct goal for each of these teams thus entails building legitimacy for the project that answers to the necessarily particularistic (with respect to the consortium's goals) agendas of these groups of experts.

While within OncoTyrol, the broader discussion of crisis in biomedical innovation played some role in its overall set-up and direction of the consortium, it was less prominent and somewhat less operationalized in the case of TRAIN. Indeed, because of direct management of research funding by the central administration, it seemed that the official narrative was not being extensively used in daily practice. Nevertheless, legitimate participation of research teams within the OncoTyrol structure depended on their compliance with collaboration and experimental practices in line with those advocated in TR rationales.

In the case of the ASC, TR had little effect on intra-network legitimacy. Since the legitimacy of the organization rests on a strong scientific rationale, it is well aligned with the mind-set of scientists and medical doctors working there. The internal governance schemes of ASC are very much driven by the experienced principal investigators leading small research groups, who coordinate loosely and without much internal differentiation. The framework of the organization is predefined by the MUV's rectorate, which conceives of the ASC as an institution for scientific excellence, where only the best research groups of the MUV should work. Accordingly, these groups were chosen by MUV in a selection procedure based on scientific output criteria only. 'Intra-network legitimacy' is of course interconnected with 'extra-network legitimacy'. The TRAIN leaders advocate to local partners the model proposed with their consortium by framing the current biomedical innovation policy landscape as threatened by a crisis with far-reaching consequences. Consortium leaders thus readily draw on debates around the legitimacy of the biomedical innovation enterprise and its relevance to civil society to justify their agendas.

Interestingly, consortium collaborators sometimes appeared to be 'phantom allies', that is partners more on paper than in practice, yet useful in order to keep current core collaborations going with the prospect of future collaborations around commercial development, for example. These phantom allies (most notably industry and patients) imbued the work blueprint provided by the consortium with legitimacy, and thus provided consortium leaders with resources to align academic members and ensure effective coordination of their work within the division of labour planned by the model. In other words, the 'presence' of these phantom allies had essentially boosted the legitimacy to alter local interpretative frameworks related to the biomedical innovation process and to marshal support from a number of policy instruments.

The ASC, for its part, consolidated an orientation towards laboratory-based research on human material that was already present at the MUV. As such, it provides a case of TR as a transformative notion being used in a non-transformative manner and to extend previously existing practices. Nevertheless the external legitimacy of ASC secured funding for infrastructure which was justified by a broader importance beyond ASC. This utilization of TR as a legitimising metaphor includes the instrumental usage of firms, which are again being used as 'phantom allies' and which in the actual daily practices of the organization until now have played a rather small role – something which may or may not change with an increasing age of the still young institution. Firms, however, were not the only 'phantom allies' – patients also tended to slip out of the roles assigned by programmatic statements. In the actual daily routines of ASC personnel, patient participation in the research process was mostly limited to tissue donation.

7.5 DISCUSSION

The material and analysis presented above provided multiple points of support for our argument that traditional STI policy analysis can benefit from closer attention to programmatic statements and their deployment in advocacy practices by change–bearing entrepreneurs.

To demonstrate this, we have drawn support from empirical cases showing how a set of socio–technical changes – that is, the closer integration of clinical experience with laboratory experimentation, investment in gap areas, new professional roles and greater coordination of projects – in some biomedical innovation systems has been recently affected by the emergence of a new policy rationale called TR. At the international level, this emergence has notably been fostered by parallel interventions and advocacy from academic leaders, academic administrations and STI policy-makers. Yet, this new policy rationale does not map out directly into a specific set of policy instruments that could be used to deploy or implement its proposals, at least not in Germany and Austria, where the networks we studied are located. We are not presented with a 'linear model of policy formulation and implementation', where one issue would be linked with one set of policy instruments, which in turn would translate to one defined set of behavioural and organizational impacts in innovation systems.

Instead, multiple issues and policy instruments co-exist in various relations, and 'impact' in innovation systems may well be achieved by new alignments of actors to long-existing instruments. Indeed, in our case studies, local entrepreneurs made opportunistic use of various pre-existing instruments. These instruments were useful for building an innovation network modelled after TR programmes, helping to enrol local allies to take on parts of the necessary labour. As such, local implementations and deployment of existing policy instruments were inflected and performed through governance processes such as the reframing of legitimate experimental practices affected by advocacy of

TR notions. New policy instruments put into place for the networks (mostly infrastructure funding) were sometimes also a consequence of previous advocacy. Furthermore, advocacy work was greatly aided by previous network building efforts. That is, building a successful collaboration to engage in multidisciplinary TR projects itself functioned as a powerful argument to enrol further allies.

Sometimes, this also meant that advocacy was constantly required to hold the emerging system together. Even in the case of the TRAIN consortium, which can be characterized as one whole and well planned policy instrument, implementation and collaboration of local actors has to be constantly maintained. Different local actors had different interpretations of the challenges facing biomedical innovation and might not join the TRAIN way of doing things.

Here, changes in programmatic orientation and deployment of classical STI policy instruments seamlessly rubbed shoulders with one another and even fed on each other. Local entrepreneurs drove these changes, supporting their contentions and actions on higher-order policy narratives made culturally available in biomedical policy networks.

In the OncoTyrol case, instead, the availability of locally yet centrally managed research money made use of programmatic TR statements with a coordinative intent less salient. That is, here the potency of a classical STI policy instrument (a centre of excellence) enabled the consortium management to ensure better, more direct coordination of the research teams. The formal programme of TR gave legitimacy and justification to an organizational model that was quite different from what participating researchers had been accustomed to in a purely academic context.

TR was used in an even more metaphoric way with ASC, where it became a recognizable symbol to link the idea of creating a new centre of excellence for biomedical research to pre-existing discussions on deficiencies in the cooperation between basic science and clinical application of research findings. Moreover, central management functions remained with the AKH/MUV, which is another factor that worked against the emergence of strong entrepreneurial and advocacy activities around the TR programme in the ASC case.

In TRAIN and OncoTyrol TR was systematically interpreted in a strong alignment towards industry collaboration. Yet, efforts by the consortium leadership to realize this seem to have fallen a bit short of the rhetoric of 'close integration'. Instead, industry partners in TRAIN, OncoTyrol, but also the ASC, often appeared as 'phantom allies' whose participation was an important signifier of success, but who ultimately made modest contributions to actual experimental activities. Similarly, patient orientation is generally considered a modus operandi of TR, also repeated in presentations of TRAIN, OncoTyrol and ASC, yet actual involvement was nowhere to be found.

Jacobsson and Lauber (2006) highlighted the role that advocacy coalitions can play in STI policy, especially in building legitimacy for given projects or programmes and aligning institutions around the corresponding goals. In other words, much like us, they find that legitimacy is a central component of innovation systems and the policies that target them. Nonetheless, these authors concentrated on high-order changes in rationale and corresponding legislative pressure as a main driver of STI policy change. What we have seen here is that legitimacy building through the formulation and advocacy of programmes is also an essential factor in the implementation of policy instruments. Deliberations about common goals, programmes or rationales can take place at the 'grassroots' level of innovation systems, especially through the work of entrepreneurs, as much as it does in parliaments and the offices of civil servants. Additionally, in the cases examined here, existing policy instruments were re-aligned and given new impacts through their use within new networks dedicated to TR. We should therefore not posit that new programmes and rationales act on the governance of STI activities only in the formulation phase of policy instruments, but that they are central determinants of policy transfer and implementation as well.

ACKNOWLEDGEMENTS

The empirical research for this paper was carried out as part of the international ELSA-GEN project 'Translational Research in Genomic Medicine: institutional and social aspects', which was active from 2010 to 2013. The Austrian research team has been financed through the GEN-AU scheme by the Austrian Research Agency (FFG) and the Austrian Federal Ministry for Science and Research (BMWF) and the German team received money from the German science ministry (BMBF) through the project management centre of the German Aerospace Centre (DLR). Etienne Vignola-Gagné was also supported by a Doctoral Fellowship of the Social Science and Humanities Research Council of Canada (grant number 752-2010-0667).

We wish to thank Susanna Borrás, Jakob Edler, Adriana Nielsson and all the other participants to the Jean-Monnet Conference.

REFERENCES

Anonymous (2012), 'What happened to personalized medicine?', *Nature Biotechnology*, **30** (1), 1.

Becker, R. and A. M. S. van Dongen (2011), 'EATRIS, a vision for translational research in Europe', *Journal of Cardiovascular Translational Research*, **4**, 231–237.

Bergeron, H., P. Castel and E. Nouguez (2013), 'Éléments pour une sociologie de l'entrepreneur–frontière. Genèse et diffusion d'un programme de prevention de l'obésité', *Revue française de sociologie,* **52** (2), 263–302.

Biegelbauer, P. (2007), 'Learning from abroad: The Austrian Competence Centre Programme Kplus', *Science and Public Policy*, **34** (9), 606–618.

Biegelbauer, P. (2013a), 'Innovation policy learning', in E. G. Carayannis and D. Campbell (eds), *Encyclopedia of Creativity, Invention, Innovation, and Entrepreneurship (CI2E)*, New York: Springer.

Biegelbauer, P. (2013b), *Wie lernt die Politik – Lernen aus Erfahrung in Politik und Verwaltung*, Wiesbaden: VS Verlag für Sozialwissenschaften.

Biegelbauer, P. and J. Hansen (2011), 'Democratic theory and citizen participation: Democracy models in the evaluation of public participation in science and technology', *Science and Public Policy*, **38** (8), 589–598.

Borrás, S. and C. M. Radaelli (2011), 'The politics of governance architectures: Creation, change and effects of the EU Lisbon strategy', *Journal of European Public Policy*, **18** (4), 463–484.

Borrás, S. and J. Edler (2014), 'The governance of change in socio-technical systems: Three pillars for a conceptual framework', in S. Borrás and J. Edler (eds), *The Governance of Socio–Technical Systems: Explaining Change*, Cheltenham, UK and Northampton, MA, USA: Edward Elgar.

Borstein, S. R. and J. Licinio (2011), 'Improving the efficacy of translational medicine by optimally integrating health care, academia and industry', *Nature Medicine*, **17**, 1567–69.

Braun, D. (2005), 'How to govern research in the "Age of Innovation": Compatibilities and incompatibilities of policy rationales', in M. Lengwiler and D. Simon (eds), *New Governance Arrangements in Science Policy*, Discussion papers Wissenschaftszentrum Berlin für Sozialforschung, Bei der Präsidentin, Projektgruppe Wissenschaftspolitik, No. P2005–101.

Cancer Letter, The (1991), 'NCI develops plan for specialized centers, but funding $67.5M program depends on new $$', *The Cancer Letter*, **17** (27), 1–4.

Castel, P. and E. Friedberg (2010), 'Institutional change as an interactive process: The case of the modernization of the French cancer centers', *Organization Science*, **21** (2), 311–330.

Clavier C. (2010), 'Bottom-Up policy convergence: A sociology of the reception of policy transfer in public health policies in Europe', *Journal of Comparative Policy Analysis: Research and Practice*, **12** (5), 451–466.

Collins, F. S. (2011), 'Reengineering translational science: The time is right', *Science Translational Medicine*, **3** (90), 90cm17.

Food and Drug Administration (2004), *Innovation or Stagnation. Challenge and Opportunity on the Critical Path to New Medical Products*, Washington, DC: U.S. Department of Health and Human Services.

Geels, F. W. and B. Verhees (2011), 'Cultural legitimacy and framing struggles in innovation journeys: A cultural-performative perspective and a case study of Dutch nuclear energy (1945–1986)', *Technology Forecasting & Social Change*, **78**, 910–930.

Gottweis, H. (1998), *Governing Molecules: The Discursive Politics of Genetic Engineering in Europe and in the United States*, Cambridge, MA: MIT Press.

Hall, P. (1993), 'Policy paradigms, social learning, and the state', *Comparative Politics*, **25**, 275–296.

Hall, P. and R. C. R. Taylor (1996), 'Political science and the three new institutionalisms', *Political Studies*, **44** (5), 936–957.

Hassenteufel P., M. Smyrl, W. Genieys and F. J. Moreno-Fuentes (2008), 'Programmatic actors and the transformation of European health care states', *Journal of Health Politics, Policy and Law*, **35** (4), 517–538.

Hedgecoe, A. and P. Martin (2003), 'Expectations and the shaping of pharmaco-genetics', *Social Studies of Science*, **33**, 327–364.

Hillman, K., M. Nilsson, A. Rickne and T. Magnusson (2011), 'Fostering sustainable technologies: A framework for analysing the governance of innovation systems', *Science and Public Policy*, **3** (5), 403–415.

Hogarth, S., M. M. Hopkins, A. Faulkner (2012), 'Personalized medicine: Renewing the social science research agenda', *Personalized Medicine*, **9** (2), 121–6.

Hollingsworth, R. (2000), 'Doing institutional analysis: Implications for the study of innovations', *Review of International Political Economy*, **7** (4), 595–644.

Holzinger, K. (2004), 'Bargaining through arguing: An empirical analysis based on speech act theory', *Political Communication*, **21** (2), 195–222.

Jacobsson, S. and V. Lauber (2006), 'The politics and policy of energy system transformation: Explaining the German diffusion of renewable energy technology', *Energy Policy*, **34**, 256–276.

Jenkins, R. (2007), 'The meaning of policy/policy and meaning', in S. M. Hodgson and Z. Irving (eds), *Policy Reconsidered: Meaning, Politics and Practices*, Bristol: Policy Press, pp. 21–36.

Kraft, A. (2013), 'New light through an old window? The "translational turn" in bio-medical research: A historical perspective', in J. Mittra and C.-P. Milne (eds), *Translational Medicine: The Future of Therapy?*, Boca Raton: CRC Press, pp. 19–53.

Lander, E. S. (2011), 'Initial impact of the sequencing of the human genome', *Nature*, **470**, 187–197.

Lasswell, H. D. (1970), 'The emerging conception of the policy sciences', *Policy Sciences*, **1** (1), 3–14.

Leonelli, S. and K. Sunder Rajan (2013), 'Biomedical trans-actions: Translational research, post-genomics and knowledge/value', *Public Culture*, **25** (3), 463–475.

Maienschein, J., M. Sunderland, R. A. Ankeny and J. S. Robert (2008), 'The ethos and ethics of translational research', *The American Journal of Bioethics*, **8** (3), 43–51.

Martin, P., M. M. Hopkins, P. Nightingale and A. Kraft (2009), 'On a critical path: Genomics, the crisis of pharmaceutical productivity and the search for sustainability', in P. Atkinson, P. Glasner and M. Lock (eds), *Handbook of Genetics and Society*, London and New York: Routledge, pp. 145–162.

Meadowcroft, J. (2009), 'What about the politics? Sustainable development, transition management, and long term energy transitions', *Policy Sciences*, **42**, 323–340.

Milne, C.-P. (2009), 'Can translational medicine bring us out of the R&D wilderness?', *Personal Med.*, **6** (5), 543–53.

Musiolik, J., J. Markard and M. Hekkert (2012), 'Networks and network resources in technological innovation systems: Towards a conceptual framework for system building', *Technological Forecasting & Social Change*, **79**, 1032–1048.

Nathan, D. G. (2002), 'Careers in translational clinical research – Historical perspectives, future challenges', *Journal of the American Medical Association*, **287**, 2424–27.

Parsons, W. (2003), *Public Policy: An Introduction to the Theory and Practice of Policy Analysis*, Cheltenham, UK and Northampton, MA, USA: Edward Elgar.

Peters, G. B. (1999), *Institutional Theory in Political Science – The 'New Institutionalism'*, London/New York: Pinter.

Sabatier, P. (1998), 'The advocacy coalition framework: Revisions and relevance for Europe', *Journal of European Public Policy*, **5** (1), 98–130.

Sabatier, P. and H. C. Jenkins–Smith (1993), *Policy Change and Learning. An Advocacy Coalition Approach*, Boulder/San Francisco/Oxford: Westview Press.

Saretzki, T. (2009), 'From bargaining to arguing, from strategic to communicative action? Theoretical distinctions and methodological problems in empirical studies of deliberative policy processes', *Critical Policy Studies*, **3** (2), 153–183.

Shahzad, A., C. S. McLachlan, J. Gault, R. J. Cohrs, X. Wang and G. Köhler (2011), 'Global translational medicine initiatives and programs', *Translational Biomedicine*, **2** (3), 2.

Swazey, J. P. and R. C. Fox (2004), 'Remembering the "golden years" of patient-oriented clinical research: A collective conversation', *Perspectives in Biology and Medicine*, **47** (4), 487–504.

Tralau-Stewart, C. J., C. A. Wyatt, D. E. Kleyn and A. Ayad (2009), 'Drug discovery: New models for industry–academic partnerships', *Drug Discovery Today*, **14** (1/2), 95–101.

Truman, D. B. (1971(1956)), *The Governmental Process*, New York: Knopf.

van Lente, H. and A. Rip (1998), 'The rise of membrane technology: From rhetorics to social reality', *Social Studies of Science*, **28** (2), 221–254.

Vignola-Gagné, E. (2014), 'Argumentative practices in science, technology and innovation policy: The case of clinician-scientists and translational research', *Science and Public Policy*, **41** (1), 94–106.

Vignola-Gagné, E. and P. Biegelbauer (2013), 'Translational research', in E. G. Carayannis and D. Campbell (eds), *Encyclopedia of Creativity, Invention, Innovation, and Entrepreneurship (CI2E)*, New York: Springer.

Vignola-Gagné, E., E. Rantanen, D. Lehner and B. Hüsing (2013), 'Translational research policies: Disruptions and continuities in biomedical research and development systems in Austria, Finland and Germany', *Journal of Community Genetics*, **4** (2), 189–201.

von Roth, P., B. J. Canny, H.-D. Volk, J. A. Noble, C. G. Prober, C. Perka and G. N. Duda (2011), 'The challenges of modern interdisciplinary medical research', *Nature Biotechnology*, **29**, 1145–48.

Wilson–Kovacs, D. M. and C. Hauskeller (2012), 'The clinician-scientist: Professional dynamics in clinical stem cell research', *Sociology of Health & Illness*, **34** (4), 497–512.

Wyngaarden, J. B. (1979), 'The clinical investigator as an endangered species', *The New England Journal of Medicine*, **301**, 1254–1259.

Zerhouni, E. A. (2005), 'Translational and clinical science – Time for a new vision', *The New England Journal of Medicine*, **353**, 1621–23.

Interviews

TRAIN case study

TRAIN Interview #1A: Staff, Twincore, Hannover; Interview in Hannover on 29 October 2010.

TRAIN Interview #1B: Staff, Twincore, Hannover; Interview in Hannover on 10 January 2012.

TRAIN Interview #2: Staff, VPM GmbH, Hannover; Interview in Hannover on 13 December 2011.

TRAIN Interview #3: Professor, Eberhard Karls University Clinic Tübingen; Interview in Tübingen on 19 December 2011.

TRAIN Interview #4: Staff, Twincore, Hannover; Interview in Hannover on 10 January 2012.

TRAIN Interview #5: Scientific Coordinator, Helmholtz Center for Infection Research, Braunschweig; Telephone interview on 18 January 2012.

TRAIN Interview #6: Staff, Niedersächsisches Ministerium für Wissenschaft und Kultur Hannover; Telephone interview on 9 March 2012.

Anna Spiegel Center case study

ASC Interview #1: Head of a research group, Professor; only located at the ASC; Interview in Vienna on 9 December 2011.

ASC Interview #2: Head of a research group; trained as biologist; Ao. Professor; only located at the ASC; Interview in Vienna on 19 December 2011.

ASC Interview #3: PhD–student; trained in molecular biology with specialization on genetics and biomedicine; in her second year; located in the research group of #1; mainly located at the ASC; Interview in Vienna on 19 December 2011.

ASC Interview #4: Head of a research group, trained as biologist, Ao. Professor; only located at the ASC; Interview in Vienna on 4 January 2012.

ASC Interview #5: Assistant head of a clinical department, Professor; responsible for a small lab team, but mainly located at the clinic; Interview in Vienna on 16 January 2012.

ASC Interview #6: Research direction at the MUV, head of department and Professor; located at the main building of the MUV/AKH; Interview in Vienna on 17 January 2012.

ASC Interview #7: Head of a research group, trained as chemist (PhD); Interview in Vienna on 20 January 2012.

ASC Interview #8: Direction, laboratory of the university clinic, located at main building; Interview in Vienna on 2 April 2012.

ASC Interview #9: Joint Interview with one chemist, responsible for a core facility, and one principal investigator; Interview in Vienna on 16 December 2012.

ASC Interview #10: Interview with administrative staff of the MUV; Interview in Vienna on 8 May 2012.

ASC Interview #11: Administrative staff, university clinic; Written answer to the interview questionnaire provided on 18 May 2012.

OncoTyrol case study

OncoTyrol Interview #1: Joint Interview with two principal investigators, Medical University of Innsbruck; Interview conducted in Innsbruck on 13 February 2012.

OncoTyrol Interview #2: Industry partner, Innsbruck; Telephone interview conducted on 23 March 2012.

OncoTyrol Interview #3: Joint interview with two administration staff, Onco-Tyrol Management; Interview conducted in Innsbruck on 21 February 2012.

OncoTyrol Interview #4: Research direction staff, OncoTyrol Office and Professor, Medical University of Innsbruck: Interview conducted in Innsbruck on 22 February 2012.

OncoTyrol Interview #5: Industry Partner, Vienna; Interview conducted in Vienna in 19 March 2012.

OncoTyrol Interview #6: Industry Partner, Zürich; Telephone interview conducted on 21 March 2012.

8. Governing radical change through the emergence of a governance arrangement

Aurélie Delemarle and Philippe Larédo

8.1 INTRODUCTION

Chapter 8 investigates the process through which radical change is governed, focusing on the activities of actors from a market perspective, from public policy makers to industrialists and to consumers. Considering the idea that markets can be organized and shaped, we follow the activities of those called 'market shapers' by Courtney et al. (1997). The literature on this topic is scattered. On the one hand, one stream of the literature deals especially with the role of a few individuals and their social and political skills to allow change (Fligstein, 1996; Fligstein and Mara Drita, 1996 on political entrepreneurs; Lawrence and Suddaby, 2006 on institutional entrepreneurs). On the other hand, another stream of the literature is focusing on the interactions between various levels (landscape, regime, niche) to explain radical change (such as the multi-level perspective (Geels, 2002, 2005) and strategic niche management). In our contribution to enlighten the debate on the governance of change, we argue that the two perspectives are complementary when we focus on the actors' activities within and across what we call 'arenas'.

Thus, we propose to follow the building of market infrastructures (Delemarle and Larédo, 2012 and Delemarle and Larédo, 2013) through the arenas that produce them. Market infrastructures are defined as a set of rules (what actors are allowed to do), of norms (what they ought to do) and of values (what they want to do). While some of those rules, norms and values are intangible (embodied in the way actors behave), most are embedded in physical equipment (communication networks or transport networks and their support systems) and in formalized processes that build on specialized certification and validation bodies and/or in legal obligations (with corresponding legislative and enforcement structures).

Such a definition assumes that there is not one single infrastructure to frame a market, but a number of them building a set of infrastructures. Accordingly, we show that there is not one single arena that produces it. We argue that the three sets of questions – through the three pillars – raised by Borrás and Edler in this volume (2014) cannot be addressed within only one single arena. On the contrary, a series of complementary/ competing arenas are developed, each being led by different actors with different interests and different targets (Bonneuil et al., 2008). We thus take a different position to Kuhlmann (2007) and Callon and Rip (1992) who would tend to argue for a single forum. Actors invest in arenas depending on the projects and views they want to defend and depending on what they think is important for the governance of markets. Arenas evolve over time: they have their own dynamics, which cannot be thought of without considering trans-arena dynamics. Our argument is that the governance of change in S&T emerges as the various arenas become aligned, into what we call a 'governance arrangement'. A governance arrangement is thus defined as the constellation of arenas and their dynamics (intra and inter arena dynamics) that are aligned in a robust manner. Until the governance arrangement is set, existing uncertainties (technical or social) do not allow actors to move forward in the development of innovations, and markets are not structured because the market infrastructures have not been agreed upon.

The chapter is organized as follows: we first review useful concepts from policy analysis (Kuhlmann, 2007) and social study of science (Bonneuil et al., 2008) that deal with settings in which strategic actors debate. We enrich these with some insights from 'hybrid forum' (Callon and Rip, 1992) and sociology of science (Vinck, 1999, 2010). We then go into details of our case, which we structure using the framework proposed by Borrás and Edler (2014, in this volume). We then discuss our findings on arenas linked to the set-up of the governance arrangement and propose a first characterization of arenas, followed by our outlook and conclusion.

8.2   FROM ARENAS TO HYBRID FORUMS: TOWARDS A FRAMEWORK TO BETTER UNDERSTAND GOVERNANCE OF S&T CHANGE

We build on the useful concept of arenas as the setting in which 'individual and collective actors interact to define the cognitive and normative dimensions of a problem' (Bonneuil et al., 2008, p. 205).

Initially developed by Strauss (Clarke, 1991) and then further elaborated in policy analysis (Kuhlmann, 2007 and Kuhlmann et al., 1999) and sociology of social problems, arenas point to a meso-level of analysis: actors negotiate within structures to reach a consensus or, in other words, to reach an alignment.

Bonneuil et al. (2008) focus on the role of these arenas in framing problems in a public debate context. They argue that one arena alone cannot encompass all problems and that several arenas co-exist, each focusing on one problem or on one framing of a problem. This way, they can compete against each other. In the case of GMOs, Bonneuil et al. (2008) counted nine arenas, each with their 'own symbolic referential, hurdles and resources i.e. its own grammar' (pp. 208-209). With each of the arenas bringing together a large variety of actors around one framing of a problem, Bonneuil et al. (2008) identify economic, scientific, expert, regulatory, legal, political, media, activist and participatory issues and problems linked to GMOs. In their study they show how trans-arena dynamics evolve over time. They explain the resulting different positioning of the GMO controversy in France and in the US with the dynamics of interactions between the arenas. In their conclusion, however, they point to the limitation of their framework: 'linking automatically orders of justification to specific types of arenas' (Bonneuil et al., 2008, p. 226) is too simplistic. This framework is useful to explain the existence of various arenas and their relationships in the context of S&T change. However, it does not help our understanding of the dynamics within the arenas.

The notion of a hybrid forum (Callon and Rip, 1992), initially developed to discuss democracy in relation to technical choices, brings complementary elements to the functioning of arenas. Both notions are equally important: *forums* as 'they are open spaces where groups can come together to discuss technical options involving the collective', and *hybrid* as 'the groups involved and the spokespersons claiming to represent them are heterogeneous, including experts, politicians, technicians and laypersons who consider themselves involved. They are also hybrid because the questions and problems taken up are addressed at different levels in a variety of domains, from ethics to economic' (Callon et al., 2009, p. 18). Hybrid forums are much more fluid[1] and less stable than arenas. Callon and his colleagues argue that hybrid forums bring together experts from three different poles (scientific, legal and socio-economic). Experts are not part of a single arena but of multiple arenas. They are 'mediators', facing multiple constraints and trying to reach a compromise that is technically robust, socially viable and legally acceptable. Their role is fluid, because constraints can change over time; as a result, this can lead to various types of compromises over time. Actors' roles are also fluid because they are part of networks of alliances across organizations that can be rearranged as new issues emerge over time or as new enrolments occur. The three poles – economic, social and legal – are interconnected and actors can move across them. The interactions between the three produce 'an expertise' and an alignment. What is interesting is that the latter cannot be known ex ante because it results from a negotiation process. The concept of hybrid forum thus brings insight into the dynamics of each arena explaining why it can grow or fall into decay. It also points to the fact that compromises need to be socially viable and legally accepted, that is, robust (Rip et al., 1995), which is a very important point in the governance of change.

So multiple arenas co-exist, some expand, some decay, as they manage (or not) to enrol new actors and mobilize around their framing of the problem. But how do they become stable? The stabilization, or 'punctu-alizing' (as proposed by Vinck, 1999, 2010), occurs when some results or products of one arena are used by others. Indeed, each result or product produces a 'before' and an 'after', in the sense that each is an endpoint reflecting an agreement between the actors, but also a materialization that can travel. It thus 'punctualizes' the previous network of actors and offers then new options for action.

We propose to build on these approaches to better understand the set-up of the governance of change in S&T systems: how does a range of arenas emerge (are they as 'simplistic' and 'mono-dimensional' as Bonneuil et al. show?); how do they evolve (what are their internal dynamics as Callon and Rip demonstrate, and how do their internal logics impact their dynamics); and how do they articulate and stabilize their relationships (how does 'punctualising' occur?)? The main argument of the chapter is that these arenas, their internal dynamics and interrelationships are what at a given point in time constitutes a governance arrangement.

We present the case study using Borrás and Edler's framework. The three pillars – purposeful actors, instruments and legitimacy – link well with the approaches presented above: indeed, the concept of arena encom-passes well the idea of a constellation of arenas with various actors and the focus on their interrelationships. The hybrid forum adds the idea of negotiation and compromise within a specific structure. Both approaches deal with actors, their interests and their heterogeneity. Callon and Rip's hybrid forum points more specifically to instruments, as hybrid forums aim at creating a consensus based on constraints, some of which are legal/regulatory ones. Both approaches – Borrás and Edler as well as Callon and Rip – deal with legitimacy issues with different emphasis: Callon and Rip's hybrid forum aims at creating some legitimacy in the context of technical democracy; Bonneuil et al.'s arenas point more indirectly to legitimacy, as each arena relies on its own grammar and mechanisms for legitimacy building.

8.3 GOVERNING NANOTECHNOLOGY BASED MARKETS

We consider the nanotechnology case to illustrate the governance arrangement, that is, the constellation of arenas and their dynamics (intra and inter arena dynamics) that are aligned in a robust manner. We know from past experience that only successful alignments stay while unsuccessful attempts disappear. This is why we prefer to test the set-up of a new governance arrangement in an ongoing case. We can thus follow the various public and private investments and how they are accounted for in the different arenas.

We chose 'nanotechnologies' to test the notion of governance arrangement because it is a dynamic case and as we argue elsewhere (Delemarle and Larédo, 2013), governance is still at a tentative stage. The case is rich in terms of the multiplicity of actors involved, the variety of spaces in which they act and the diversity of concerns they push forward.

Nanotechnologies are generally considered to represent a radical technological shift. Working at the nanoscale enables scientists to develop new properties that do not exist at larger scales, either to add new functions to existing products (like water-repellent glass to keep windows continuously clean) or to design completely new products (like complex high speed chips in which transistors are only nanometres in size). Nanotechnologies are present in multiple markets (from leisure, to electronics, food and pharmaceuticals), mostly to add new functionalities to existing products, but they also open up radically new avenues to address numerous prevailing issues (from boosting energy conversion for solar panels, to drug delivery and new structural materials) (Larédo et al., 2010). This is the first time countries outside the Triadic group have made such massive R&D investments. It has led to the creation of multiple S&T niches in which national programmes have developed and tested new technological demonstrators/prototypes. This hype has also driven private sector activity, with most of the large global firms now owning nanotechnology patents from chemicals and materials, to health care and pharmaceutical industry, and electronics and telecommunications, to cite just a few application fields (Larédo et al., 2010). Nanotechnologies are indeed considered as a 'general purpose technology' (Bresnahan and Trajtenberg, 1995) that promises to impact all fields in a pervasive manner. Lastly, civil society at large is participating in this movement: NGOs have drawn attention to uncertainties about the environmental and health effects of nanomaterials – and indeed, we know little about their long term effects on human beings or the environment, as matter at the nanoscale does not always have the same physical, chemical, electronic or structural properties as it does at the micro scale (The Royal Society & The Royal Academy of Engineering, 2004; Aitken et al., 2004). Below, we characterize the five chosen arenas in turn.

8.3.1 Arena 1: ISO nanotechnologies technical committee on nanotechnologies TC229

Box 8.1   Arena 1 in the Nutshell of the Borrás/Edler Concept

Objective: market structuring by defining terms (WG1), by the selection of recognized HSE process (WG3) and by the definition of technical specifications for B-to-B (WG4)

Actors: companies, public laboratories, specialized agencies and governmental bodies (both technical ministries (labour, health, and so on) and strategic (industry and commerce))

Instruments: technical standards

Legitimacy: technical expertise and rules of consensus for each technical standard developed

---

The International Organization for Standardization (ISO) creates standards in all fields. 'ISO is the world largest standards developing organization. Between 1947 and the present day, ISO has published more than 18,500 International Standards, ranging from standards for activities such as agriculture and construction, through mechanical engineering, to medical devices, to the newest information technology developments.'[2] The Technical Committee 229 'nanotechnologies' (TC229) was created in 2005 with the objective 'to develop science-based standards for the field of nanotechnology in order to promote its commercial applications in a secure manner'.[3] As nanotechnologies are transversal, it was initially decided that the TC would develop high-level standards that can be used in all applications while application-based standards would be developed in industry specific committees.

ISO TC229[4] has been successful in attracting many types of experts (Table 8.1[5]): from high-level scientists with management positions in industry, to scientific agencies who felt that something needed to be done to support the development of nanotechnologies, while others, in contrast, were specialists in standards but had, at the start of the Committee, no knowledge of nanotechnologies. Whereas the first meeting of the committee in 2005 was attended by 40 delegates, the latest meetings attracted between 120 and 200 delegates. The core of the group is made up of 30 to 40 delegates while the rest of the delegates join the meeting mainly depending on its location: the biannual meetings are organized alternatively in America, in Europe and in Asia, which demonstrates the attractiveness of the TC at a global level. The membership is worldwide: in 2006, there were 28 participating countries (P) and six observing countries (O); and 34 P and 11 O in 2012, respectively. In addition to the national delegates, TC229, like any other ISO technical committee, includes representatives from various bodies, called liaisons. The establishment of liaisons in the standardization system is a way of formalising a contact between activities that are believed to have mutual benefits. This is seen both as a way for efficient communication, which in turn prevents duplication of work and as a way to promote sensible demarcations between areas. The increase from six internal liaisons in 2005 to 30 in 2013, and from no external liaison at all to nine in 2013 also shows the attractiveness of the committee and the strong position as a coordination entity built by the TC over the years. For instance, ISO TC229 received the mandate from CEN (European Standardization Committee) and from the OECD to develop terminology standards, while it has co-developed terminology and characterization standards with the IEC (International Electrotechnical Commission – international standards and conformity assessment body for all fields of electrotechnology).

TC 229 initially focused its activities around three themes that structured the TC's organization in three Joint Working Groups (JWG). These were discussed and decided among the experts present during the first two meetings.[6]

JWG 1 'terminology and nomenclature' aims at creating 'a common language for scientific, technical, commercial, and regulatory processes' (TC 229 Business Plan, 2007). Its mission is 'to establish a taxonomic terminology framework for describing and defining nanotechnologies in a clear and unambiguous manner; and thence to explore possible models for a nomenclature framework that could be the basis for appropriate regulatory systems'.[7] It is a joint working group with the International Electrotechnical Commission IEC.

Table 8.1   Membership of TC229

Date	Meeting location	Number of permanent countries members	Number of internal liaisons	Number of external liaisons
End of 2005	London, UK	23	6	0
Mid 2006	Tokyo, Japan	27	7	2
End of 2006	Seoul, Rep of South Korea	28	15	4
Mid 2007	Berlin, Germany	29	18	4
End of 2007	Singapore, Singapore	30	19	4
Mid 2008	Bordeaux, France	30	21	4
End of 2008	Shanghai, China	32	19	4
Mid 2009	Seattle, USA	32	25	7
End of 2009	Tel Aviv, Israel	32	25	8
Mid 2010	Maastricht, the Netherlands	33	26	8
End of 2010	Kuala Lumpur, Malaysia	36	26	9
Mid 2011	St Petersburg, Russia	24	27	9
End of 2011	Johannesburg, South Africa	34	27	9
Mid 2012	Stresa, Italy	34	29	9
March 2013	Queretaro, Mexico	34	30	10

JWG 2 'measurement and characterization' is also a joint working group with IEC TC113. It aims at developing standards in measurement that are 'internationally accepted for quantitative scientific, commercial and regulatory activities'.[8]

The objective of JWG 3 'health, safety and environmental issues' is to ensure 'occupational safety, and consumer and environmental protection, promoting good practice in the production, use and disposal of nanomaterials, nanotechnology products and nanotechnology-enabled systems and products'.[9]

TC229 increased its activities in 2008 with a fourth JWG 'Material specifications', which aims at establishing nanomaterials specifications for professionals and thus at easing B-to-B exchanges on the market. There were pressures to include this fourth working group because China was the first country to release a national standard on the subject and the Chinese delegation wanted to translate this national advantage to the global market.

In 2008, two transversal task groups (TG) were added as the TC recognized the need to take into consideration societal concerns. The task of TG 'Nanotechnology and sustainability' is to identify areas in which standards can be developed to speed up the process for innovations that are linked to sustainability and that are close to the market. It is actually aiming at setting priorities for new work items being directly linked to sustainability. An exemplary case is water purification.[10] TG 'Consumer and Societal dimensions of nanotechnology' was created to take into consideration all non-technical aspects of nanotechnology including ethical issues such as the participation of countries from the Southern hemisphere, of underrepresented groups and of the consumers.

TC229 grew over time both in size, as the number of members and liaisons shows, and in number of projects, as Table 8.2 illustrates.

Table 8.2   Activities of TC229

Date	Total number of standardization documents published	Number of projects discussed*
November 2005	0	0
June 2006	0	1
December 2006	0	3
June 2007	0	10
December 2007	0	23
May 2008	0	29
Nov 2008	0	33
June 2009	2	40
Oct 2009	2	41
May 2010	2	44
December 2010	7	39
May 2011	11	34
November 2011	15	32
June 2012	23	24

Note: Projects are standardization documents under development. It takes 24 months to develop a draft that is submitted to vote. Documents need to be published within 36 months.[11]

TC229 became a central actor in the governance of nanotechnologies: its leading role in defining the terms related to nanotechnologies (JWG1) and characterising/measuring it (JWG2) is illustrated by the number of standardization and standardization-like organizations that rely on it for this work (Table 8.3). TC229 even plays a role as coordinating entity:[12] general definitions and characterisation methods/measurement are carried out by TC229, while specific work on applications is carried out by existing industrial TCs, even if this involves working outside the ISO structure. In 2011, for example, TAPPI, the worldwide Technical Association for Pulp, Paper and related Industries, which is in charge of standardization in those fields, contacted ISO TC229 to coordinate the standardization activities in relation to nanocellulose materials, and it was agreed that ISO TC229 JWG1 would work on definitions related to nanocellulose and that JWG2 would work on the corresponding characterizations and measurements. To give another example: in 2007, ISO TC229 and the IEC (the International Electrotechnical Commission – in charge of standardization activities in electrotechnology) decided to avoid redundancy by creating joint working groups to manage their nanotechnology-related activities.[13]

Table 8.3   Details of some of the external liaisons

Acronym	Full name
EC-JRC (IRMM)	European Commission – Joint Research Centre (Institute for Reference Materials and Measurements)
VAMAS	The Versailles Project on Advanced Materials and Standards
ANF	Asia Nano Forum
BIPM	Bureau International des Poids et Mesures (International Bureau of Weights and Measures)
ECOS	European Environmental Citizens Organisation for Standardisation
IUPAC	International Union of Pure and Applied Chemistry
OECD – WPMN	Organisation for Economic Co-operation and Development, Working Party on Nanomaterials
ETUI	European Trade Union Institute
TAPPI	Technical Association for Pulp, Paper and related Industries

TC229's development pattern shows the progressive enrolment of new actors and the enlargement of its scope of activities. This is illustrated by the growing number of liaisons but also the increasing activity (as an indicator of the increasing number of experts mobilized to work on the standardization documents). Its extended scope is illustrated by the development of WG4 and by the set-up of the two TGs in 2008 which both introduced new themes in a technical committee.

TC229 shows its appeal as, in 2013, it proposed the first standardization projects that are not directly technical in JWG1 (with the support of the OCDE), covering 'economic indicators for nanotechnologies' and 'terminology – nanotechnologies in plain English'.

8.3.2 Arena 2: Working Party on Manufactured Nanomaterials (WPMN) at the Organisation for Economic Co-operation and Development (OECD)

Box 8.2   Arena 2 in the Nutshell of the Borrás/Edler Concept

Objective: 'safety evaluation and assessment of manufactured nanomaterials'

Actors: OECD, governmental agencies and ministries, companies

Instruments: recommendations, reports, good practices

Legitimacy: international organization whose mission is to 'promote policies that improve the economic and social well-being of people around the world'[14]

In 2006, the OECD set up the Working Party on Manufactured Nanomaterials. It 'involves OECD member countries, as well as some non-members economies and other stakeholders to pool expertise and to fund the safety testing of specific Manufactured Nanomaterials'.[15] The Working Party on the safety of Manufactured Nanomaterials (WPMN) was created 'to ensure that the approaches for hazard, exposure and risk assessment for manufactured nanomaterials are of a high quality, science-based and internationally harmonised'.[16] Its terms of reference state ten points among which the first is:

> to elaborate and implement a program of work (...) to promote international co-operation in the health and environmental safety related aspects of manufactured nanomaterials ... The main topic areas to be included in the

program of work will include: Definitions, nomenclature and characterization (physicochemical properties, uses) where not otherwise available; Environmental fate and effects (hazard identification, hazard, exposure and risk assessment methods); Human exposure and health effects (hazard identification, hazard, exposure and risk assessment methods); Exchange of information on regulatory and risk management frameworks (limited mainly to the chemicals sector) as well as environmental benefits. (OECD, 2010, p. 1)[17]

Table 8.4 presents the 37 documents that constitute the outputs of WPMN's work. First, it shows that that their work on 'definitions, nomenclature and characterization' was not carried out by the OECD itself, rather it was transferred to the ISO TC229 in 2008. It is thus an acknowledgment from the OECD that ISO was legitimate to fulfil this task. It then shows a change in focus in relation to the objective of developing methods: the four 'guidance' documents produced describe 'how to do things' rather than 'what to do'. Last, most documents (25) are actually reviews and summaries of what other actors have been doing. This is why the WPMN developed a database regrouping governmental activities linked to EHS issues of nanomaterials. There is thus an important move away from what was expected – that is, to assess manufactured nanomaterials. The failure of the arena's activities can be explained by the fact that the OECD WPMN relied on national and private support for developing the R&D processes implied for the characterization of the nanomaterials. The initial idea was to work first on 13 selected manufactured nanomaterials as a test, which would then be replicated to other nanomaterials. However, due to the definition process of the nanomaterial characteristics being slow and to the R&D costs, the WPMN recognized that it could not be reproduced.

Table 8.4   List of OECD WPMN outputs at 2 July 2013

Type of document	Number
Gathering of the opinions and activities of participating members	11
OECD work program	7
Reviews (including 2 workshops)	14
'Guidance' documents	4
List of regulated nanomaterials	1
Total	37

The pattern of development of the OECD WPMN thus shows a failure in coordinating activities at the global level and in assessing manufactured nanomaterials. It evolved to become an arena that disseminates information produced by others.

8.3.3   Arena 3: International Council on Nanotechnology (ICoN)

Box 8.3   Arena 3 in the Nutshell of the Borrás/Edler Concept

Objective: to share knowledge on health, environmental and safety issues

Actors: a few companies and governmental agencies gathered within the International Council on Nanotechnology

Instruments: knowledge database and journal

Legitimacy: openness of the database

ICoN is a non-governmental organization that defines itself as 'an international, multi-stakeholder organization whose mission is to develop and communicate information regarding potential environmental and health risks of nanotechnology, thereby fostering risk reduction while maximizing societal benefit'.[18] Founded in 2004: 'ICON is a knowledge-driven organization [that] does not engage in advocacy or commercial activities... It is composed of members from academia, industry, government and non-governmental organizations[19] from France, Japan, the Netherlands, Switzerland, Taiwan, the United Kingdom and the United States.'[20] It was initially supported by a National Bureau of Economic Affairs grant and by Rice University, as well as by industrial sponsorship from DuPont, Intel, Lockheed Martin, L'Oreal, Mitsubishi Corporation, Procter & Gamble and Swiss Re insurance.

ICoN aims at providing transparent and high quality technical information on health and environmental risk issues in nanotechnologies. Initially, it created a database – the ICON Environmental, Health and Safety (EHS) database – to collect as much data as possible on these issues. The database has been upgraded into a virtual journal, which contained (as of 5 November 2013) 8092 summaries (abstracts) and citations of research papers related to the EHS implications of nanoscale materials covering the period 1962-2013.[21] Anyone can propose online the inclusion of a new summary, provided the paper has already been published in a scientific journal. The database/virtual journal can be searched under nine specific criteria: method of study, particle type, paper type, risk exposure group, production method, exposure pathway, exposure of hazard target, content emphasis and target audience.

It is difficult to assess its use: apart from the virtual journal/database, the website has not been updated since 2010 and carries no data about its use. Moreover, almost no one involved in standardization knows about it or has used it as a source of information (Delemarle and Larédo, 2013).

ICoN's development pattern thus shows a failure to become the reference repertory for EHS issues related to nanotechnologies. It materializes the initial interests from global actors in the field, bringing public and private partners together under a non-profit organization form. However, the membership has not evolved, pointing to a lack of attractiveness. The number of abstracts in the virtual journal is still increasing, but it results from a process that is not transparent and the choice of abstracts and their referencing is unknown. Moreover, Porter et al. (2008) indicated that their database covers 54 900 EHS publications up to the end of 2007. The coverage of the ICoN database seems thus very limited.

8.3.4   Arena 4: The European Code of Conduct for Responsible Nanosciences and Nanotechnologies Research

---

Box 8.4   Arena 4 in the Nutshell of the Borrás/Edler Concept

Objective: to shape 'responsible' practices

Actors: EU commission, nanotechnology company association, Responsible NanoCode supporters, NGOs

Instruments: voluntary Code of Conduct (CoC)

Legitimacy: co-development with companies and research organizations involved in nanotechnologies. Surveys on its use to foster learning and to provide updates of Code of Conduct

---

The focus of the EU Commission was to provide guidance for undertaking research – not for commercializing products. The European code of conduct (CoC) initially resulted from another initiative: the nano-responsible code, which was the output of a joint initiative of the UK

Royal Society, Insight investment, the Nanotechnology Industrial Association and the UK Nanotechnology Knowledge Transfer Network, who collectively warned about the risk of inaction for business, as technical, social and commercial uncertainties were rising (Sutcliffe and Hodgson, 2006).[22] On this basis, the European Commission produced the EU Code of responsible research in nanotechnology with the support of large European companies.

The European CoC Code of Conduct 'encompasses seven general principles on which Member States are invited to take concrete action to ensure that nanotechnologies are developed in a safe manner'.[23] These are: (i) meaning; (ii) sustainability; (iii) precaution; (iv) inclusiveness; (v) excellence; (vi) innovation and (vii) accountability. It was proposed as a voluntary approach without certification or accreditation requirements, but companies were expected to embrace the CoC because they had been involved in the creation process and it was not regulatory related.

The code was publicized in specific conferences organized by the EU Commission. We investigated the actual use and diffusion of the EU CoC, which is the only way to follow the success or failure of the arena. We selected a sample of 37 companies located in Europe, which were identified using the work done on nanotechnology dynamics (Delemarle et al., 2009).[24] We visited their websites to characterize their 'nanoresponsible' practices: 60 per cent do mention such practices, but, of these, nine out of ten develop their own approach (their own code of conduct or specific guidelines) and none explicitly referred to the EU CoC (Table 8.5).

Table 8.5   Use and diffusion of the EU CoC in a sample of firms in nanotechnologies

Number of companies who:	do not mention any specific guidelines linked to nano-technology	mention specific guidelines linked to nano-technology	refer to the EU CoC	develop their own CoC or have a written position	refer to industry practices in relation to nano
Total 37	22	15	0	14	3

Notes: 1 entity refers to the EU CoC in the list of references. The last two columns are not exclusive. Some companies developed their own CoC and also refer to industry specific practices.

The EU CoC development pattern thus also shows a failure to become a reference in shaping practices at the European level. The OECD did not develop this aspect either. It was partially developed within the ISO TC229 via the development of a framework on risk management. But, rather than a failure of one arena, what we see is the failure of an arena to generate interest and support for its concern: less than half of the companies mention specific guidelines linked to their use of nanotechnologies.

8.3.5   Arena 5: nanoREACH (Registration, Evaluation, Authorization and Restriction of Chemical Substances at the Nanoscale)

Box 8.5   Arena 5 in the Nutshell of the Borrás/Edler Concept

Objective: to register nanomaterials as chemical substances

Actors: EU Commission, European Chemicals Agency (ECHA), chemical companies and their association

Instruments: regulatory framework enforced by the EU Commission

Legitimacy: legal enforcement by the EU Commission

The REACH framework is a regulatory framework enforced by the EU commission in 2007. It aims at 'ensur(ing) a high level of protection of human health and the environment from the risks that can be posed by chemicals, the promotion of alternative test methods, the free circulation of substances on the internal market and enhancing competitiveness and innovation'.[25] It is thus a mode of regulation for the chemical industry. The principle that underlies the framework is that manufacturers and importers of chemicals are responsible for the substances they manufacture or import. They must identify and manage risks linked to them.[26] It is thus the actors themselves who are responsible for saying what they are using and how they are handling the nanomaterials. For each substance manufactured or imported in quantities of one ton or more per year per company, manufacturers and importers have to fill in a registration dossier and submit it to the European Chemicals Agency (ECHA) (registration step). For selected substances of high concern the company may be asked to provide more information (the evaluation step); and some substances, considered of very high concern, are subject to authorization (the authorization step). Finally, the EU authorities can put 'restrictions on the manufacture, use or placing on the market of substances causing an unacceptable risk to human health or the environment'.[27]

Concerns due to uncertainties related to nanomaterials' toxicity led actors to question the relevance of the REACH framework to handle nanomaterials.[28] While the European Commission stated in 2008 that the 'current legislation covers in principle the potential health, safety and environmental risks in relation to nanomaterials' (European Commission, 2008, p. 11) and that 'the protection of health, safety and the environment needs mostly to be enhanced by improving implementation of current legislation' (ibidem), several voices were raised against REACH as being able to capture the specificities of nanomaterials.

In a nutshell, the controversy lies in the definition of nanomaterials.[29] REACH (and the EU Commission) do not use the definitions set out by ISO for identifying a nanomaterial.

In 2011, the EU Commission adopted the following definition:

'Nanomaterial' means a natural, incidental or manufactured material containing particles, in an unbound state or as an aggregate or as an agglomerate and where, for 50 per cent or more of the particles in the number size distribution, one or more external dimensions is in the size range *1-100 nm* [emphasis added].

In specific cases and where warranted by concerns for the environment, health, safety or competitiveness *the number size distribution threshold of 50 per cent may be replaced by a threshold between 1 and 50 per cent* [emphasis added].

By derogation from the above, fullerenes, graphene flakes and single wall carbon nanotubes with one or more external dimensions below 1 nm should be considered as nanomaterials. (European Commission, 2011)

The ISO definition is: 'Nanomaterial: material with any external dimension in the nanoscale or having internal structure or surface structure in the nanoscale',[30] 'Nanoscale: size range from approximately 1 nm to 100 nm.'[31]

The ISO definition is more flexible concerning the size range. Experts working on nanoREACH (among which CEFIC members)[32] are arguing that the scale effect may not only appear between 1 and 100 nm and that a product having 45 per cent of matter at 95 nm and 55 per cent at 105nm is not considered as a nanomaterial (while a product that has

50 per cent of matter between 1 and 100 nm is defined as a nanomaterial). In other word, size cannot be a unique identifier for nanoscale effect.[33]

The NanoREACH development pattern shows a mixed result. While the chemical industry had been very reluctant vis-à-vis the adoption of REACH, in the case of nanomaterials, industry representatives have been involved from the start, producing position papers and reference documents that are central to ongoing developments. We find an overall position that favours 'local' adaptations (for specific couples of products and use), rather than a transversal approach (for example, a nano-REACH) regulation). Note however that the discussions are still ongoing.

8.4. DISCUSSION

We have analysed the dynamics of five arenas connected with the shaping of nanotechnology markets, using a very classical approach in the field of STS (Science, Technology and Society) for evaluating their success: their capacity to enrol new actors and the taking over of circulated 'outputs' by other arenas.

8.4.1 Trans-arena Dynamics

The more an arena is growing both in scope and in size, the more successful it is, because it becomes relevant for a growing number of actors and is trusted to address and re-address complementary issues. This is the case for the ISO, which enrols, aggregates and renews the issues it is proposing. For example, it enrols new actors upon receiving the mandate from the OECD and the EU Commission (via the Vienna Agreement between ISO and CEN) to establish a common vocabulary. It is aggregating when, for example, it also encompasses the issue of risk management,[34] which has been partly the objective of the EU Code of Conduct, or when it develops external liaisons with other standardization bodies. It renews its ways at looking at market uncertainties when it includes subjects that were not initially in its scope, as illustrated by the creation of the two task groups on sustainability and societal issues of nanotechnology, or when it develops standardization documents on economic indicators on nanotechnology.

The second classical criterion of success lies in the ability of an arena to impose its viewpoints to others. When looking at our cases, a first indication for this is the ability of the arena to embed its outputs into other instruments, may these be tangible or not, like a definition, a method or a standard. The EU code of conduct is a good counter example of this: it is just a discourse tool with no 'operational' translation and no third party to apply it and in doing so signals credibility to firms. This may well explain why few firms refer to it and no firm ever mentions applying it.

Arenas are successful if their outputs are adopted by other arenas. This is, for example, the case of the definition of nanotechnology by ISO which has been taken over by other standardization bodies or the OECD; however, this success is limited, as another important arena, REACH and the European Commission, has developed its own definitions and de facto re-opened the debate about what nanotechnologies are.

We consider these two dimensions: (1) managing to enrol new actors and enlarging their initial remit while (2) seeing their 'outputs' taken over by other arenas, as indications of the notion of output legitimacy as proposed by Borrás and Edler (2014). They are central to trans-arena dynamics since they imply both a circulation of actors and artefacts between arenas. We assume that actors by their presence ensure inter-arena coherence in the ways problems are selected, defined and addressed; and that by being used in other arenas, artefacts transfer and embed the solutions promoted by the arena that produced them.

Taking these two criteria as a reference point, we can now consider the conditions that favour or hinder the ability of an arena to succeed. From the analysis of the five cases, we derive a first exploratory list of four key aspects to consider, which would have to be further validated in a wider set of situations. The four aspects are: (1) the degree of specificity; (2) the degree of openness; (3) the level of transparency and (4) the structuration of the arena. We shall address them in turn.

8.4.1.1 The degree of specificity of the arena

We clearly face two types of arenas in our five cases: those that focus on one aspect of nanotechnology (ICON and toxicology) or one group of actors (the EU code of conduct and firms, or OECD and governments), and those that address the issue at large, whether within one large industry or sector (REACH and the chemical/materials industries) or globally, as ISO does for all industrial sectors. While one may consider that it might be easier for a 'targeted' arena to be recognised as such and to receive its specific task, our cases seem to show the reverse. It has been very difficult both for the OECD and ICON to broaden their partnership and even to deliver the initially targeted objective. From the outset, they represented two very different configurations, with the OECD benefiting from a high level 'input' legitimacy, being a global reference for all issues dealing with research and innovation, and having worked on chemical safety for decades, while ICON was a *de novo* creation. The ability for an arena to enlarge its composition and broaden the topics it covers seems to be linked to a limited degree to the specificity of the arena. This does not mean that an arena does not focus on certain aspects when it is created, but rather that its embedding leaves open the possibility to address other topics: this limits the costs of investment for participating actors and makes room for learning.

8.4.1.2   The degree of openness of the arena

How easily can actors join an arena? What are the cognitive prerequisites to participate in debates? These are the two questions that are considered under this aspect. For instance, both OECD and ISO require formal membership for representatives of governments and for members of national delegations. Participation in the OECD WPMN is initiated by existing members through invitation to partake in specific work. In the case of ISO, national delegations are supposed to include actors from diverse environments: firms, public research, government representatives and consumer representatives. Similarly, within ISO, actors are liaising in and out of the committee, both to get information from what others are doing but also to give information about what TC229 is doing. This way, they avoid the fact that the arena develops a product in a vacuum, but rather takes other products under development elsewhere into account. It is thus important to consider the 'degree' of closeness or openness, through the established rules for participation and the connections established with other arenas.

The other aspect of openness is linked to the degree of technical expertise needed to participate in the arena: to what extent is the participation in the arena conditioned by a specific expertise? The participation in debates within REACH requires a technical expertise in nanomaterials, while the participation in the creation of the European Code of Conduct does not require this kind of expertise.

8.4.1.3   The level of transparency

Transparency relies on the existence of rules of functioning, on the ways the working process is formalized. For example, an outsider who wishes to consult the ICoN virtual journal knows little about how papers are selected. Similarly, the OECD has produced four 'guidance documents', the production process of which remains unknown to the outside user. The situation widely differs for ISO, because its work and adoption processes are codified in a series of steps. For each step there is a different formal process of adoption. This provides what could be considered 'process' legitimacy to the outputs coming from ISO.

8.4.1.4   The organizational features of arenas

We were struck by this fourth aspect. Four out of five identified arenas have developed within the boundaries of existing organizations, while the fifth one was created de novo. Two features seem to matter here: the first is the fact that activities are eased by the existence of stabilized processes that enable the organization of the work and the production of robust compromises that generate the outputs. The second important feature is the mobilization of existing processes to shape outputs and organize their circulation. This is exemplified by OECD WPMN and ISO TC229. Both rely on internal structures based on dedicated secretaries and standard member bodies. In the case of the code of conduct, both aspects are missing, while the case of ICoN shows that it is not enough to have a legal form with an executive board, working groups and activities. Those that have succeeded, at least partly, also have employees, means of implementation, mechanisms to develop activities, and so on. This organizational aspect is central but has been missing in existing research on arenas. The existence of an organization to support the arena is thus considered as an important element to consider.

We suggest that these four aspects are a way to further disentangle the notion of 'input' legitimacy proposed by Borrás and Edler (2014). It might be useful to further refine the 'input' notion and separate the dimensions that constitute the arena, from those that characterize its working processes and, as with innovation studies, distinguish between 'input' and 'process' legitimacy.

Below we provide a first attempt to characterize the five arenas along the lines of the four aspects that determine the success of the arenas as defined above. Table 8.6 shows two main results: on the one hand, there is no arena that addresses all four aspects positively; on the other hand, there seems to be a connection with multiple negative features and failure. Still, there is clearly more work needed on how these four aspects are interconnected and related to the deployment of performative arenas.

Table 8.6   Characterization of arenas

Criteria	ISO TC229	OECD WPMN	ICoN	EU CoC	REACH
Degree of specificity	–	–	+	+	–
Degree of openness	–/+	–	–	–	–
Level of transparency	+	–/+	–	–	+
Degree of structuration	+	+	+/–	–	+

8.4.2   From a Multiplicity of Arenas to a Governance Arrangement

The move from a multiplicity of arenas to a governance arrangement relies on the alignment of arenas. The cases present two kinds of alignment. First, an alignment exists when others, outside of a given arena, use the product of this arena, for example, when ISO TC229 develops definitions that are used by others. This type of alignment is based on the circulation of arena products. The products that circulate 'punctualize' the work of the arena without having to consider it again (Vinck, 1999, 2010). However, the cases also illustrate another type of alignment between arenas: an alignment based on the mandate given by one arena to another to develop a given product. An example of this is the OECD or TAPPI giving a mandate to ISO TC229 to develop terminology and characterizations for nanotechnologies. We can trace the degree of alignment or misalignment, for example between ISO (and its enrolees) and REACH (or nanoREACH) on the definition of nano-materials. The apparent misalignment is central because it relates to the organization's vision of markets for nanomaterials. On the one hand, there is the vision that there are different markets for nanoproducts while, on the other hand, there is the vision that there is one market. This misalignment does not allow yet the set-up of a governance arrangement and this is why it currently leads to the re-opening of a debate on the definition of nanomaterials.

   More generally then, what are the conditions of alignment? In other words, how is consensus that has been reached within individual arenas shared and diffused? This remains an open question. Our present hypothesis, looking at the empirical work conducted (but not presented here, Delemarle, 2012) is that actors belonging to several arenas play a critical role. These actors may act as gatekeepers (a member of a group who is at its boundary and controls access of outsiders to the group) or brokers (a member of a group that makes a link between two arenas that otherwise would not have been in contact, thus providing access to information). The success of ISO TC229 is linked to the existence of in and out liaisons with other ISO TCs and with external organizations. Its success is also linked to the fact that many national delegation members are also members of other arenas such as the OECD WPMN or the EU CoC. Most often, within ISO TC229, members are not only technical experts recognized in their fields; they are also high level experts in their country and within their companies or public organizations reaching multiple other (political) arenas. Indeed, we should not forget that actors are first of all strategic players. They invest in arenas according to their interests.

A second hypothesis is concerned with the respective positioning of arenas: arenas can be complementary (that is addressing different issues and aiming at producing different outputs) or competing amongst each other (around the same output). This notion of complementarity is important because as arenas recognize the relevance of other arenas, they can delegate the development of certain outputs to them (as we have shown, at least partly, for the definition and characterization of nano-technology products). Complementarity thus fosters alignment. On the contrary, competition fosters uncertainty. We hypothesize that a governance arrangement cannot be stable as long as competition between arenas remains.

8.5 CONCLUSIONS

We started Chapter 8 with the aim to better understand the process through which radical change is governed. We chose to focus on actors' activities within and across arenas to do so. Using current situations and on-going developments in the field of nanotechnologies, we have looked at five arenas in which actors invest. We propose a two-stage approach: at a first stage, 'concerned' arenas are identified and their internal dynamics are studied; and, at the second stage, the articulations between the arenas and their alignment are scrutinized. Thus to understand the governance of change means to follow the construction of *governance arrangements*.

Actors invest in specific arenas to try and influence the future governance arrangement. We have defined successful arenas as those that manage to enrol new actors, enlarge their initial remit while seeing their 'outputs' taken over by other arenas. This makes it clear that arenas have various degrees of success or failure. We have proposed a first attempt to delineate four aspects that contribute to the success of an arena: the degree of specificity, the degree of openness, the level of transparency and the degree of structuration. These aspects enable us to disentangle the notion of input legitimacy proposed by Borrás and Edler in their introductory chapter. While the first three have already been studied, we were struck by the importance of the fourth, the structuration of arenas and the critical role of organizational dimensions, not only in its legal aspect, but even more so for favouring work processes, for shaping 'outputs' and for ensuring their circulation. One initial reflection is that in four out of the five cases the arenas existed before the issue of nanotechnologies and that their success was linked to their ability to adapt to the new issue. This point clearly needs to be further explored and more research on the organization of arenas is needed.

Another interesting phenomenon is that the five arenas we considered developed directly at the international level, even driving a reversal of established approaches in the case of ISO. Why is that so? Is it only because expertise has been distributed or is it an example of a deeper change in S&T governance?

NOTES

1. This is in line with Callon's framing and overflowing concept developed in 1999.
2. www.iso.org/iso/home/about.htm (accessed 13 October 2011).
3. ISO TC229, General Assembly, 12 June 2009.
   The group produced this first definition of its activities in 2005: 'Title: Nanotechnologies; Scope: "Standardization in the field of nanotechnologies that includes either or both of the following: (i) Understanding and control of matter and processes at the nanoscale, typically, but not exclusively, below 100 nanometers in one or more dimensions where the onset of size-dependent phenomena usually enables novel applications; (ii) Utilizing the properties of nanoscale materials that differ from the properties of individual atoms, molecules, and bulk matter, to create improved materials, devices, and systems that exploit these new properties"'. Source: ISO TC229 archives – N41.
4. This paragraph is based on one of the authors' experience (and observation) as technical expert in the committee between 2007 and 2012.
5. Based on ISO TC229 secretariat's reports.
6. Each national delegation presented its vision of the structure of the TC and the works that TC229 should focus on (a deeper analysis can be found in Delemarle, 2013). The three themes at the core of TC229 were easily acknowledged by the delegations. The core of the discussion was on the structure of the committee, that is, an organization in sub-committees or without sub-committees only based on WG.
7. Clive Willis, presentation to the general assembly, 21 November 2008.
8. TC 229 archives, Business Plan, 2007.
9. TC 229 archives, Business Plan, 2007.
10. Water purification was especially highlighted in the dinner speech by the convenor of TC229 during the Tokyo meeting in June 2006. This is one of the few publicly available documents of TC229 on the ISO website, accessed 13 December 2012 at www.iso.org/iso/fr/iso_technical_committee?commid=381983.
11. www.iso.org/sites/directives.html#toc_marker-21, accessed 30 January 2014.
12. So TC229 is transversal across many industries – in 2013, its members came from multiple industries and application committees: biotechnologies, forestry, textiles, electronics, materials and so on.
13. ISO TC229 WG1 and WG2 are Joint WGs between ISO and IEC, bringing together experts from both organizations and producing documents that are published jointly by ISO and IEC.
14. www.oecd.org/about/, accessed 2 July 2013.
15. www.oecd.org/science/nanosafety/sponsorshipprogrammeforthetestingofmanufactured nanomaterials.htm, accessed 27 March 2014.
16. www.oecd.org/science/nanosafety/, accessed 2 July 2013.
17. Terms of reference for the working party on manufactured nanomaterials, 2006. Liaison report from OECD to ISO TC229, 10 April 2010.

18. http://icon.rice.edu/about.cfm, fact sheet, accessed 13 December 2012. This document was last updated on 1 July 2010.
19. ICoN 27 members 2012 (based on ICoN website).

	2012
Public admin. /Govt lab	33%
University	15%
Company	37%
Other	15%

The most recent changes to the executive board occurred in 2009 when five new members joined (two companies, two public administrations and one other). Since then, there has been no change in the membership: both individual and organizational members have been very stable over the years.

20. http://icon.rice.edu/about.cfm, fact sheet, accessed 13 December 2012.
21. On 8 March 2013, the database contained 7014 summaries, showing that the database is updated.
22. They brought together members from eight companies, four scientific organisations/universities and three NGOs to produce seven principles (illustrated by examples) and a benchmark after numerous public consultations. The targets of the Code of Conduct are companies' boards because they are said to be the ones able to impose change in companies. 'The Code will be designed to establish a consensus of what constitutes good practice in businesses across the nanotechnology value chain (that is, from research and development to manufacturing, distribution and retailing) so that businesses can align their processes with emerging good practice and form the foundation for the development of indicators of compliance.' (The Responsible NanoCode, 2008, accessed 15 April 2013 at www.responsiblenanocode.org/documents/ theresponsiblenanocodeupdateannouncement.pdf.
23. http://europa.eu/rapid/pressReleasesAction.do?reference=IP/08/193&format=HTML, accessed 18 April 2012.
24. We selected the top five companies in the main European clusters. This led us to a sample of 37 companies that have activities in Europe but they can be companies from other continents.
25. http://ec.europa.eu/enterprise/sectors/chemicals/reach/index_en.htm, accessed 1 July 2013.
26. http://ec.europa.eu /enterprise /sectors/chemicals/reach/how-it-works/index_en.htm, accessed 1 July 2013.
27. http://ec.europa.eu /enterprise/sectors /chemicals/reach/how-it-works/index_en.htm, accessed 27 March 2014.
28. For a recent comment on this issue see, for example, Schwirn et al., 2014.
29. Own interpretation based on discussions with chemical experts at ISO TC229. Three projects are developed by the chemical industry and the European chemical association to determine whether a specific nanoREACH needs to be developed in addition to REACH:
    1. IP-oN 1 (Substance Identification): the existing REACH registration dossier is considered relevant by industry experts, accessed 27 March 2014 at http://ec.europa.eu/environment/chemicals/nanotech/pdf/report_ripon1.pdf.
    2. RIP-oN 2 (Information Requirements): the existing REACH registration dossier is relevant with a few adjustments. The report concludes: 'A comprehensive

synthesis of findings, implications, issues and advice has been developed and integrated through the Task Reports and the Final Project Report. Where considered relevant, feasible and justified, specific advice for updating guidance has been provided.' (Hankin et al., 2011, xii)

3. RIP-oN 3 (Exposure & CSA): the existing REACH registration dossier is relevant with a few adjustments.

The main limit identified was expressed as follows: 'For issues which are not currently technically/scientifically mature for developing detailed guidance, the need for further research and development has been indicated' (ibid.) and experts expect results from OECD work and ISO standardisation work within TC 229 to provide answers in the future, accessed 27 March 2014 at http://ec.europa.eu/ environment/chemicals/nanotech/pdf/report_ripon3.pdf.

30. ISO/TS 80004-1:2010, 2.4.
31. ISO/TS 12805:2011, 3.2.
32. CEFIC is the European Chemical Industry Council. Its membership entails around 29 000 companies.
33. Results of RiP-oN 1 accessed 12 July 2013 at www.cefic.org/Documents/ IndustrySupport/REACH-Implementation/Workshops/REACH-and-Nano-Workshop/ 2011-06-23/Nano%20REACH%20Workshop%20-%20RIP-oN1%20industry%20pers pective%20-%20Morris%20Cole.pdf.
34. Project 7 in WG3 with Environmental Defense (NGO) and Dupont Chemicals.

REFERENCES

Aitken R. J., K. S. Creely and C. L. Tran (2004), *Nanoparticles: An Occupational Hygiene Review*, Sudbury, UK: HSE Books RR274.

Bonneuil, C., P. B. Joly and C. Marris (2008), 'Disentrenching experiment: The construction of GM crop field trials as a social problem', *Science Technology Human Values*, **33**, 201–229.

Borrás, S. and J. Edler (2014), 'The governance of change in socio-technical systems: Three pillars for a conceptual framework', in S. Borrás and J. Edler (eds), *The Governance of Socio-Technical Systems: Explaining Change*, Cheltenham, UK and Northampton, MA, USA: Edward Elgar.

Bresnahan, T. F. and M. Trajtenberg (1995), 'General purpose technologies "engines of growth"?', *Journal of Econometrics*, **65** (1), 83–108.

Callon, M., P. Lascoumes, and Y. Barthe (translated by G. Burchell) (2009), *Acting in An Uncertain World: An Essay on Technical Democracy*, Cambridge, MA, USA and London, UK, 2009: MIT Press, 283 pages.

Callon, M. and A. Rip (1992), 'Humains, non-humains: morale d'une coexistence', in J. Theys and B. Kalaora (eds), *La Terre Outragée. Les Experts Sont Formels*, Paris: éditions Autrement, pp. 140–156.

Clarke, A. E. (1991), 'Social worlds theory as organizational theory', in D. Maines (ed.), *Social Organization and Social Process: Essays in Honor of Anselm Strauss*, Hawthorne, NY: Aldine de Gruyter, pp. 119–158.

Courtney, H., J. Kirkland and P. Viguerie (1997), 'Strategy under uncertainty', *Harvard Business Review*, **75** (6).

Delemarle, A. (2012), 'Organizing markets for nanotechnology products: Investigating firms' collective actions in ISO and the European Code of Conduct', paper presented at the SCORE Workshop on 'Organizing Markets', Stockholm, 18-19 January 2012.

Delemarle A., B. Kahane, L. Villard and P. Larédo (2009), 'Geography of knowledge production in nanotechnologies', *Nanotechnology Law & Business*, **6**, 103–122.

Delemarle, A. and P. Larédo (2012), 'Governing markets for radical products by designing market infrastructure. Market infrastructures – towards a market paradigm?', paper presented at the 4S-EASST Conference 2012, Copenhagen Business School, Denmark, October 2012.

Delemarle, A. and P. Larédo (2013), 'Tentative governance for new markets by creating market infrastructures', *IFRIS Working Paper, http://ifris.org/publications/*.

European Commission (2008), *Communication from the Commission to the European Parliament, the Council and the European Economic and Social Committee Regulatory Aspects of Nanomaterials*, COM (2008) 366 final, Brussels: European Commission, accessed 27 March 2014 at http://ec.europa.eu,nanotechnology/pdf/comm_2008_0366_en.pdf.

European Commission (2011), *Commission Recommendation of 18 October 2011 on the Definition of Nanomaterial (2011/696/EU)*, OJ L 275/38, 20 October 2011, Brussels.

Fligstein, N. (1996), 'Markets as politics: A political-cultural approach to market institutions', *American Sociological Review*, **61**, 656–673.

Fligstein, N. (2001), *The Architecture of Markets: An Economic Sociology of Capitalist Societies*, Princeton, NJ: Princeton University Press.

Fligstein, N. and I. Mara Drita (1996), 'How to make a market: Reflections on the European Union's Single Market Program', *American Journal of Sociology*, **102**, 1–33.

Geels, F. W. (2002), 'Technological transitions as evolutionary reconfiguration processes: A multi-level perspective and a case-study', *Research Policy*, **31** (8/9), 1257–1274.

Geels, F. W. (2005), 'The dynamics of transitions in socio-technical systems: A multi-level analysis of the transition pathway from horse-drawn carriages to automobiles (1860–1930)', *Technology Analysis & Strategic Management*, **17** (4), 445–476.

Hankin, S. M., S. A. K. Peters, C. A. Poland, S. Foss Hansen, J. Holmqvist, B. L. Ross, ... R. J. Aitken (2011), 'Specific Advice on Fulfilling Information Requirements for Nanomaterials under REACH (RIP-oN 2) – Final Project Report', (reference: RNC/RIP-oN2/FPR/1/FINAL), 1 July 2011, accessed at http://ec.europa.eu/environment/chemicals/nanotech/pdf/report_ripon2.pdf.

Kuhlmann, S. (2007), 'Rationales and evolution of public *"knowledge policies"* in the context of their evaluation', paper presented at the Seminario Internacional CGEE, Rio de Janeiro, 3-5 December 2007.

Kuhlmann, S., P. Boekholt, L. Georghiou, K. Guy, J.-A. Héraud, P. Larédo ... R. Smits (1999), *Improving Distributed Intelligence in Complex Innovation Systems. Final report of the Advanced Science and Policy Planning Network (ASTPP)*, Karlsruhe: Fraunhofer Institute.

Larédo, P., A. Delemarle and B. Kahane (2010), 'Dynamics of nano sciences and technologies: Policy implications', *STI – Science, Technology Industry Review*, **1** (1), 43–62.

Lawrence, T. and R. Suddaby (2006), 'Institutional work', in S. Clegg, C. Hardy, and T. Lawrence (eds), *Handbook of Organization Studies, 2nd edition*, London: Sage, pp. 215–254.

Porter, A. L., J. Youtie, P. Shapira and D. Schoeneck (2008), 'Refining search terms for nanotechnology', *Journal of Nanoparticle Research*, **10** (5), 715–728.

Rip, A., T. J. Misa and J. Schot (eds) (1995), *Managing Technology in Society: The Approach of Constructive Technology Assessment*, London: Pinter.

Schwirn, K., L. Tietjen and I. Beer (2014), 'Why are nanomaterials different and how can they be appropriately regulated under REACH?', *Environmental Sciences Europe* **26** (4), accessed 27 March 2014 at www.enveurope.com/content/26/1/4.

Sutcliffe, H. and S. Hodgson (2006), 'An uncertain business: The technical, social and commercial challenges presented by nanotechnology', *Ancona briefing paper*, accessed 28 March 2011 at www.responsiblenanocode.org.

The Royal Society & The Royal Academy of Engineering (2004), Nanoscience and nanotechnologies: Opportunities and uncertainties, *The Royal Society & The Royal Academy of Engineering Report*, (July), 127, *116p*.

Vinck, D. (1999), 'Les objets intermédiaires dans les réseaux de coopération scientifique. Contribution à la prise en compte des objets dans les dynamiques sociales', *Revue française de sociologie*, **40** (2), 385–414.

Vinck, D. (2010), *The Sociology of Scientific Work*, Cheltenham, UK and Northampton, MA, USA: Edward Elgar.

9. The who, what, how and why of governing change: first lessons and ways forward

Susana Borrás and Jakob Edler

9.1 INTRODUCTION

This book brings forward a focus on the governance of change in socio-technical and innovation systems. In Chapter 1 we defined the governance of change in ST&I systems as the way in which societal and state actors intentionally interact in order to transform ST&I systems by regulating issues of societal concern, defining the processes and direction of how technological artefacts and innovations are produced, and shaping how these are introduced, absorbed, diffused and used within society and the economy. While our approach to the governance of change acknowledges the normative dimensions of 'governance', it emphasizes its analytical dimension for studying these complex societal and political processes. In order to do so, we have first proposed a simple typology of governance situations and then developed a conceptual framework based on three interrelated pillars: the opportunity structures and capable agents, governance instrumentation and democratic legitimacy. These three pillars constitute the theoretical foundations from which a set of specific questions are formulated in order to focus the study of system's change on the study of the underlying governance processes and dynamics. The starting point for this book was the observation that the literature has not provided a well-organized focus on the underlying processes and conditions for governance of change in socio-technical and innovation systems.

We organized the analytical questions posed at the beginning of this book around these three pillars. When considering the first pillar, the role of and interaction between the opportunity structures and capable agents, our conceptual framework looks specifically at the role of agency. Hence, the overall issue here is to define *who and what* drives change. This leads to the analytical questions:

- Who are the primary agents of change?
- What is their capacity to induce/inhibit change?
- What capabilities do they have (resources and interpretative abilities)?
- What is the distribution of the agents' capabilities within the socio-technical and innovation system, and how does this affect the action of these agents?

Regarding the second pillar, instrumentation, the main issue we turn to is *how* change is influenced. From this, the following concrete analytical questions were identified at the onset of this book:

- What are the instruments used?
- By whom are they used?
- How are they implemented?
- How are the instruments shaped?
- How do public and private instruments interact?
- How and why do they 'work' or not work, and how do they interact with other instruments?
- What are the instrumental tensions, and how are they resolved (if at all)?

Last but not least, democratic legitimacy as the third analytical pillar asks to what degree and why change is accepted. The concrete analytical questions here are:

- What are the actor arenas and the poly-centrality of governance, and what are the resulting tensions and challenges for legitimacy?
- What is the cultural embedding of governance instruments and how does it change over time?
- How socially accepted are the governance processes and outcomes, and why is this?
- How is contestation of processes and outcomes dealt with?

Using this framework, we finish this book with first conclusions drawn from the cases presented in this volume. We first characterize the nature of governance of change in socio-technical systems as presented in those case studies. To do so, we apply our two-dimensional typology of modes of governance elaborated earlier in Chapter 1. This is followed by a more in-depth synthesis for each of the three pillars, reflecting on the theoretical implications drawn from the empirical analysis in the different chapters. Following from the overall findings of this book, we conclude with some thoughts on a future research agenda that works towards a theory of governance of change in socio-technical systems.

9.2 GOVERNING CHANGE: WHAT GOVERNANCE?

In a first step in our theoretical approach, we have outlined a typology of governance modes, differentiating the type of actors and the form of domination along two dimensions. Naturally, this is a simplification of the complexity of governance, but it nevertheless allows for a first characterization of different key features in the concrete empirical cases, as a basis for understanding governance of change more deeply.

Table 9.1   Stylized typology of governance modes

	Driven by state actors	Driven by societal actors
Hierarchical, dominated	Command and control	Oligopoly
Heterarchical, non-dominated	State as primus inter pares	Self-regulation

The examples in this book show different types of governance at play, and these differences have different consequences for change. In Barberá-Tomás and Molas-Gallart's analysis of the governance of medical devices we see a case of predominant command and control through regulation. These authors show the interplay of regulation and technical change and how regulation influences the direction and rate of change over time, which leads to undesired outcomes. We see the shortcomings of a governance situation that is dominated by command and control in a case where a technology has reached maturity, and regulation assumes (wrongly) that incremental innovation is safer for the patients. This points towards the contrasting meaning of regulation as trigger and inhibitor of change: while regulation can certainly lead to change and is often used to induce firms to innovate more radically (most pronounced in the field of eco-innovation), it can also cement the lock-in of socio-technical systems if it is defined to allow for too much incremental innovation in a specific search trajectory where technological solutions are exhausted. In other words, command and control governance can be strong in triggering change if it is deliberately designed to open for alternative technological trajectories (as is the case for example for some eco-innovation), but not when it is deliberately designed to force agents to stay in established technological trajectories. In order to avoid lock-in, regulatory systems dominated by command and control have to allow for opening up the debate to incumbent stakeholders on the supply and demand side, and for challenging and altering regulation in view of systems' transformation and technological change.

Two other chapters in this book represent the governance type of 'state as primus inter pares', where transformation is driven primarily by state actors, but the governance process and its effectiveness are entirely dependent on the interplay between state and non-state actors. The case of the governance of discontinuation presented by Stegmaier, Kuhlmann, and Visser shows that in order to change radically, old systems and practices must go, and that this discontinuation requires purposeful state actors and a conscious discontinuation governance. This does not work through command and control alone, but needs consensus building and interaction with societal actors. A very different case of state-driven governance in heterarchical settings is the case of change in translational research in biomedicine, as analysed by Vignola-Gagné et al. The authors show how the implementation of translational research (TR) programmes at biomedical RTD sites located in Austria and Germany, while driven by state actors and preferences, is strongly dependent on a range of stakeholders and their learning over time.

The three other cases in this book represent governance that is dominated by societal rather than state actors. Interestingly, all three examples are concerned, in one way or another, with market creation and standard setting. Daemmrich's analysis of the role of technical standards in the development of biodegradable plastics is an excellent example of oligopolistic societal governance. It shows the role of a limited number of strong societal players who by setting standards in fact perform anticipatory market building and thus shape the direction of change of the system.

Delemarle and Laredo have a similar approach when discussing arenas of societal and state actors who create a set of market infrastructures for an emerging technology (nanotechnology). They show how the governance of infrastructure creation is dispersed across multiple arenas, preventing the dominance of one group of societal actors in what we can label as a multiple oligopoly. Thus, their case could be situated half way between self-regulated and oligopolistic governance. Their micro analysis of the arenas and their interplay sheds light on the fact that societally dominated, polycentric governance mechanisms need certain preconditions to work, and only if we understand those preconditions can we understand the opportunities and limits of social-actors' driven market creation.

Finally, Loconto and Barbier represent an example of self-regulation, with minimal involvement of traditional state regulatory actors in the definition and implementation of agro-food standards. Here, the authors highlight the preconditions and limits of those self-regulated mechanisms, ranging from appropriate framing of the issue to the build-up of credibility and legitimacy as a crucial condition for compliance.

As we have seen, the chapters in the book represent the four fields in our governance matrix above. What are the lessons for our three pillars that can now finally be drawn from those cases and types of governance in this first, exploratory discussion about the who, what, how and why of governing change in socio-technical and innovation systems?

9.3 GOVERNANCE OF CHANGE: LESSONS FOR OUR PILLARS

In this section we look at the three interrelated pillars: the opportunity structures and capable agents, governance instrumentation and democratic legitimacy.

9.3.1 Opportunity Structures and Capable Agents

Our first pillar is concerned with the question of who and what drives change, focusing on actors and their governance capability and intentionality in the system. Across the case studies in this volume, the agents driving change have displayed a high level of organizational capability, mobilizing and combining other actors' knowledge, contributing strongly to framing the problem, and having the endurance needed for promoting system change. A closer look across our chapters allows some further differentiation as for the capabilities relevant for our question of system's change.

A first conclusion of the cross-reading of cases in this volume is that the capability of actors in the governance of change is strongly based on their ability to manage heterogeneity. Arthur Daemmrich's chapter on the governance of change in the socio-technical system towards biodegradable plastics shows the mobilization of interdisciplinary and inter-organizational cooperation, moderated by capable agents towards the establishment of a new standard. However, in spite of this capable agent and the opportunity structure offered by new technical solutions, change of the socio-technical system did not materialize because consumers did not respond to a sufficient degree. Thus, although BASF, standard bodies and environmentalist groups were capable agents in the governance of change, the anticipated market reaction did not correspond to expectations and behaviours across the range of affected stakeholders.

A second example for the importance of managing heterogeneity is presented by Alison Loconto and Marc Barbier in their case of sustainable standards in the agro-food system. This case is about one central institutional actor, the inter-organizational ISEAL alliance. In many ways, this analysis shows that this alliance is the most relevant capable actor in the international sphere when it comes to defining the transnational standards for the certification of sustainable agro-food products. The pragmatic approach of this central actor has given way to a successful strategy fostering the growth of sustainable certified products world-wide. However, the success of the standards largely depends on the successful framing of credibility not only locally, but transnationally. This, in turn, is very much dependent on the ability of the capable agents to mobilize and bring different kinds of knowledge (expert, experiential) in line with its own core values and image as a credible promoter.

In contrast to the prominence of one central association of actors as change promoter, Delemarle and Laredo demonstrate that system change can be a product of the interplay of a multiplicity of capable actors. They conceptualize change as the creation of a market infrastructure defined as a set of rules (what actors are allowed to do), of norms (what they ought to do) and of values (what they want to do). Using the example of nanotechnology, they stress that a whole range of very different actors are engaged across a number of related arenas. They point towards the capabilities of arenas as ensembles of actors who are tasked with the production of specific elements of market infrastructure. Thus, creating market infrastructure through a variety of different instruments is not only about the capabilities and drive of individual actors to initiate and contribute to market infrastructure creation, it is about the organizational capabilities within and of arenas to mobilise and moderate discourses and deliver on outputs that contribute to the market infrastructure. Change in socio-technical systems, particularly when it comes to the creation of markets, can only be understood if we broaden our concept of capabilities and also think about capabilities of collectives to prepare for and enable that change. This is especially true in the absence of meaningful state actor influence or command and control governance, in particular in situations where the opportunity structures are not well defined yet, typically in emerging and enabling technologies which have many possibilities of being used in a broad range of sector and products (like the case of nanotechnology).

In the case of discontinuation, conceptualized and empirically illustrated by the chapter of Stegmaier et al., we learn that even though there was an overwhelming societal consensus across Europe and some initial national initiatives, for a long time this consensus was not strong enough to initiate system change. It took the lead of the EU Commission as the supranational body to regulate the discontinuation in a meaningful way. The reason for this is probably that the EU Commission combined its regulatory power with a range of discursive instruments, thus linking powering and sense-making. The Commission designed a multi-step process with different degrees of openness and inclusion. This case is an illustration of the importance of agents' capabilities to design a process, particularly in complex, contested situations of change.

A different kind of institutional entrepreneurship is analysed in the case of change in biomedical research towards translational research. Here, individual institutional entrepreneurs, such as scientists convinced of the inner logic of translational research (TR), in conjunction with international advocacy coalitions took the main initiative. The resources they could draw on were partly organizational (for example scientists in important management positions) and partly intellectual credibility and the ability to create win-win situations to underpin the visions of change.

9.3.2 Instruments for the Governance of Change

Our second pillar is concerned with how change is influenced, which instruments are used by whom, how instruments interact, to what extent they work and why, and how potential tensions between instruments are resolved.

Three chapters in this book have impressively shown the importance – and limits – of standardization processes and standards as instruments to govern change through enabling market creation. Daemmrich's case emphasizes that standards are not just a means to create uniformity and predictability related to new products, but in doing so have a much broader role to play. As a tool for anticipatory market creation they coordinate technology and social institutions within heterogeneous actor landscapes. In Daemmrich's case of biodegradable plastics, voluntary standards were a crucial instrument for change because they enabled the firms to differentiate a product category (biodegradable plastics) relative to other synthetics, they established a market based on further criteria beyond price alone, and they informed about the new market. Further, the development of the standards was organized in an interactive manner to include a broader perspective from the outset, such as involving user groups. However, these functionalities of standards have limits. The standard on the biodegradable products worked only in conjunction with other regulation which internalized externalities of the product that was supposed to be replaced and which shifted the economic argument in favour of innovation. Further, once the standards were set, they were initially less effective than expected, as consumer's behaviour did not change in line with the underlying expectations embedded in the standard itself. The involvement of user groups in the development of the instrument was not sufficient for the standard to be widely effective. However, as a tool for change, standards have subsequently worked as they allowed flexibility in other product specifications to accommodate user's preferences without violating the spirit of the standard itself.

Barberá-Tomás and Molas-Gallart bring forward a very strong case regarding the role of regulation as an instrument for the governance of change in socio-technical systems that induced a technological failure. Their study on the hip prosthesis defect case shows how regulation of medical devices can shape particular search trends that foster and lock in incremental rather than radical innovation. The assumption implicit in this command and control regime in the health sector, that incremental technical change is safer than radical technical change, proved to be wrong, with unintended severe consequences for patients' safety. The burdensome regulatory framework imposed on radical innovation discouraged radical change vis-à-vis incremental change. This case shows that the outcomes of governing change in a socio-technical system are not only dependent on socio-political factors like assumptions underlying the regulations or social legitimacy, but also on the technological features of the products subject to regulation.

Alison Loconto and Marc Barbier shed further light on standards as governance instruments of change in their study of the development of sustainability standards in the agro-food system. Here, the process of standardization, largely driven by non-state actors, is first and foremost a process of knowledge framing, capability building and norm setting. The case of the meta-standards of the ISEAL alliance demonstrates the different but complementary processes to build up necessary capacities and a common stock of knowledge in the standardization process, for example through negotiations to define the auditor competencies, the auditing sampling and the technical credibility of the standards. Further, sustainable standards have implications for socially responsible investing and organizational buying and accounting, and hence they embody specific normative and moral dimensions. Second, standardization processes not only re-frame knowledge and norms, but do so through changing the relationships between market, state and civil society. In this particular case, this was driven by the multi-stakeholder initiatives and transnational alliances.

An even broader and more holistic view on instrumentation is taken by Delemarle and Laredo in their analysis of market creation as vehicle of system change. The authors conceptualize change in socio-technical systems that is driven by emerging technologies as the successful creation of market infrastructures. They demonstrate convincingly that there are many different kinds of instruments that contribute to the overall emerging market infrastructure (standards, guidelines, policy reports, knowledge databases/journals, code of conduct and regulatory frameworks). Those instruments are constructed simultaneously in different public-private arenas. The authors discuss the conditions under which the various instruments become effective. Most importantly, those conditions have to do with the structural and procedural conditions of the arenas that produce the instrument and with the conditions for interconnections between the arenas. The main lesson here is that the question of instruments, therefore, cannot be tackled without understanding the arena of their origin (and the legitimacy of that arena, see below), and change in socio-technical system is driven by sets of instruments rather than individual instruments.

Traditionally, instrumentation in socio-technical systems is associated with the idea of supporting positive change, that is, supporting activities and capabilities that positively generate something new in the direction of desired change. Stegmaier et al. show that when we are faced with a discontinuation problem, we need to identify what the underlying problem in the previously stabilized system is. In addition, we need to find instrumentation to adjust and discontinue existing framework conditions and governance practices that had stabilized the socio-technical system that is to be discontinued. This is essential if we want to understand the governance of change, because creating something new might often require proactive initiatives to discontinue the old. Stegmaier et al. show that command and control instruments alone are not enough; to discontinue also means to alter routines and practices of suppliers and users of technologies.

In their analysis of change in biomedical research towards translational research, Vignola-Gagné et al. take a functional perspective and discuss how different instruments, with quite different functions (research grant funding, infrastructure funding, professionalization of education, organization building), together pulled in the same direction in order to change research orientations. Interestingly, not all of those instruments were new, but rather, purposeful actors (see above) took advantage of existing instruments and re-defined their rationality. The combination of various (new and old) instruments created incentives and framework conditions conducive to the new policy paradigm and in doing so allowed a re-alignment of actors in novel ways.

9.3.3 Legitimacy

Our final pillar is focusing on the question of the extent and nature of social acceptance of governance of change, asking about the challenges for legitimacy arising from poly-centrality of governance, the importance of cultural embedding of governance, the conditions for output and input legitimacy, and the way conflicts about legitimacy of governance are dealt with.

A main lesson across our cases is that governance of change relies strongly on input legitimacy. This is due to the high level of uncertainty and the long term nature of effects (and thus the output dimension) of change in the system. Uncertainty increases the need to search for ideas and knowledge that can support and direct governance of change. It also works towards a broader inclusion of actors to mobilize stakeholder views and broadly identify opportunities and challenges. The long term nature of effects in many instances of change of systems seems to reduce the relative importance of output legitimacy for the actual process of governing change. The examples in this book indicate that the legitimacy of governance is related to the ideational and organizational sources of change, to the credibility of the agents of change and of the technical solutions proposed; and to the processes related to governing change. For example, in Daemmrich's discussion of biodegradable plastics, legitimacy stems from the discourse arrangement in the standard setting arrangement as well as the credibility of the standard setting body and complementary institutions providing scientific underpinning. Thus, the final effectiveness of the standard can only be understood in conjunction with the credibility of its production and the capabilities and strategies of the main agent of change that pushed for the standard. The negotiation over technical aspects, for example in standardization processes, is at the same time a process of re-framing and joint sense-making. The 'what' and 'how' in those technical discussions is intimately interlinked to the 'why' and 'what for', and if those questions can be aligned, new standards are rendered into powerful tools of change in the socio-technical system.

When it comes to legitimacy in terms of the ideational and cognitive sources, national practice often draws on international discourse. International cognitive and normative ideas are taken up and transferred in national contexts. In their discussion of attempts to re-orient biomedical research and innovation activity towards more user involvement (translational research), Vignola-Gagné et al. show the two ways in which new international legitimacy claims affect local change. First, local communities are part of the broad international epistemic and policy discourse, embedded in the re-definition of cognitive and normative claims. Second, legitimacy claims are proactively constructed and instrumentally used by transnational and localized advocacy coalitions in favour of change. However, the authors demonstrate that despite the programmatic and normative legitimacy of the claim for translational research that emerged in the Austrian cases, there was no broad re-orientation of practices. This was partly due to the fact that the operational requirements, such as provisions for the inclusion of patients into the research programme design, were not in place, and partly to the fact that the legitimacy claim was instrumentally used by local entrepreneurs to capture existing instruments, rather than to live up to the normative core of translational research. More deeply, though, the international epistemic and policy discourse does not seem to have led to a broad and deep enough re-orientation of actor's behaviour.

The critical issue of input legitimacy is further highlighted by Loconto and Barbier's case of ISEAL alliance standard setting for sustainable agro-food products. The authors show the complexity of legitimacy issues in the governance of change in socio-technical systems. The technical credibility of the standard is a key aspect for its legitimacy at different levels (e.g. producer, consumer), but the framing of that technical credibility into specific knowledge is not easy. The case shows that the pragmatic approach of ISEAL is to put forward a vision of conformity assessment that is based on the idea of appropriateness or 'fit for purpose' rather than an ideal type of credible guarantee. This pragmatic and flexible approach is strategic, because it enables the scaling up of activities that would ultimately allow ISEAL to gain terrain over competing (non-certified sustainable) agro-food technical systems. But it might turn out to be problematic in legitimacy terms as ISEAL members are raising the question of who accredits the accreditors. This again corresponds to questions about input-legitimacy (who makes the decisions and how) rather than to output-legitimacy (how effective are the collective actions) which is based on the technical knowledge embedded in the sustainable standard and in the certification of individual products.

In their discussion of market infrastructure development through multiple arenas and governance arrangements, Delemarle and Laredo demonstrate the multiplicity of legitimacy sources in one technological area. As different arenas have different contributions to the development of market infrastructure for new technologies, each arena has slightly different legitimacy foundations. All of those claims are mainly about the procedural aspects of input legitimacy in the governance of change – such as self-organized participatory processes and openness of expert knowledge and data. In addition, legitimacy is based on the credibility of international organizations. In this case this refers to the regulatory framework of the EU (hard law regulations) and to the OECD's mandate to promote policies globally. However, the way the legitimacy claims pan out depends in addition on the credibility and operational effectiveness with which agents of change in the respective arenas can deliver.

The legitimacy of governing change towards the discontinuation of socio-technical systems has its specific challenges. As Stegmaier et al. show, discontinuation is normally a very long term process, during which various vested interests are affected, and long established routines and practices as well as normative and cognitive beliefs have to be changed. Thus, not only is a strong and convincing normative and cognitive argument to be made for a new problem perception and a credible solution, but those initial legitimacy claims also need to be put forward by credible advocacy coalitions and need to be upheld both in terms of the credibility of the underlying rationale and knowledge, and in terms of the governance process and practices themselves.

Finally, Barberá-Tomás and Molas-Gallart remind us about the potential loss of legitimacy in socio-technical systems and their key institutions if they fail to deliver appropriate solutions. This is what we call output legitimacy. In their case, a strong regulatory regime prevented radical technological change because it was based on unsuitable assumptions about risk. The result was a failure to deliver appropriate solutions, in this case patients' safety. This example shows how the governance of change, biased towards incremental rather than radical change, produced outputs that were not legitimate. Finally, and perhaps most importantly, it reminds us that governance of change in socio-technical systems is after all about improving social well-being through better solutions.

9.4   ACHIEVEMENTS – AND A FUTURE RESEARCH AGENDA

This book started with the observation that despite the vast literature about change in socio-economic systems, the way change in socio-technical systems is actually governed is still poorly understood. The framework that we have developed in this book is a first step towards a theory of governance of change which has governance at its core, focusing on the three main pillars of governance and looking at them together: purposeful actors and the opportunity structures they create or take advantage of, the instruments that are used in governing change, and the nature and conditions for the legitimacy of change and its governance.

As the analysis of each case and the cross case analysis above have shown, to look at governance of change through our lens does allow us to better understand the nature of and hurdles associated with the three pillars of governance of change. For each pillar, this analysis has allowed a first abstraction, first lessons towards a more holistic theory building. We have seen that system's change is not mainly determined by socio-cultural context conditions or by market forces, but by a combination of the two, greatly influenced by purposeful actors, the instruments deployed, and the legitimacy claims that are made and sustained. At the same time, the cases have shown that it is not agency or institutions, but agency and their capacity within (changing) institutional frameworks that drive or hinder change.

As we have seen across the cases, the dynamics related to the governance of change have a lot to do with the way actors interpret the system and the value it generates, and how they assess the value of system's change, triggered by technological change or by change in societal preferences. This is not only a highly reflexive process, but a highly political process as well.

A next step towards a theory of governance of change in socio-technical systems should involve a more systematic look at the conditions and processes within the three pillars, and a more systematic development of how the three pillars interact, and how this interaction in turn is influenced by the prevailing governance type and socio-technical conditions in the system. This next step would allow us to make predictions about what modes of governance are associated with different forms of system change (or lack of change).

Our journey towards a theory would allow us to analyse the governance of change in socio-technical and innovation systems in a holistic way. The cross case analysis performed in this concluding chapter induces one basic idea towards a comprehensive theory, which is the relation between basic properties of the system and the change under question (the level of uncertainty, the degree of transformation and the heterogeneity of the actor landscape in a (changing) socio-technical system) on the one hand, and the characteristics and dynamics within and the interplay of our three pillars in the governance of change, on the other hand. This is only possible now that we have conceptualized and understood the pillars themselves. The ultimate destination of our journey would be a middle range theory about the governance of change in socio-technical and innovation systems. To get closer to that destination will be the core of a new and collective research agenda ahead of us. You are welcome to join us in that journey.

Index